Barb,

Thanks so much
For your hospitality —
You really made my
trip special.

I hope you enjoy
our book.

Stay in touch!

— Jonathan

How Not to Greet Famous People

the best stories from
ducts.org

edited by jonathan kravetz and charles salzberg

LIBRARY OF CONGRESS
Control Number: 2004112360

ISBN 0-9759760-0-1

1st Printing   *   500 Copies   *   August 2004

Ducts Webzine Association, Inc.
P O Box 3203
Grand Central Station
New York, NY 10163
(718) 383-6728

Jonathan Kravetz, Editor-in-Chief

Printed in the United States by Morris Publishing
3212 East Highway 30 • Kearney, NE 68847
1-800-650-7888

We would like to thank the following individuals and organizations. This book would not have existed without their invaluable support:

The New York Writers Workshop; The Frederick Douglass Creative Arts Center of New York; the Council of Literary Magazines and Presses; Denis Woychuk of KGB Bar, New York; Alice Elliot Dark; Cody Dennison, Web Designer; Jeff Labrecque, Book Designer; Tim Tomlinson, Fiction Editor; Ryan Van Winkle, Poetry Editor; Cindy Moore, Art Gallery Editor; Daniel McCoy, Humor Editor; Anne Mironchik, Business Manager; Kara Murray, Marketing Director; Stephanie Hart, former editor and our biggest fan; and the many contributors who could easily have earned a place in the book, but did not because space was limited.

CONTENTS

CHAPTER 1: HUMOR

[15]   **Jonathan Kravetz** Opiate

[17]   **Bill Bilodeau** It's All in Their Heads

[19]   **Mark Goldblatt** Ricki Does the Heights

[23]   **Gideon Evans** Explaining Enron as a Sports Metaphor

[24]   **Kathleen Boland** My Sinister Neighbor's Journal

[25]   **Ross Klavan** King of the Far Out, Groovy, Wild Frontier

[29]   **Kathleen Boland** From a Forgotten Cousin in a Distant Land

[31]   **Nick Bhasin** Amsterdam? Amsterdammit!

[36]   **Laura Buchholtz** How Not to Greet Famous People

[37]   **Daniel McCoy** Rally the Flag Around Stuff, Boys

CHAPTER 2: ESSAYS

[39]   **Eric Gillen** Welcome to New York City

[41]   **Anonymous** The Tunnel

[46]   **Robert Flanagan** Twenty Guns and Booze

[50]   **Helen Zelon** Snow in Summer

[55]   **Jennifer DeMeritt** Now That It's Over

[58]   **Stephanie Hart** A Letter to My Father

[63]   **Harilyn Rousso** Buying the Wedding Dress

[65]   **Elliot Ravetz** Of Philosophy, Pentimento and Precision

[73]   **Katrina Markel** The Bill Riley Talent Competition

[79]   **Patricia Kinney** Blood and Water

[84]   **Tom Fast** Naked Man

[90]   **Domenick Angiello** The Store

[111]   **Hillery N. Borton** Absolutely, Totally, and in All Ways, Inconceivable!

CHAPTER 3: **FICTION**

[115]   **Margaret Hundley Parker** I Ain't Proud

[125]   **Mitchell Levenberg** The Cat

[129]   **E.B. Gallardo** The Waiting Room

[134]   **Thaddeus Rutowski** Little Bee

[135]   **Maud Newton** Why I Still Think of Marisol

[140]   **Tony Whiteside** How'd You Catch This Thing?

[143]   **Charles Salzberg** The Duke Steps Out

[155]   **Philippe Stessel** A Fly

[159]   **Jonathan Kravetz** Such a Perfect Day

CHAPTER 4: **PROFILES**

[169]   **Charles Salzberg** Pat Cooper

[176]   **Richard Goodman** William Burroughs

[182]   **Ryan Van Winkle** The Streaker

[186]   **Cynthia Ehrenkrantz** Betsy

[195]   **Domenick Angiello** Cindy

[199]   **Jonathan Kravetz** Principal Trumpet

[207]   **Rachelle Meyer** Buskers on the Bowery

POETRY

[22]   **Ryan Van Winkle** Maria

[38]   **Susie Armitage** Records

[83]   **Nic Darling** the day my grandpa didn't die

[124]   **Mehmed Begic** IDENTITY

[154]   **Summer Copeland** Western Haikus

[206]   **Joelle Hann** Gutting Trout

[211]   Contributors

the universe demands it: more DUCTS!

Why Ducts?

I'm glad you asked that question. Lets begin with an anecdote: Ducts Co-founder Philip Shane and I were walking down 10th Avenue in New York City one spring day, discussing the meaning of life, gorging ourselves on ice-cream bars and trying to come up with a good and proper title for our new online magazine. I suggested, "The People's Court," but Phil told me that it had already been taken.

Then Phil said, "The title should suggest that this is a way for people to connect to the world."

"Yes," I agreed. "And more than that, it should suggest that this is a way for Us (and I capitalized that word) to reach out to the masses."

"It's about connections," Phil said.

"Connections that make sense of the world," I said, but then added, "Or non-sense."

Then, suddenly, my cookie dough vanilla ice cream bar fell off its stick onto the sidewalk. I bent to pick it up, but stopped when I saw what was in front of me. Phil stopped as well.

A long, tubular duct ran up the side of a warehouse, took a sharp left turn, and then ran into an adjacent building, a nightclub. How absurd, we both thought. And what a wonderful metaphor for the strange, funny, sad, exciting, tragic and clever ways that human beings connect to one another.

"Perfect," I said.

"Yes, perfect," Phil said. Just then Phil's peanut butter/chocolate ice cream bar fell to the pavement.

We spent the next hour or so watching birds eat ice cream off the pavement and discussing what sort of material we would offer you (we discussed it, not the birds). After much debate, we decided that Ducts would be a free online gallery focusing on the art of personal narrative. But, we knew, personal stories take many forms. Thus, we divided our literary journal into multiple "ducts," although we hoped our writers would often blur the line between one category and another. We wanted to be subversive, when it was called for. And versive when that was called for. If anything, Ducts would be about point of view. It would be a diverse collection of personal opinions and ideas.

Ducts has changed a great deal since that fateful spring in 1999. At the time we thought it would simply be an interesting side project, something to take our mind off the numbingly bad New York winters. Of course, we believed there was a need for a quality online magazine, but we really had no idea: writers and artists, professionals and amateurs, immediately embraced us. And to my surprise, so did an ever growing, dedicated audience. There was and is, it seems, a tremendous need for a venue like Ducts. Corporations grow larger, more powerful, buying up music companies, book publishers, television stations, making it more difficult than ever for the average Joe and Jane to find that unique sound in the universe: a well-written, personal story.

Today Ducts fills a unique and highly necessary niche in the literary community. Look around and you won't find that many magazines, online or otherwise, devoted to personal narrative. The exceptional staff at Ducts.org unearths the very best personal essays, memoir, fiction, art and more to create a beautifully designed home for both established writers and emerging talent.

Our first issue had fewer than ten contributors. Our summer, 2004 issue had over forty-five. Our reading series is going on its sixth season. We've incorporated and launched our first writing contest. After five years of an increasing demand for more Ducts, we finally began to see that our little side project was here to stay and that it was time to put something a little more solid into the world. Thus, this book. We hope you enjoy it half as much as we enjoyed creating it for you.

--Jonathan Kravetz, Editor-in-Chief, Ducts.org

JONATHAN KRAVETZ
OPIATE
jesus visits midtown

Conyers, Georgia (CNN)--*An estimated 100,000 pilgrims crowded onto a Georgia farm Tuesday to hear what they believed would be a final message from the Virgin Mary, delivered by a woman who claims to have received hundreds of such visions. Nancy Fowler, 47, has attracted huge crowds since she said the Virgin Mary told her to buy a farm in 1990 and pass on her messages to the faithful.*

Personal journal: Jeffrey Carlson.

Thursday
Arrive home from work. Turn on television and drink Budweiser. Watch Derek Jeter hit a triple. Hear a soft buzzing sound that grows louder. It's Jesus. He is hovering over the television. I lean closer to understand what he is saying. But he is only making a soft buzzing sound. Assume this is his way of telling me to stop leaning so close. Finish Bud and watch Jeter boot routine ground ball.

Friday
Jesus follows me to work. My boss asks me to stop making that annoying buzzing sound. I tell him it's Jesus. He calls me a liar and fires me. I leave building with cardboard box containing three years worth of junk. Jesus steals a pen from supply room. I get mugged on the subway. Suddenly, I have a revelation: Jesus wants me to preach his gospel. I get an idea for my first sermon. Jesus loans me his pen.

Saturday
Jesus and I attend aerobics class at the local YMCA. Jesus bags it after ten minutes and goes out for a smoke. Later, I call Channel 7 News. Bill Beutel takes my statement. We have to pray more and dedicate ourselves to God, I say. And we should all wear brightly colored underwear. Nothing else. It's the real thing, Bill declares. Jesus flies around the room making helicopter sounds with his mouth.

Sunday
Jesus gets up early for church. Go without me, I say from bed. Bill Beutel and a film crew arrive at 10 a.m. I stand on my front stoop and describe the miracle. How do we know it's really Jesus? Bill says all of his viewers want to know. I describe the helicopter sounds and Bill nods gravely. Jesus buzzes in after church and turns on the television. We watch Bill's interview of me on

the 6 o'clock news. Jesus laughs because I forgot to comb my hair. "At least you remembered your pink undies," he remarks. Mayor Giuliani promises to keep the streets "Jesus free" and posts twenty-six policeman outside my apartment building.

Monday

A large crowd of religious zealots assemble outside my apartment. When I exit to begin hunting for a new job, the people cheer and three 14 year old girls pass out. I deliver my sermon. A young man points to a puffy cloud above and yells, "It's Jesus!" Jesus looks up and is more puzzled than anyone. "That doesn't look anything like me," he says. The Mayor schedules a parade for Jesus and me. No one wants the gays, particularly Jesus, but I say, "what the hell," and the city council reluctantly caves in.

Tuesday

I interview at an employment agency for a secretarial position, but my typing is too slow. "And you'll need some more clothes," the woman says. Jesus gets a job working at a law firm in mid-town, $18 an hour, but we decide he should march in the parade instead. I ride on the first float. I wave to the thousands and thousands of people gathered along Fifth Avenue who wave and scream my name. Most wear yellow underwear. Jesus sulks. He is upset that he is relegated to the ninth float (after the Dallas Cowboy cheerleaders). Later, at home, we share an order of moo shu chicken and swap family stories. His are much, much longer.

Wednesday

Calvin Klein offers me a job pitching brightly colored underwear. Martin Scorsese wants to make a movie about me, but Jesus and Martin come to blows during our production meeting. The deal falls through and Martin cites, "religious differences" as his reason. I am awarded the Nobel Prize and the Pulitzer ("just in case"). I go home after hawking orange boxer shorts on the David Letterman Show. I turn on the television and drink a Budweiser. I watch Derek Jeter hit a triple. Jesus elbows me in the ribs. "His bat is corked," he says. I ask who corked it and Jesus smiles. "George Steinbrenner. Who else?" I shake my head. Damn Yankees.

BILL BILODEAU
IT'S ALL IN THEIR HEADS
our intrepid columnist surveys the political landscape
from an (ahem) unique perspective

Let me just say this, right off the bat: Size matters.

I'm speaking, of course, about politics. It's true. There have been studies that show the tallest candidate in a race has the best chance of victory, and I can tell you from first-hand experience that in newsrooms across the country, journalists--those paragons of virtue and intellect who largely dictate the issues (healthcare) and positions (squatting) that shape the political landscape of our fair nation--are laughing themselves silly every time they even think of the phrase "President Gary Bauer."

It's not because he's not intelligent; he surely is. It's not because his views on how Americans should live their lives are slightly to the right of Benito Mussolini's; they are, but lots of people think that way. More than anything, it's because he's vertically challenged, inauspiciously heightened, the runt of the presidential litter. There hasn't been a successful politician who was really short since the mayor of Munchkinland (and he only got elected through the support of the Lollipop Guild).

Think about it. What kept Michael Dukakis out of the White House? Not Willie Horton. Not Kitty's drinking or the fact that he had what would have been the funniest-sounding name for a president since, um, well, you get the idea. No, it was the Dudley Moore factor. It was the goofy picture of Dukakis, wearing a helmet, peering out the turret of a U.S. Army tank, looking like Dudley Moore or a little kid trying on his dad's hat.

Now, Ted Kennedy, another Massachusetts would-be president once upon a time, who also had an alcoholic wife, would have done fine in the helmet and tank. Why? Because his head is HUGE! He has enough head for two people. He looks like a Saturday-morning cartoon of a famous adult—adult head on a tiny child's body.

I saw Kennedy at a political breakfast (scrambled eggs, bacon, broiled red potatoes, coffee) about eight years ago. He's not particularly tall, although tall enough. His aides, of course, were very large, and it was hard to see him at first. Then the group parted, and this enormous gray-haired head popped out and started speaking in that caricature of a New England accent.

I realized then that his head made him seem larger than life, more impressive than those around him. I think this makes a difference.

Now, of course, we are once again in the grip, or maybe the throes, of political fever. This fever, or fervor, has swept the nation over the past two months. At least, it's swept New Hampshire, Iowa, and a few other states that have already held their primaries and/or caucuses. Anyway, this heightened political season has given me an opportunity shared by very few of my fellow Americans: the chance to share a restroom with possibly the next leader of the free world.

It's true. My latest political brush with fame came on the job, where I am an editor at a small daily newspaper in New Hampshire. Although it had nothing to do with my wanting to be here, I'm told working in such a place is something almost all serious journalists envy for exactly this reason—potentially standing shoulder to shoulder (or, more accurately in my case, shoulder to elbow) with the likes of Bill Bradley.

During their New Hampshire primary campaigns, I met with Bradley, Al Gore and John McCain, who all visited our paper to get their positions across to our readers. Bradley was, by far, the most impressive. Being an ex-college and professional basketball player, he was also the tallest. During his visit, he spoke at length in our conference room. Afterward, I visited our smallish men's room, only to find Bradley taking up most of it (pit stops are sometimes few and far between on the campaign trail). If you think he looms large during TV debates, you really must see him in a tiny bathroom.

Gore's visit was also impressive, but for other reasons. Because he's vice president, he's accompanied everywhere he goes by bomb-sniffing dogs and people-sniffing Secret Service agents. When he visited, he took the time to shake hands with virtually everyone in the building, which was very friendly and warm. He changed from his business suit to casual clothes in one of our interview rooms (okay, our only interview room), which had been co-opted by his people the day before. They put in a new phone line that we suspect was a direct line to the White House (although at an early-morning meeting in the room that day, none of us had the balls to call. I wonder if Bill or Hillary would have answered?).

On that topic, the other great race going on now in American politics is, of course, Hillary's bid against Rudy Giuliani for a New York Senate seat. On this topic, I can only say, as someone born and bred in the shadow of Boston (we are bred to despise all things New York): Ha Ha! New Yorkers are going to be stuck with one of these losers no matter what!! This is great! I hope Hillary wins and Rudy stays as mayor and you're stuck with BOTH of them!

Besides, I think her head is bigger.

The news that Ricki Lake was at work on her first novel, tentatively titled SOPHIE'S REVENGE, called to mind an obvious question: would this sudden literary turn affect her afternoon talk show? So I tuned in last week, and there, sure enough, sat the four principal characters of Emily Bronte's 1847 classic WUTHERING HEIGHTS. Dressed in period attire, they were seated in canvas-backed chairs lined up across the stage: Isabella, Heathcliff, Cathy and Edgar. Off to the side, just in view of the camera, sat a woman in a business outfit whom I did not recognize.

I hit the volume just in time to hear Edgar declare: "The man is no gentleman, Ricki. He will not bow out gracefully."

"BOW OUT GRACEFULLY!" Heathcliff shouted. "Can the earth bow out of its orbit? The morning out of its day? How, therefore, can a soul bow out of its flesh?"

"She is married to ME," Edgar shouted back. "You abandoned her!"

Heathcliff narrowed his eyes. "I was with her always."

"He was, Edgar," Cathy said, emotionless. "Always."

"Even as she lay beside you, I was with her!"

Edgar rose from his chair and began to storm off stage, but Cathy caught him by the arm. "Oh do sit down, Edgar!"

"I didn't come to be subjected to such . . . insinuations. I won't abide them."

"Let the poor fellow leave, Cathy," Heathcliff said, his voice liquid with sarcasm. "It's all too much, I fear, for his constitution."

"No, I'll remain. I won't give you the satisfaction—"

Heathcliff and Cathy erupted, simultaneously, with laughter.

Ricki, at this point, joined the conversation. "Now let me make sure I've got this straight. Heathcliff was Cathy's first love, but then, POOF, he just disappeared for two years, out of the picture. So Cathy, thinking he's gone forever, married Edgar. But then Heathcliff came back—and that's when things got really weird. When Heathcliff found out Cathy had married Edgar, he got back at both of them by marrying Isabella, Edgar's sister. Is that about right?"

"I shan't deny it!" Heathcliff cried.

The audience hissed at Heathcliff.

Ricki then continued. "The person I want to hear from is Isabella. You've been sitting there so quietly on the end. What do you think about all of this?"

"Please, I don't want to be here. . . . "

"Yet you agreed to come on our show," Ricki said.

"He compelled me!" Isabella pointed at Heathcliff, then, an instant later, began to sob.

Her tears elicited Heathcliff's laughter. "Do you see, all of you, the wretchedness to which I am wed?"

"Forgive me for asking this, Isabella," Ricki said, "but if you know how Heathcliff feels, why do you stay with him? Why don't you just move out?"

"Yes, Isabella," said Cathy, snidely, "why don't you JUST?"

"He would not permit it," Isabella wept. "He is not a man but a fiend—"

"What do you mean he won't permit it?" Ricki asked. "Has he threatened you?"

"His threats are his kindnesses," she replied.

"Has he physically abused you?"

"What of it?" Heathcliff snarled. "I have no pity!"

A man from the audience jumped to his feet, and Ricki thrust her microphone under his chin. "You don't ever raise your hand to a woman!"

Next came a comment from a woman several rows back. "I think Mr. Heathcliff, or whatever his name is, needs to get respect for himself. Unless you have respect for yourself, you can't respect anyone else."

"Madam, it is the WORLD I do not respect," Heathcliff stated, "How can I respect a world in which a creature such as Edgar Linton might come between Cathy and myself?"

He was answered by another woman in the audience. "All I want to say is I think you're being very judgmental, and if I were the woman on the end—Isabella— if I were you, I'd dump him in a minute."

The audience applauded the suggestion.

Ricki then turned back to the stage and gestured towards the woman off to the side, the one in the business outfit. "At this point, I'd like to introduce Dr. Allison Greenberg-Vaughn, a relationships expert. Dr. Vaughn, you've been listening to all this—I noticed you taking notes before. Can you help us straighten things out?"

Dr. Vaughn leaned forward in her chair. "I hope so, Ricki. I think it's clear there are many issues here—which is okay. Everyone has issues. However, I do have a simple question to ask. Cathy, do you love your husband?"

"Edgar has been very kind to me," she answered.

Dr. Vaughn frowned. "That's not what I asked, Cathy."

"Yes, of course I love him. He's my husband."

"And what about Heathcliff?" the doctor inquired.

Cathy's eyes suddenly welled up. "I AM Heathcliff."

"So if I hear you correctly," Dr. Vaughn said, "what you're saying is that you LOVE Edgar, but you're IN LOVE with Heathcliff. Am I right?"

"Yes, yes," Cathy sobbed. "Only don't force me to utter the words."

Dr. Vaughn paused, giving Cathy a moment to compose herself, then continued. "This situation is actually quite common, Ricki. You see, Cathy is what I call a NEED-MONSTER. She's grown accustomed to having her own needs satisfied, no matter what. It's not her fault. She wouldn't be the way she is if there weren't always people around her ready to satisfy those needs. Edgar is a good example. He's what I call a CARETAKER. He feels a need to take care of those closest to him—"

"In other words," Ricki broke in, "he's afraid to let go—afraid that if he does let go, he might be abandoned."

"Exactly," Dr. Vaughn said. "But it's important to remember that we're not here to cast blame. It's no one's fault—"

"POSH," Heathcliff sneered. "It's Cathy's fault—hers alone. Together, she and I would have braved Satan's legions. She, alone, could have sundered us. She has killed us both, though we live and breathe."

Dr. Vaughn was unfazed. "In that case, may I ask you a simple question, Heathcliff: Why do you feel this need to manipulate those around you?"

"He IS a bit of a control freak," Ricki agreed.

"Words!" he cried. "I talk to you of the death of souls, and you reply with WORDS?

It is not words that matter. It is WORMS. Do you understand me, woman?"

Now a young woman in the front row leapt up and snatched the microphone from Ricki's hand. "I just want to say that the guy in the middle, the loud guy, he's a pig, and the lady sitting right next to him, her, Cathy, she's nothing but a HO, plain and simple."

"You GO, girl!" called a woman behind her.

Heathcliff glanced from side to side. "What does she mean by HO?"

Ricki smiled mischievously. "Trust me, Heathcliff, you don't want to know."

"I insist," he said, rising ominously. "What is the woman's meaning?"

The answer came from the woman herself. "You don't scare me. It means she's a slut."

The words were no sooner spoken than Heathcliff lifted up his chair and hurled it into the audience. Three beefy security guards rushed the stage—knocking Edgar head over heels before he could get out of their way—and began to grapple with Heathcliff. It was at this point that a dog food commercial suddenly appeared on the screen, and I turned off the television.

Ryan Van Winkle | **Maria**　　　　　　　　　　　　　　　　*Poem*

The Heineken tastes like electric tin in Scotland.

It's a brutal blow to our youth.
A kick in the nuts of our 17-year-old selves.

A blowtorch to the tits of every
cavalry ride we made to New Haven.

Spanish Maria
didn't care if we were 21 or 12.

Mom's green Taurus parked in the ghetto.
The MGD and Heineken in her trunk.

We'd fly out of the urban degradation like
*　heroes.*
We rescued the beer and were bringing it to the
*　'burbs.*

It was going to have a better life.

We drank some on the bridge towards home.
*　Tossed*
the empties on Scabby Maggie's lawn, howled
*　all nights*
loving those green necks.

And here this beer tastes like shit.

And this is why I drink beer:
because the memory of you, Pete,

your hand on the tape deck and
Clark's head out the window tossing his bottle,

Paul tearing up the mail in the back seat
and me wondering if the folks will notice the
*　dent.*

I drink for the memories.
I drink this shit beer because it's cheap here.

The copper penny taste is a wolf fang straight
*　through the heart*
of our only great love,

Maria.

GIDEON EVANS
EXPLAINING ENRON AS A SPORTS METAPHOR
if those guys in the Bronx...

While everyone is up in arms about the Enron debacle, many Americans are having trouble understanding the complicated details of what happened. Therefore, as a service to the "layperson," I am going to explain the Enron situation as a sports metaphor. I like sports a lot, and I find that using sports terms to represent other things helps make things easier to understand. I hope this clears things up.

Okay, let's say Enron is the New York Yankees...

So the New York Yankees started in Houston from the merger of two pipeline companies in 1985. It quickly become a profitable company, however, as competition grew, the Yankees started to get into other areas of business, including energy trading, broadband, metals, and steel, as well as advertising time and space. There were various problems with some of the Yankees' foreign projects, like its 1998 investment in a British waterservices business, and its 65% stake in the $3 billion Dabhol power plant in India. Financial problems arose, so the Yankees hired Andrew Fastow, a financial Wizard at leveraged buyouts, who along with former CEO Jeffrey Skilling allegedly created partnerships with names like Jedi and Chewco, where The Yankees' debt was hidden. Liquidity was also an issue since much of the money that changed hands among companies and employees was in stock options rather than hard currency.

Because of the murkiness of all these dealings, nobody outside of the Yankees knew that they were losing money, and brokers and business writers continued to recommend Yankees' stock. As a result, the Yankees' stock was up 87% in 2000. The company was rated sixth worldwide, and yet it was actually failing miserably. To compound matters, accountant Arthur Anderson, whose independence is questioned since it is employed by the Yankees and paid millions of dollars by the Yankees, never accounted for any of the debt that actually existed.

In the midst of all this confusion, the Yankees top brass, namely Fastow, Skilling, and Lay, began to cash out on their stock options while they prevented employees from cashing out on their own retirement plans. Therefore, many of the Yankees employees in Houston and around the world could only sit by and watch as the 401k plans that they worked for years to establish lost all of their value. The Yankees finally declared bankruptcy in December, laid off many employees, and are now embroiled in numerous hearings in Congress and governmental regulatory bodies. With the exception of former CEO Jeffrey Skilling, most of the witnesses are "taking the Fifth" and not testifying. Now, the questions are, "Who among the Yankees knew what and when?" and "Will any of the Yankee top executives go to jail?", and "How can another Yankees be avoided?"

KATHLEEN BOLAND
MY SINISTER NEIGHBOR'S JOURNAL
keeping it loud

Dear Journal,

I did not smoke enough cigarettes in front of skinny neighbor girl's apartment door today. I run out after smoking second pack. I ask wife Yetna to go buy more. Yetna shouts at me. She tells me to go [Russian Expletive] myself.

I wait and wait for Yetna to break down and buy cigarettes. Finally at 1:00 pm I am climbing walls. I walk to 7-11 and buy cigarettes. I will not share them with Yetna. I come back to apartment building and smoke three cigarettes in front of skinny neighbor girl's apartment door.

At 3:00 pm my cell phone rings. It is Pavel. I do not want Yetna to hear my conversation, so I go outside and talk in front of skinny neighbor girl's apartment door. Skinny girl does not speak Russian, so I am safe. I light up cigarette.

I yell at Pavel for calling me on cell phone. Anyone can trace call. Pavel yells back and calls me a bald [Russian Expletive.] He tells me to meet him at Long Beach Pier tomorrow at midnight. He wants me to bring trash bags and a saw. I yell at him again. How can he be so stupid to ask me this on cell phone? Anyone can be listening!

In rage, I pound fist on skinny neighbor girl's apartment door. Skinny girl opens it and glares at me like scared, angry deer. She needs to gain 20 pounds. She looks like skeleton.

At 5:00 pm I find Yetna standing outside wearing fuzzy pink bathrobe. She is smoking cigarette. I ask her where she gets cigarette and she tells me to go [Russian Expletive] myself with a [Russian Expletive.] I want to hit her, but I yell at her for 40 minutes instead.

If I hit her, police might come and find human fingers stored in freezer.
-T.

ROSS KLAVAN
DAVY, DAVY CROCKETT, KING OF THE FAR OUT, GROOVY, WILD FRONTIER
how davy crockett formed the counter-culture of the 1960s

"The West is the best." *Jim Morrison*

As a fledgling historian, I've been plagiarizing some very interesting work lately on the origins of that bizarre and elusive national psychosis known historically as "The '60s." Much has been written. Even more has been televised. Some evidence resides in the recorded annals of radio and some is still on 8mm film waiting to be developed. Among the causes suggested for this national and personal turmoil: a downward shift in demographics combined with an upward shift in the economic cycle, the pill, drugs, anything that happens on the pill or on drugs, the war in Vietnam, Las Vegas architecture, the writings of Herbert Marcuse and Norman O. Brown, and a delayed celebration for the end of World War II.

No one, however, except for Bleatman and Himmler (1999)—from whom I cribbed this report—has stumbled upon this central fact: the generation that participated in the social, cultural, political, psychological and emotional uprising commonly known as "The '60s" was influenced in early childhood by the national mania over Walt Disney's "Davy Crockett." This phenomenon had deep and long lasting unconscious effects.

According to "The Davy Crockett Craze," by Paul F. Anderson (R&G Productions, 1996) the nation's mania over the then all but forgotten buckskin clad, coonskin clad, moccasin clad mensch (marvelously portrayed by Fess Parker) began the week of December 16-22, 1954, just days after ABC broadcast episode one, "Davy Crockett, Indian Fighter." The continuation of this epic saga came in January of 1955 with the politically sensitive, "Crockett Goes To Congress" and the following February with "Crockett at the Alamo." Hunger for Crockettania, was sudden and almost as voracious as the nineteenth century hunger to steal any land then occupied by non-whites. Anderson writes that the craze ultimately meant sales of $300,000,000 in Davy stuff or over $1.8 billion in 1996 dollars or as Crockett might have said, "Many pelts." It was oddly brief, however. According to Anderson, the love of things Crockettish lasted only about a year with some residual effects into 1957. Disney himself is quoted as saying he was taken by surprise at the uproar. Had he foreseen it, Disney said, he wouldn't have killed off his hero in episode three. The entire series, writes Anderson was re-broadcast later in 1955 to make the most of the sudden euphoria and then two more episodes were added, broadcast in 1955 and early 1956. Naturally, massive plans were undertaken to extend the Crockett story, but soon the craze cooled and Parker was hustled off to be utilized in Disney feature films.

During those Davy days, the Crockett character was viewed as exemplifying all that was good about wholesome, solid, mainstream American values, including the fact that he'd helped cause several million Latinos to ask, "Hey, who stole northern Mexico?"

Disney was known as an active Conservative who wanted to promote a marketable and mesmerizing American hero. When a Crockett backlash began—Crockett's real story bursting into public awareness with a Clinton-Lewinski lewdness—no less than arch-conservative William F. Buckley railed that the debunking campaign was partly due to "resentment by liberal publicists of Davy's neurosis-free approach to life," (quoted in Anderson.)

Yet, years later, as the children of Crockettaria came of age, it seems Crockett's values fueled not the crumbling edifice of the conservative mainstream, but the burgeoning counter-culture which had unconsciously adopted Davy's values, haircut and mode of dress. As Freud wrote to Jung in 1928: "If there's ever such a thing as television, don't watch too much and don't sit too close."

First, Crockett's physical presence. As stated in Bleatman and Himmler (1999), "Only an idiot could miss the similarities between Davy Crockett's clothes and those of various counter-culture sects such as hippies, yippies and diggers. Long hair, fringed jackets, wide belt buckles and moccasins. It's as pronounced as Paladin's influence on current New York fashion."

But the influence doesn't end there. A careful analysis of the three Davy Crockett episodes reveals actions and dialogue that had the unintended effect of driving millions of young people wild in the streets, forcing an overhaul of contemporary America. Crockett's most famous historically verified quote echoes through the '60s and even up to the more recent era of post-modern commodification. Said Davy: "Be always sure you're right, then go ahead." Had he bypassed the Alamo and thus lived until 1968, Crockett might just as well have stated: "Dig your head, do your thing, be your thing," as did Abbie Hoffman or the more abbreviated, "Do it," in the words of Jerry Rubin (later to be bastardized into "Just do it," in the name of Nike.) Likewise, the popularity of the guitar—which was later to make such a strong impression on a bewildered generation—is foreshadowed by Crockett's sidekick, Georgie Russell (played to a toady T by Buddy Ebsen).

Throughout the series, Georgie follows Davy on horseback literally narrating Crockett's every move with a new verse of "Davy Crockett, King of the Wild Frontier." Davy rides his horse and hears Georgie sing behind him, "Davy rode a horse." Then Davy crosses a stream and hears behind him, "Davy crossed a stream." Then Davy shoots his gun and hears behind him, "Davy shot his gun," all to the ballad's well-known, hypnotic tune. This clearly speaks to the importance of music during the period known irritatingly as "The 60's," but one wonders when Crockett will turn in his saddle and say, "Hey, Georgie. Why the hell don't you SHUT UP!" In fact, quoting a verse of the Davy Crockett Ballad referring to the first episode, ("Davy Crockett, Indian Fighter,") the song itself proclaims an outlook that would make its way more than 130 years into the uncertain future:

> "He give his word and he give his hand
> That his Injun friends could keep their land
> And the rest of his life he took the stand
> That justice was do every Redskin band."

If we quickly but gingerly skip over the ugly, hateful, disgusting, paternalistic and patriarchic racist references to Native Americans, this beautiful acceptance of "Indian" culture was to become an important part of the decade known increasingly as "The '60s." So was resistance to authority. This is a mainstay of Crockett's outlook as (again, episode one) he refuses to bow to the crushing power of the U.S. Army, following only his own creed and what is good for the welfare of his men. Interestingly, the Army itself is pictured as a top-heavy, clanking, stupefying formal military organization which is no match for the wily, guerrilla fighting Creek Indians. American soldiers can only avoid ambush in the jungles of Tennessee if helped by Crockett, a man of the woods. As Bleatman and Himmler write (1999) "Only an idiot would miss that obvious critique."

This strong theme of rebellion against authority includes not only the Army but extends to the political establishment, as well. In episode two ("Crockett Goes To Congress") the Davy-depiction is of a man who:

> "Went off to Washington and served a spell,
> Fixing up the government and laws as well.
> Took over Washington so I hear tell,
> And patched up the crack in the Liberty Bell."

This approach, including the mention of Crockett's revolutionary leanings ("took over Washington") mark a clear connection between the latter day counter-culture and what obsessed young minds watching TV in the '50s regardless of the intended purpose. Crockett's presence in Congress is marked by humor, drinking and a decided lack of "speechifying," a stated refusal to dress properly, a distrust of campaign promises as well as a stated fight for the small farmer (read "commune.") In his introductory speech to Congress, Crockett asks that whiskey be allowed in the congressional chamber and states that his father is the toughest man alive "and I can lick my father," a clear pointing towards the Oedipal conflict which so marked the period known by some as "The '60s."

Also in Washington, Crockett criticizes President Jackson face-to-face, then meets up again with his former military commander, Tobias Norton who is presented as so much the martinet it's as if he sat down naked on a long steel rod. Both Norton and Jackson double-cross Crockett attempting to secretly pass a bill that will rob land from the Indians. Learning of this government deception, Crockett shouts at Norton, "Here's what I think of your kind of politics!" then punches him as the uptight Norton goes careening floorward. Next, during an impassioned plea to Congress, Crockett demands that Washington hold sacred its promise to the Indians and blames himself and his political colleagues for letting the bill get so far. "We all have a responsibility to this strappin', fun-lovin', britches-bustin', young bar cub of a country," declares Davy. This speech might just as well have come out of "Revolution For The Hell Of It."

Finally, searching for a peaceful plot of land, "the man who don't know fear" wanders to Texas and ends up buying the farm at the Alamo. This final episode is largely a battle scene, the Alamo situation depicted in mythic manner as the brave fight of a small band of heroes against an overwhelmingly large and evil force. On the way to the fight, Crockett makes a nearly Kerouacian statement about his nomadic ways saying, "A man keeps moving around his whole life looking for his particular paradise." And the night before he goes to Crockett Heaven, swinging his rifle against his enemies, he is pictured singing a quiet ballad called "Farewell to the Mountains" in which the word "bosom" is heard as a metaphor for "soul."

According to Bleatman and Himmler (1999) "Only an idiot would miss the fact that this was the first time the word "bosom" was heard on television by an entire generation which couldn't stop snickering until it started breathing heavily over Annette Funicello." Thus, the sexual revolution. This final episode ends with a shot of Davy Crockett's Journal, the words he's written shown on screen: "March 6, 1836. Liberty and Independence Forever!"

More could be said, much, much more. And even more than that. But to go on would be to violate the backwoods brevity of Crockett himself, a man of few words who didn't learn until age 30 that the word "bar" was actually pronounced "bear." This accounted for his famous hand-to-hand match with a grizzly whom he openly claimed had stolen a very expensive jug of his best corn "likker."

And so we must end with paradox: No Crockett, no '60s. No '60s, no drug culture. No drug culture, no music (which we've been hearing now, over and over, for what? almost 40 years?) No drug culture and music, no widening of consciousness and creativity, no women's rights, no gay rights, no volunteer military, no computers, no Internet. No long hair, short skirts, or modernity.

Ergo: No Crockett, no America. We'd still be a nation of short-pants and clip-on bow ties, fighting in Vietnam.

KATHLEEN BOLAND
FROM A FORGOTTEN COUSIN
IN A DISTANT LAND
americans have it so rough

January 2

Dear Cousin,

Today I went hungry once again. There was nothing left in our cupboard but some flour that was infested with maggots. I poured it onto the counter and picked out the maggots one by one. Maggots, fleas, lice—you name it, we've got it!

After I picked out the maggots, I mixed the flour with a little water. We've had no water since the bombing, so I walked to the drainage ditch this morning to fill up some buckets. The children were so excited about the flour and water concoction. They said they loved my cooking! Unfortunately, there was not enough left over for me. I tried filling my stomach with water, but it's hard not to think about food.

To distract myself, I read that book you sent me last year from America, "The Power of Positive Thinking." I'm really feeling good right now. I hope one day the postal system in my country will be reinstated and I'll finally be able to mail these letters.

I'm so glad you fled our country and became a "career gal" in America. I hope you're doing well.

Sincerely,
Ana

January 12

Dear Cousin,

It's so very cold today. I burned our last chair in the fireplace in order to keep the children alive. Tonight I plan to burn the table. What use is it? It only reminds us of the food we do not have.

Bombs were falling all around us yesterday, so I was unable to go to the market and beg for chicken bones. I saw a cockroach scurrying across the room, and luckily I was fast enough to make a meal of it. The children were excited. You know what they say when you see a roach, "There are thousands more where that came from!"

I couldn't sleep last night so I read by the light of the burning chair. I picked up that book "Bridget Jones' Diary," that you sent me last year. It's very sad. That poor Bridget can't find a husband. I feel blessed. At least I had a husband before he was murdered by guerrilla rebels in front of his children.

Love,
Ana

Jan 19th

Dear Cousin,

I'm concerned about my youngest child, Abdekar. He looks very thin. I wanted to take him to the doctor, but the doctor was murdered by guerrilla rebels in front of his grandchildren yesterday. I'd hoped he could cure Abdekar's relentless vomiting. I worry that the cockroaches we've been eating still carry poison from back in the good old days when we had poison to keep them under control.

I wish you could still send me packages the way you did before the war. We could use some nourishing food, dry clothing and of course, good books. Everything was taken from us during the siege and we don't know when or if our lives will ever get back to normal.

I finished "Bridget Jones" the other day. I was happy she finally found a man and a career that she enjoyed. I started another book by a woman named Sandra Tsing Loh who suffers from terrible bags under her eyes. I thank God every day that the undersides of my eyes are smooth and youthful. That is why my life was spared by the guerilla rebels.

Tomorrow I'll read your book, "Creating a Life Worth Living" and make a five-year plan.

Love, Ana

Feb 10

Dear Cousin,

I buried Abkebar today. The other children were abducted from me earlier in the week by rebel slave-traders. I hope they end up in a sweatshop where they'll at least be warm.

Now that it's just me in the house, I've got plenty of time for reading. Sadly, I was forced to burn the other books I read, but I saved a few to keep me occupied. As your Dr. Phil in America says, "What am I gonna do, go cry on Mama's shoulder?" That's a laugh. I have not seen my parents since they disowned me for dishonoring the family name after our elderly neighbor got drunk and made a pass at me. Time to "get real" I guess. It's just me now.

I know I'm going to be okay. I finished reading "The Seven Habits of Highly Effective People," and I've been "Sharpening the Saw," both figuratively and literally. A sharp saw will come in handy when the guerilla rebels try to attack me again.

Love, Ana

NICK BHASIN
AMSTERDAM? AMSTERDAMMITT!
getting high as a turkey on the weed smoke

I believe it was someone who once said, "Nothing gives man perspective like getting high as a turkey on the weed smoke." And so, during a two week jaunt with my brother through seven of Europe's finest cities, I visited Amsterdam, a city famous for its weed smoke. Now, anyone who's ever done drugs will tell you that, in Amsterdam, some of those drugs are legal. And anyone who's ever done anything legal will tell you that, you can't get arrested for doing it. I hoped the layover would give me enough perspective to get me through the lonely haze of desperation that I live in every day.

But it wasn't all pot and/or brownies from the start. After we landed in Paris, my brother and I never got over jet lag, probably due to some conspiracy on the part of the Parisians to be rude to us at odd hours. It was hell from there on in. We couldn't sleep at night and we could barely stay awake during the day. One night in Prague, we slept from 12 midnight to 5:30 in the evening the next day. I felt like the man in that fable, "Fable Man," who woke up after sleeping for a long time and had a great white beard and a pumpkin head! "Where's my head!? Where is my head!?!" Then he laughs and laughs.

We didn't sleep the night before in Brussels, and the train ride to Amsterdam pitted us against a pack of squealing Spaniards armed with lisps. It seemed like every word these people used had an "s" in it, because the lisping was non-stop. I could have murdered them all and felt okay about it, but finally we arrived in Amsterdam.

At our hotel, the desk clerk looked us over, making note of our brown skin and lack of a shave. I knew exactly what the bastard was thinking: "Gorgeous

Mexican razor blade models. Typical." I just hate that attitude. Look, people, I'm not a model and I'm not Mexican. All handsome people with brown skin are not Mexican models! When is the world going to learn? When are you going to learn? Jerk.

We went up to our room, which consisted of two hard, slim twin beds and a bathroom and everything else. But these beds were slim. How slim? Imagine the slimmest thing you know and multiply that by a lot more slimness. That's how slim they were. Whenever I tossed and/or turned in these slim beds, I almost fell off them. That's how slim they were! Goddammit, if I live to be 300, and I will, I'll never understand the European slim bed phenomenon. Jerk.

I don't know if it was my inability to stop thinking about bed slimness, but my brother agreed that we should split up for the evening. I was anxious to taste the perfectly legal green candy Amsterdam is famous for selling. And I wanted to smoke a lot of marijuana too. I also had my friend's novel with me to peruse. My brother, a trumpet player, wanted to take in a concert of the Amsterdam Philharmonic. He agreed to meet me at the hash bar if he couldn't get into the concert. Otherwise, we planned to meet back at the hotel.

So we parted ways. I went to a coffeeshop called The Noon, which "Let's Go Europe" described as American-owned. "Ask the owners how they got their US flag," the travel guide playfully suggested. The "Let's Go" people also made sure to caution visitors to Amsterdam to experiment with drugs in moderation. "Thanks," I thought to myself. "But no thanks." I was going to put this town out of business with all the weed I was about to smoke.

I marched into the The Noon like Russell Crowe marching into the rehab clinic, ready to teach those savages a thing or two about recreational drug abuse. I took a moment to appreciate the sweet aroma of burning marijuana, then stepped up to the counter, where I said to the Counter Man, "I'd like to see a menu." I was under the impression that the coffeeshops in Amsterdam offered extensive menus, detailing the cost and strength of different kinds of marijuana and hashish. Well the Counter Man/Licensed Dealer just giggled at me. He looked at his friends, who also started giggling. At first, I thought they were laughing at "Who's The Boss" on the TV in the corner, but I knew that would have been completely impossible.

So I laughed a little bit, then looked around awkwardly, which helped them realize that I had no idea what I was doing. Then they raised the volume on the stereo, which was playing Eminem's latest album. They started bobbing their heads, playing it very cool. Then I looked closer. Red eyes, the giggles, an over appreciation for angry American music—these people were Democrats! And they were high! I finally understood where the expression, "High as a Democrat" came from. Then I did what I always do when I meet people who play it very cool. I tried harder to fit in. I started bobbing my head to "Stan" and mouthing the words, as if to say, "Hello. Amazingly, I am also familiar with this tremendously popular song that is played on the radio over and over again. I'm just as cool and obvious as you." Then I thought, "Why would Stan [in the song] write a letter while he's driving? I don't buy it." Then I thought, "Will I seem cooler if I ask them where they got their US flag, even though I can't see it?"

More giggles.

The Counter Man brought out a huge, beautiful Ziploc bag full of marijuana. He let me smell it. Very nice.

"I'll have some of that," I said.

"A joint?" he said.

"Okay," I said.

Then he said something in English that sounded like "Seven dollars."

"I'm sorry?"

"Seven dollars," he said again, I think.

"I have to pay in dollars?"

More giggles.

"Yes," he said. "Dollars."

More giggles.

I thought, "Isn't this a different country? Don't they use different money here? Where the hell is that flag? Damn you, 'Let's Go Europe.'"

I stood there silently, waiting for this stoned Dutch wizard to make sense when a baked, balding Spaniard asked me if I spoke Spanish. Whenever people ask me that I like to play it safe. So, in Spanish, I said, "A little." When I've been out of practice, I can hold a conversation if the speed is kept low. Not that it mattered to this bastard, because he spoke as fast as he could. He talked to me for about ten minutes, asked me a few questions in super-fast Spanish. As far as I could tell, he suggested a joint mixed with tobacco, as the marijuana by itself was very strong. I was insulted, but I was also tired of standing and not smoking marijuana. So I paid for the mixed joint and a Coca Cola Light (it's a tough Marijuana Guy drink in Amsterdam) and sat down at a nice, little table with a large, frightening, stone-carved ashtray on it.

I took out my friend's novel and a red pen, and prepared to help him immeasurably with his career. I took a sip of the Coca-Cola Light, a few puffs of the joint, and started to read.

Well, friends, I hadn't slept in 32 hours or eaten in 14. Eminem was blasting and Tony Danza was saying something unfunny in Dutch when the drugs took hold.

Suddenly, the reading got a lot harder.

Then the music got a lot louder and so did the giggling. Paranoia set in, as it can when you puff the weed smoke.

"Oh, God," I thought. "I'm drinking a Coca-Cola Light. It's even wussier than Diet Coke! My legs are crossed funny! What do I look like!?! A Democrat? Do I look like a Democrat!?!" My inner freak-out contrasted sharply with my calm exterior. Enough to make me feel like I was going completely insane. "This place is getting too small for all of us!" I said to myself, even though it was practically empty. I quickly packed up my friend's novel and my pen, put my coat on, grabbed the Coca-Cola Light, my only connection to the real world, and headed for the door. I was almost out when the Counter Man and the Spaniard offered a stoned, "Good-bye." Without stopping, I turned my body enough to give a big salute and a "Take care."

Finally, I escaped. I escaped into the fresh, cool air that was vast and endless. "Dear Jesus, I don't know where I am," I thought. Then I started to walk. All I had to do was get back to the hotel and wait out the storm. But then I remembered that I was supposed to meet my brother outside the hash bar if he didn't make it into the concert. "He's going to get there and see that I'm not there," I thought. "Then someone is going to kill him and leave his body in a tulip garden or a windmill and I'll never see him again!" I visualized meeting my parents at the airport back in the US. They see me come out alone, with extra bags. "Where's your brother?" they ask. I tell them that he's in the bathroom. They're fine with it; then they give me my entire inheritance.

Maybe I wasn't being realistic.

I was sweating now.

I got to the hotel and decided to wait for my brother outside while I read my friend's novel. But the reading problem came up again. Suddenly, the "Let's Go Europe" book was laughing at me, the wind blowing through its pages and highlighting "Be Responsible. Be Responsible. You're A Fuck-Up. Be Responsible."

I started to remember what sweet times my brother and I had as kids. We used to double up on a dirt bike and ride around at night on my grandmother's street in Puerto Rico. Once we accidentally knocked over the neighbor's garbage can and some local street toughs accosted us. My brother cursed at them and ran away, leaving me to get my ass kicked. Hmm. That wasn't so sweet. Still, if I hadn't wanted to inhale that evil plant weed smoke monster, my brother would have been alive and standing right next to me, playing his loud trumpet and cleaning the spit valve. Goddammit, shut up! Where does that spit go!?! I need to sleep! Shut up! Shut up! Oh, God, I was going insane.

And I developed the most severe case of cottonmouth I've ever had. I started to gag and headed straight for the hotel bar. I politely asked the bartender for some water. He complied. I looked at the people casually chatting. Didn't they realize that I was freaking out? Why weren't they helping? I spent what felt like four hours going to and from the bar, asking for more and more water. "What if my brother doesn't come back to the hotel?" I thought. "What if he's waiting for me outside the pot joint? Wouldn't the Counter Man tell him that I had left? No, he hates me. There was so much giggling. I can't go back there. They'll eat me alive because they probably take the munchies more seriously here!"

I went back outside the hotel and looked right and left over and over again. I thought, "I can do this for three hours, right?" Wrong again. Then I thought, "If he's dead now, and I wait three hours for him, that's three hours we could have had the police looking for his carcass. They should be combing the canals and lakes with nets. Call out an APB! How do you say that in Dutch!?! Oh, God, I'm going to die in Amsterdam looking for my brother! Why did we split up!?! Damn you, Amsterdam! Damn your fine quality marijuana and regularly tested prostitutes! I wish I'd never heard of you!" I was on the verge of tears, short of breath, light-headed, leaning against the hotel, wishing my brother would come back, hoping someone would stop and help and call the police and give me something to eat and put me to bed.

Then I had to pee. Didn't I read somewhere that a heart attack frequently starts in the bladder? Yes, definitely. I wanted to spend my last moments on Earth in the hotel room, but I didn't have the key. My bastard brother had it. So I asked the asshole behind the desk if I could have the key to my room. He gave me some bullshit about how my brother was supposed to leave it with him. "He's dead, you insensitive coward!" I wanted to say. "Who cares about your precious hotel rules! Have you forgotten that I am a Mexican razor blade model?!" Then he had the bartender get me into my room. I was scared, because I got five glasses of water out of that bastard and never gave him a tip. I got into the room, peed, and got into bed, planning to watch TV until my brother came back or the police arrived with the bad news or I slipped into permanent slumber. I started to fall asleep. "What if my brother is dead and while I'm asleep he comes back to li…"

I woke up when my brother walked into the room, happy as a gopher. He said he went to the concert, walked around, and ate twice, the glutton.

I fell back to sleep and dreamed about leaving Amsterdam on a weed smoke free flight, while my brother played taps on his trumpet. Good times.

And that's the story of the best marijuana I've ever had.

LAURA BUCHHOLTZ
HOW NOT TO GREET FAMOUS PEOPLE
our humor editor meets bill clinton (sort of)

I'm sure, when asked the question, "what famous person would you like to be able to meet–living or dead"?, someone somewhere would answer: Bill Clinton. I'm also sure that someday, someone in the future might even answer this question by saying, "I would like to meet Bill Clinton during the week the World Trade Center attack occurred." Surely this person would have many, many smart questions or things to say to the former US president. For example, some smart things to ask the president during this time might be:

1. Would resolution of the Palestinian/Israeli conflict help to reduce international terrorism?

2. How do you think the currently forming international coalition against terrorism will impact US foreign policy in the future?

3. In light of the current volatility in the Middle East, would you now support drilling for oil in the Alaskan Arctic Refuge?

I'll admit it. I had a brief, fortuitous chance to meet our former US president last week. While riding my bike up the West Side bike trail in Manhattan last week, I happened upon a heliport at which two helicopters had just landed. The scurrying and bustle surrounding the scene caught my attention and like any self-respecting hanger-on, I stopped to watch. Who are these people getting out of the choppers? Why that looks like....could it be....yes, yes it is! Rudy Giuliani and Bill Clinton! For God's sake, there are two very important and historically relevant men right in front of me! I suddenly feel a rising excitement and a vicarious connection to the world outside myself! What will happen next?!

Rudy quickly got into his car, which drove off to applause. Bill Clinton then magnanimously stepped in to greet the crowd of fifteen or twenty onlookers, including myself, who had stopped along the nearby bike path.

Here he comes. Here comes my chance. I'm going to shake the hand of the former president. What's that red thing on his nose? His eyes are steely grey slits. He's shaking children's hands. I'm lurking behind the children like a suspicious teenager who continues to trick-or-treat despite her obviously inappropriate size. What do I say? What do I do? The children scurry away, and time slows down. Clinton reaches out his hand and I extend mine, our eyes meet, my brain locks down, and I say—at this moment of immense historical significance celestial significance (as far as I'm concerned)—

Hey, how are you doing?

And he smiles and shakes my hand and says hello and moves on, and time speeds up and my face flushes and I get back on my bike and scenery flies by as I curse myself. Hey, there, Mr. Former President. Your country just suffered a brutal attack! How's it going? What's new, Mr. Former President? Oh yeah, Afghanistan has promised to launch a Jihad against us. Well, how are you? Troops are heading overseas, and at home we're finding ominous crop-dusting manuals in terrorist hideouts. Wow, Mr. President—what's up? Stupid stupid stupid.

It's not fair. I wasn't ready. I want another chance. So Mr. Clinton, as you're reading this fantastic new issue of DUCTS, just pretend that I asked you one or all of the first three questions. And the next time you're hanging out on Friendster, send me your response along with a statement of unbelievable insight and worldly wisdom. And by the way, how's it going? I'm fine.

DANIEL MCCOY
RALLY THE FLAG AROUND STUFF, BOYS
the pig in your blanket

Patriotism is the new black, and as a part of this nationwide trend, people are wrapping things in flags like never before: war heroes, government documents, and suspicious legislation are just a few of the many things to be swathed in the flag. But what can we, mere citizens, do if we wish to be a part of the Patriotti? In the interests of style and national pride we offer this handy primer for people trying to decide what *they too* might wrap in the American flag.

* Delicious chocolate candies
* Patriotic undies
* The hopes and dreams of a nation
* A short poem about water lilies--more of a haiku, really
* The single version of Harvey Danger's "Flagpole Sitta"
* Toast

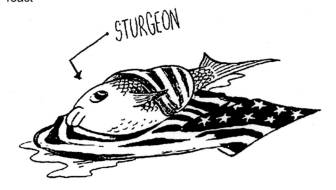

STURGEON

- John Williams
- All the small things
- Yesterday's papers
- The collected footnotes of acclaimed author David Foster Wallace
- Bits and pieces
- Dribs and drabs
- Schadenfraude
- Laura Palmer
- A very small piece of cheese, such as one might enjoy atop a cracker
- Fooseball instructions
- Sandy Duncan's glass eye
- Butter
- The "It" possessed by original "It Girl," Clara Bow
- The "It" possessed by *Rocky and Bullwinkle* star, Piper Perabo
- My appendix
- The appendix to The Riverside Shakespeare
- Limericks
- Most of half a sandwich
- 10 high-density discs
- Irony (dead)
- A Wyndham Hill sampler
- Whys and Wherefores
- Sturgeon
- Blind Pew
- The heavens' embroidered cloths/
  Enwrought with golden and silver light/
  The blue and the dim and the dark cloths/
  Of night and light and the half-light
- The last thing you said to your mother before leaving the house that fateful morning oh-so-many years ago, when it seemed as though your whole life lay ahead of you and the world was bright and new, and you needed only to dream something to make it happen, before the rains came.

Susie Armitage | **Records**

My sister lost her virginity to the White Album
and even now she thinks Bungalow Bill
is a love song. How music photographs
a moment: I was thirteen, dancing

with a boy I wanted to kiss
when Al Green told us to stay together.
For three minutes and eighteen seconds
I believed, but over the summer
he moved to Wichita. Nights, much later
I fell asleep with someone else
to Dark Side or Kid A, until that afternoon

driving home the day after he left.
Bob Dylan's It Ain't Me, Babe
was in my tape deck—maybe even worse
was the low rush of cars
going over the bridge
after I cut the sound.

CHAPTER 2: ESSAYS

ERIC GILLEN
WELCOME TO NEW YORK CITY
through a night, darkly

Last night I turned to my friend Rahul and said, "If this NYU party is lame, then we need to go somewhere different and exciting." He smirked, knowing full-well that the New York University dorm party would be one of the worst parties since the Donners got to the mountains. "Somewhere different, eh? Sure. Sure. Just put your trust in me."

"Okay, let's go to this party then."

At NYU, students can only sign in three people a night and the security keeps your ID, which means that in order to leave, the person who signs you in must sign you out. Then security must flip through a billion IDs, a complete pain in the ass. We enter the dorm on the corner of 3rd and 11th. After calling down a fleet of people to sign in four people and haggling with the NYU security to get in the building, we ascend in the elevator.

I enter the apartment first, since I know absolutely nobody and I cannot believe how packed and tiny the apartment is. I turn to Rahul and Chris and say, "Thirty minutes."

They nod.

It's like a comic book convention. These are the social dregs at the bottom of the social melting pot. Clad in a simple blue shirt, khakis and shoes I look like a god. I'm not wearing a snow-cap indoors, my pants aren't ripped, drawn-on or shredded and I have styling product in my hair. I immediately run the gauntlet down a cramped hallway for the booze, some social lubricant. The card table features a cake that someone grabbed a handful of, as opposed to the more conventional slice. The missing bit looks like a crater, making the round chocolate chip cake look like a gigantic muffin on a desk somewhere. Next to the cake is a girl who struggles to hold her eyelids open under the weight of all that eye shadow. She apparently made this cake.

"Want cake! Want cake! Have cake!"

"Uh—no thank you. Want booze. Want booze."

The spread is lackluster. Two empty bottles of Absolut, three inches of Bacardi and a nearly-depleted handle of Tanqueray. I pick the gin. For my troubles, I am given the worst gin and tonic of all time. They poured in the tonic first, had no ice cubes and then dumped in two shots of gin. It tasted like Drano and not in the good "burny down-the-hatch" way.

I sip it. And when I say sip, I mean I wet my upper lip with the foul concoction and then lick it off with my tongue. Drinking directly would've killed me.

I talk to Rahul and we decide to play a game. On the count of three we start laughing for no reason, pretending that someone said something hysterically funny.

"One. Two. Three," we whisper in unison.

Insert hysterical laughter here, followed by bewildered, longing stares.

Clearly, we are having the best time at the party. Which is pathetic, considering we were lying.

After what seems like the better part of Post-Modernism, we leave.

Rahul grins as we hail a cab.

"Division and Orchard," he tells the confused cabbie.

"Where?" a soft Pakistani voice lolls through the partition.

"Division!"

"Okay," he says unsteadily. We're about to get lost.

We get lost, zig-zagging in the broken grid of lower Manhattan. I mention that I need to hit an ATM, which elicits a collective "Fuck" from my travel partner. When the cab finally lurches to a halt on a darkened corner in the fringe of Chinatown, I understand why. It's like a ghost town there. Nothing is lit up. There's no neon. No flashing anything. No people. No cars. It's quiet and I'm not used to this quiet.

We spot a deli three blocks away. It's called "Moe's Deli." As I use the ATM, which charges the odd fee of $1.60, I giggle picturing an Asian man named Moe, who owns the only Deli still open left of 1st Avenue after midnight. Moe, you know an Asian guy named Moe.

The bar is called "The Barber Shop." Next to the deli, it too is the only thing open in and around Division Street. People are milling around beneath the awning, which is almost entirely in Chinese characters except for a rim of white English text that says "The Barber Shop."

I get carded at the door, which aggravates me since my compatriots walked in unscathed. I grab a beer. And then I see it.

There's a woman out front, clad in all black, topped by a black watch cap. Finally, I realize why people are milling around out front. She's whirling flaming disks around in the middle of the street. As in flaming oily rags on the end of chains that spin around her black body in huge quick arcs.

Like some crazed Polynesian, she is lighting up the night with fire. Only she's standing in the middle of the street, not at a beach luau. Her friends are trying to climb the light pole behind her to knock out the street lamp. They fail. She keeps whirling, taking a break, only to dip her chains back in the concoction of lighter fluid and God knows what else. Fifteen people stare, unquestioning.

Why is there a woman performing tricks with flaming oily rags on the end of spiraling metal chains in front of a bar on the edge of a vacant Chinatown street on a Thursday night at 1:36 in the morning?

Welcome to New York City.

ANONYMOUS
THE TUNNEL
a mental health worker reveals a deep secret

I pulled my blankets off in slow motion. My knees all but buckled under me as I put one foot and then the other on the floor beneath me. I dragged myself to the shower, trying without success to turn the spigot. I barely managed to put tooth paste on my tooth brush. My clothes closet loomed in front of me, one big blur. I felt like I was sinking into a deep black tunnel. I had been gradually descending into this abyss for days, but I wanted to pretend it wasn't happening.

One hanger after another was thrown on the floor or bed. What skirt matched what blouse? What dress went with what shoes? Anger rose up inside me. The greater the anger, the harder the clothes landed on the floor.

"What had I done to deserve this?"

"Why me?"

As I threw the discarded clothes on the floor or bed my husband picked them up, putting them all back in the closet. He begged me to stop.

"You have to stay home," he said. "There is no way you can function at work today... For my sake, stay home. I'll stay with you. Please..."

He didn't get it. Mental health professionals couldn't show their own weakness. We aren't supposed to have a mental illness.

Thirteen years before, I had been diagnosed with Bipolar Disorder. But in the throes of my irrational thinking that morning, I had decided my job depended on my appearance at work. I thought if I didn't show up my supervisor would discover my secret, and fire me.

My job meant everything to me. I'd decided to change professions after many years, gone to college and received a Masters in Social Work. Now I was in the last year of my training, my final field placement before graduating. In my mind, my whole career was on the line. I was afraid I would lose my identity as a professional.

I felt every bit of energy trickle through my body and out my toes. I wanted to be sensible: return to bed, survive the day. But thirteen years after my original diagnosis, the paralyzing fear that my secret would be discovered was greater than all the good sense I had that day. I imagined my coworkers, when I returned to work, pointing fingers at me, saying, "She couldn't come to work because she is one of them." I probably should have been more afraid that my illness would be obvious to my colleagues. But I was not thinking rationally. I would go to work. They wouldn't know.

Without a word to my hysterical spouse, I shuffled outside, one foot at a time, dragging myself to the car, opening the door and thinking that my husband was right. As I placed my hands on the wheel I was gripped with fear. What if I got into a car accident? Or I couldn't concentrate enough to find my way? I sat for what seemed like hours without turning the key. I cried. I wanted to feel my husband's arms around me. But the fear of being found out was still greater than rational thought. I turned the ignition and put my foot on the gas pedal.

It's still hard to know why I acted as I did. Perhaps I was trying to prove to myself I could get away with it. But I realize now that if I saw someone in my condition walking down the halls, I would know immediately that something was wrong. It was irrational of me to think I could hide my problem.

I started driving to work. I felt like someone else was in control. Soon my destination was in front of me. My legs carried me from the car to the elevator in the facility. The elevator lifted me to the third floor, the doors opened wide, my heart pounded, and my eyes filled again. I wanted to die.

It's not too late to turn around and go home, I told myself. But my legs started on their own. I found myself walking to the psychiatric ward where I was expected to be a stable, collected, clinical social worker.

With eyes lowered and a softly mumbled, "Good morning," I began the day. I pulled myself down the gray halls. Voices came to me from a distance. I heard a patient say, "Hi, can we talk?" Nodding, I automatically answered, "In a little while." I heard an authoritative voice saying someone named John was being discharged the next day. I heard orders to refer him for community resources, and to provide the family with a list of possible signs of suicidal ideation...

But would I myself live long enough to complete the task? I didn't want to. I kept thinking, "Why bother living. After all, soon my secret will be out and ruin my life." Even with all my training, I'm not sure what kept me alive that day. Somewhere in the deepest recesses of my unconscious a voice was whispering, "Keep breathing and remember your loved ones."

A fellow social worker approached. "What's wrong with you?" she said. "Your mood and affect is worse than the patients."

I was taken back by the comment. Had I been a patient on the unit I would have been asked "How are you feeling? You look rather anxious and sad. Why don't we talk for a while?" That's what and how the patients would have been asked, with sympathy and understanding. But a social worker is not allowed to get sick. I was scared and angry at them and myself. They felt I had no right to act like I did, I thought.

The gray halls became longer, fuzzier.

It's strange now to remember that the patients were coming to me with their problems. Because, on that day, I needed help too. Many questioned the sadness on my face. I was surprised to find myself feeling closer to the patients than the staff, and even found them to be more compassionate. They recognized the symptoms.

My terrible secret was out, I thought. I needed to escape from the unit. I ran to the cafeteria, going off into a corner to be rid of questions. How was I going to make it until 5:00 p.m.? Did I want to make it? Yes, I thought. My career was on the line.

After lunch, my supervisor called and requested to see me in her office. Pushing the button for the elevator, I held my breath. This was the end. I could feel it. I entered my supervisor's cold office. I faced a tall woman with a cold stare. I didn't know if I'd walk out of there with my job intact, but I was oddly relieved she was about to find out. I just hoped she'd understand.

Without a hint of concern for me, her student, she said: "Staff on the unit have complained about your performance and lack of competency today. They don't understand your change in behavior and are feeling extremely uncomfortable around you."

She then spoke the words that fulfilled my worst possible fear. "The nursing staff has told me that you are looking and sounding like the patients, and have been for the past week."

My world came tumbling down.

I knew I couldn't hold it in anymore. I decided to drop the bomb and confide my secret. My supervisor trained social work students to be empathetic, respectful and understanding. She had to understand that mental illness was not a crime. Maybe there was still hope. How could she not care about one of her own? I felt cold, like the temperature in the room was plummeting. Why couldn't I get warm? I told my supervisor everything.

The bomb exploded in my face. "Go home and call your doctor," she said.

She was openly hostile, I thought. Of course, I knew enough from all my training that my judgment might be impaired; I might not be reacting to my supervisor but, rather, to my own despair. Was her aggression real? And yet, even through the black clouds, I could sense her anger. Yes, she was hostile. It was so palpable that day that I knew it wasn't a figment of my imagination.

I shuffled out, crying. Should I take pills or cut my wrists? That's what I was thinking. The car was on automatic pilot. Somehow I made it home.

I don't remember who called the doctor, me or my husband. It would have been so easy to take my life. To live was harder.

Suddenly, I found myself in the hospital, a patient, not a clinical social worker.

I'd been placed in a hospital before, but I was an undergraduate at the time and hadn't yet worked with patients. This was my first hospital stay as a professional. It was humiliating and I tried to let everyone know I wasn't really a patient. I just needed my medicine adjusted, I told them. I knew as much as they did!

But they still treated me badly. They were condescending.

The experience changed me. I was able to think, "this is how my patients are being treated." I'd never really understood that before. I learned to question myself. Was I being as condescending as the hospital staff? Did I ever treat my patients as badly as the staff was treating me?

After that troubling week in the hospital, listening to staff members jingle their keys ready to lock a door at any moment, I was discharged. My medication had been adjusted and I felt stable.

It was time to return to work. I wondered, "Could the social worker and the patient ever become one?"

The drive to work was pleasant; the sun was bright and shining. The grass and trees were green and the flowers were beginning to bloom. Why couldn't I see those things before? I walked leisurely to work. I felt lighter. It was almost a relief that my secret was out, at least in part. My supervisor and school liaison knew, but no one else did. I decided my first stop that morning would be to greet my supervisor.

A few patients waved and smiled as I headed toward the elevator. That was a good sign. Perhaps I hadn't lost the trust of the patients and staff. Nonetheless, I was overcome with shame. Did they know I had Bipolar Disorder and where I'd been this past week?

As I walked out of the elevator and neared my supervisor's door I was overcome with that paralyzing fear again. My throat began to close. My supervisor asked me in and beckoned me to a chair.

She said, "If I had known you had Bipolar Disorder I never would have accepted you as my student for the year. Don't ever take a job in a psychiatric hospital. It is not the place for you."

For the second time, I left her office with a sinking heart and took the elevator up to the unit as I had done the week before. I was deep in thought, contemplating my supervisor's words. Maybe she was right. Maybe having Bipolar Disorder did eliminate me as a psychotherapist.

My patients welcomed me back and I didn't sense that they knew. My day was exhilarating. The halls were brighter. I saw how the patients were treated through different eyes than I had one week before; the distinction, within myself, between social worker and patient was gone.

I realized that I was not only a good clinician, but I had the advantage of wearing two hats: patient and professional. "Empathy" and "respect" are important words which are often spoken in mental health settings. But they should be reflected in actions, too.

I knew my supervisor was wrong. This was exactly the right place for me. And yet, even many years later, I continue to live in constant fear of being found out. On rare occasions, I have confided in a colleague. But I am guarded. Most colleagues would react as my supervisor did ten years ago, I fear.

The professional and patient in me are one most of the time. Years can race by without an episode. When they do recur, I find myself wondering if this will be the time that I won't be able to pull myself out of that black tunnel. And yet, sometimes I feel I am lucky to have my illness. It has made me a stronger person and provided me with courage and insight I would have never possessed. When a patient tells me they are feeling suicidal I can honestly say: "I know how much pain you must be in to want to die."

ROBERT FLANAGAN
TWENTY GUNS AND BOOZE
a visit to the louisiana state penitentiary rodeo

Two hours ago we were sitting on the elegant porch of The Columns Hotel in New Orleans desperately drinking Bloody Marys, each of us battling our demon hangovers. Now we just drove through the gates of the Louisiana State Penitentiary in Angola, Louisiana.

My girlfriend Christine softly strokes my hand and whispers words of encouragement. Our friends, Maggie and Bill, in the back seat are too quiet, probably silently concocting lies about how we picked them up hitchhiking.

The Angola Prison Rodeo is held each October at the Louisiana State Penitentiary. Christine read about it in the local newspaper. Maggie snatched the paper and read aloud, gesturing emphatically. Last night it seemed like a wonderful idea.

We bought a bottle of tequila on the road, planning in our college/sporting event type minds, a little tailgate drink before the rodeo. As we approached the prison gate, we saw a guard handing out little slips of paper. The paper listed the prohibited items we must surrender before entering the prison. Upon seeing the sign "Louisiana State Correctional Facility" and the guards, all thoughts of trying to smuggle anything in, like at a concert or ball game, vanished quickly. I slowed the car, frantically searching for an elusive nail file, scissors, aspirin or glue. Of course, the only prohibited items were firearms, alcohol and drugs, but I got this paranoid feeling that the gates would slam shut behind us and I would be suddenly confronted by the crazy crooked smiles of a dozen correctional officers.

The prohibited item in our car was the tequila, which we quickly surrendered. I fully expected it to go in the trash, but instead the guard smiled, tagged it and placed it on one of the most frightening tables imaginable.

Apparently, our fellow rodeo fans were a wild-eyed bunch. The table was covered with guns and booze; silver plated, feminine derringers sitting next to high-powered automatics. Boxes and boxes of bullets were scattered all over, interspersed with bourbon bottles.

Angola was once rated the worst prison in the United States. The prison grounds, with the exception of the phalanx of guards at the gate, are actually quite pleasant. There are no huge walls, no guard towers. It looks like a well tended farm, not a prison. The only indications of its purpose are the disciplined groups of men, marching in close formation with hoes on their shoulders.

We drive past the fields and after a mile can finally see the buildings and gleaming, polished glint of the razor wire fences. Around the rutted field where we park the car, camouflaged-dressed guards patrol on horseback, heavily armed with rifles and shotguns. The black suited guards at the gate were intimidating enough but they look like some sort of public-affairs squad compared to these horsemen.

It's oven hot when we step out of the air-conditioned car. The air is a thick heavy thing and it moves with you. The smell of farm animals mingles with the scent of cooking meat and open sewer ditches. The arena is packed, though the rodeo is just starting.

The two cinder-block bathrooms by the gate have already overflowed and are pouring out in front of the ticket booth. At the gate, the woman selling tickets is flanked on either side by two guards. I step over a wad of toilet paper, mashed with a boot print, and wince slightly when I see the guards looking at me.

They approach quickly, snatch Christine's camera bag without a word, and search it thoroughly.

I recall seeing a rodeo on Wide World of Sports or ESPN or something. Then again, I also recall watching The Best Lumberjack Competition. Since I would not understand Lumber-Jacking, I don't know why I expect to understand this.

It appears they are all riding bulls and horses. Apparently the goal is to stay on the animal as long as possible. Seems simple enough in theory, but almost all of the inmates are thrown off in the first second and then get stomped. This elicits great squeals of delight from the small children next to us. Several inmates try to scramble off their animals before they get out of the gate. All around us the more knowledgeable parents are busily trying to explain these rodeo nuances to their kids while the men are getting smashed.

"Gotta move with the bull, be the bull, not fight it," one says.

Be the bull? This kid is four years old. The bull's scrotum is like two cantaloupes in a stocking.

These first few events seem prolonged, painful to watch and violent. The inmates, torn, bloody and holding their ribs, move with glazed looks from one fiasco to the next. They don't look like I remember from TV. Those swaggering, cocky cowboys, and frantic, talented clowns. No one seemed to be getting hurt on TV. No one bled.

"Shouldn't they be...um...better at this?" I ask Christine. She is alternately glaring at a grease smear on her sleeve and a leathery woman next to her who is eating fried dough and smoking.

"I want a divorce." She growls.

"Baby...we're not married." I stammer.

"I'm practicing." I have heard four different women say that since we got here. It's like a mantra. That and 'suck it.' I've heard at least a dozen children yell 'suck it' in the past half hour.

Bill and Maggie are sitting in front of us. They are readers, the type of people who get a new piece of equipment, TV, VCR, whatever and it sits in the box for at least a day while they studiously pick apart the instructions. Not me. I tear the thing out and break every rule of fragile equipment, shoving in plugs where it looks like they go, forcing pieces when they don't move. I don't even open the book until something starts smoking.

They are reading the rodeo program I didn't know existed.

Confused, I lean down and ask Bill. "Is this what it is supposed to be like? They all look really hurt."

"They're supposed to get hurt. Apparently that is the shtick. It says in the program that none of these guys know how to ride horses. That's why everyone comes here."

"They know how to rape though, don't they." Maggie says. She has been saying this since we arrived, convinced all the inmates are in here for rape.

"I think...um...some of them might be in here for drugs Maggie. Or, you know, like... assault?" I say.

"Don't kid yourself, wiseass."

We have only been here for a few hours but already the mood of our group is getting black. Yesterday, during cocktails on the porch we were different.

"Guys. Do you want to go? I think...um...I would really like to leave." I say. Bill's eyes show definite relief, but Maggie grabs his arm roughly.

Next to me Christine is on the edge of her seat. She turns slowly and stares at me. The big event of the rodeo is starting.

"No." Maggie says softly.

In the last event a red poker chip is taped between the horns of a bull. The bull is then whipped into a frenzy and turned out in the ring. Ten convicts try to snatch the poker chip. The winner gets 100 dollars. I mentally evaluate my checking account and consider offering all ten of them 100 dollars each to limp back to their cells.

The bull charges out and goes for the closest man, flipping him over the wall in two seconds flat. The remaining nine fan out around the bull and begin making dashes in toward the horns. No one even gets close. The bull charges left and right just nicking inmates who go shooting off into the dirt.

Two men go in from opposite sides, one taking a horn in the stomach, the other, the one with the shaved head, is blasted backward by the bull's shoulder, his right leg folding under his body at a sickening angle. The remaining inmates scatter and the bull turns slowly.

The man with the shaved head's leg is obviously broken as he stands, wobbling on the other. There is no one within twenty feet of him. The crowd around us makes a collective and surprising sound, not bloodthirsty cries or vindictive howls from before, but a low groan of compassion and sickened realization.

The bull has plenty of room for a running start and the man's sad, pathetic hopping still leaves a virtually unmoving target. His right leg is twisted, dragging, foot turned outward in the dust. He is looking over his shoulder. I can see his face, even from way up here. There is no more false bravado, no more posing for his fellow convicts. His face is terror and bewilderment.

He is hit squarely from behind and folds backwards over the bull's head, then shoots straight up, limbs flapping like they are barely connected, and the bull is on him before he hits the ground. Through the cloud of dust his body twists and whips back and forth in the slashing horns and hooves.

A few inmates try to distract the bull, no funny clowns and no guards. No one on a horse rides up to stop this.

He is pushed violently through the dirt towards the wall, lifted into the air repeatedly, his body totally limp, flopping like a rag doll. Back down, pushed through the dirt some more. In the air again he hits the wooden wall with a dull thump and the bull's horns thrash at his unmoving body until finally some unseen hands pull him underneath the boards.

Somewhere on a microphone, the warden is calling an end to the rodeo.

Walking back to the car I ask Christine softly if she will drive home.

"Suck it." She says.

We inch slowly, silently through the gate, leaving the tequila behind.

HELEN ZELON
SNOW IN SUMMER
peace, war, snow, new york and the inexplicable past explained
Snow in Summer was later published in Ms. Magazine, *Spring 2003*

My family landed in a spanking-new stucco bungalow in Holly Park Homes, in Gardena, California, after the construction of the San Diego Freeway leveled our first house. Our new house had been built along with hundreds of close cousins, all promptly sold off to a generation of young families striving to inhabit the American Dream—three bedrooms, two baths, eat-in kitchen, two-car garage. Block after block, laid out on a grid as predictable and contained as the houses themselves. Controlling the interior environment, the terrain of memory and emotion, was the peculiar art my parents sought to refine every day.

Banked by the commercial avenues Van Ness and Rosecrans and the abyss-like 135th Street drainage ditch and sandy Rowley Park, the Holly Park kids biked, skated and ran, stripping hydrangea bushes for pretend-bride bouquets and cycling the endless loop of Ardath, 141st Street, Daphne, 139th Street as summer mornings stretched past noon into lazy, hot, white-sky afternoons.

The summer I turned eight my mother returned to full-time work and my life took on an air of autonomy. Our babysitter, Mrs. Mozell Rollins, an Ozark Baptist quilter, was so besotted with my toddler sister—she of the long ringlets and liquid eyes, the spider-web eyelashes and sweet baby scents—that I had comparatively free rein. Her benevolent indifference was my opportunity for adventure.

Summer afternoons, I hopped on my bike and rode the three-quarter miles to Purche Avenue School, where Mrs. Owens, the school librarian, waited—for me alone, I knew it. Her first name was Charlotte. Charlotte, my mother's name! Her newest name, that is, after her birth name Tsirla and her nickname Cesia, which became Czeslawa when she went underground on Aryan papers, in Warsaw, in 1941. Now her friends and my father called her Cesia again, but at work, where my parents strove to keep the facts of their lives a secret, she was Charlotte. That she shared the librarian's name was an omen to me; Mrs. Owens stood in for the grandmothers whose faces I had never seen.

Every weekday was the same: Ride to school, get a book. Read the book overnight, go back. Biographies, novels, mysteries, series--I ate the Bobbsey Twins and Nancy Drew for breakfast. Fridays were the best, because I could keep the book until Monday, and because Mrs. Owens often had something special put aside for me. One Friday in July, she gave me "A Cricket in Times Square," and my life changed forever.

New York! Lively, loud, vibrating city! People from all kinds of different places, with faraway names and strange accents confusing their speech. California was sameness to me, even then, and I did not fit in. My friends were blonde and fair,

I am dark. They had patent-leather cases filled with blonde Barbies and red-headed Midges; my Auntie Celia gave me my brown-eyed, black-haired Barbie, a mini-misfit among her 11-inch peers. All my girlfriends had -ee names—Vicky, Kathy, Debbie, Ruthie, Randi—and I was stuck in the old world, with a name for aunties and old maids. My sister lucked out: she was named Edith, but became Edie (that -ee ending!) right away. Me, I am Helen, named for my grandmother, named for a dark and foreign place, for a time lost to fire and history.

Our neighbors bought their houses with GI loans. The fathers had gone to college on GI bills. Mothers stayed home, or worked as school aides or secretaries while Grandmas baked cookies and marshmallow treats. My parents were in the war, too, but not as soldiers. Now, they were American. They were engineers. Their work was rocketry and war planes; they knew top secrets and wouldn't tell, even when I begged to know just one tiny confidence. The friends that they played poker with on Saturday nights had numbers tattooed on their arms. Nobody, but nobody, knew from marshmallow treats.

If the land of the Beach Boys and eternal summer was not for me, I decided, I was not for it either. In New York, my book promised, you could be different—dark, foreign. I realized I had been born in the wrong place, a tragic error in my parents' epic saga of war, survival, immigration and resettlement. The phoenix had risen from the ashes, yes, but had wound up on the wrong coast altogether. I was a New Yorker meant to be. I was eight, and I was moving East, as soon as I could manage it.

It snowed in New York, it said so in my book. Great white blizzards of snow, banking up on the streets, going gray with street grit, drifting into the ravines of Central Park. It confettied down the subway grates, and newsstand vendors had to bundle against the cold, damp white. It said so in the book.

On Monday, I rode to the library as usual, but didn't check out a new book. Instead, I renewed "Cricket," and read it through again, looking for a secret recipe for snow, a hint, any clue. At night, I punched my pillow up to make a bolster while I read. A tiny white down-feather pricked my cheek through the cotton ticking. I pulled it out, puffed it off my fingertip with an easy pah! of breath and watched it drift and settle onto my lavender bedspread. It lay there, balanced on a tuft of chenille, and the thought exploded in my 8-year-old brain. I had my plan.

The next morning, as usual, my father rose before the sunrise, with ample time for his habitual meticulous toilette—shaving three times with a clean razor blade, twice against the grain of his beard and once, with it. Cleanliness was how he survived the camps, he said. He respected himself more than the others, and it showed. A fine appearance remained a principal talisman for success in his new country, where he could once again afford worsted wool suits and leather shoes with laces. His rinsed-clean shaving brush stood on the porcelain rim of the bathroom sink as my mother began her own catechism, of cosmetics and perfumes, that allowed her to present her professional self to the world.

Max Factor pancake makeup and rosy creme blush, light-blue powder eyeshadow, Maybelline pencil eyeliner, then mascara. Bouffant beauty-parlor hair tamed into a buoyant flip by a shower of Aqua Net hairspray. A burst of Chanel No. 5—my mother's homage to her idol, Marie Curie—and Revlon's Love That Red lipstick finished her face. She bent across me, perched on the back of the toilet tank, to tear off a single square of toilet tissue. Carefully separating the paper along the perforations, she folded it precisely in half and blotted her lips. On school days, she often tucked that square of tissue into my lunch sack, a loving kiss from an absent mother. But now, in summer, she gave it to me. I tried to match my lips to hers, on the paper, and carry some of the vivid color to my own small mouth.

My father left for work in his sporty white Monza. My mother, after her customary morning repast of rye toast, smoked cod, coffee and unfiltered Herbert Tareyton cigarettes, welcomed Mrs. Rollins, then drove off in her big bronze Buick Skylark. In my mother's absence, Mrs. Rollins' distaste for me was unfettered by any concern for How It Looked. She took care of me, saw to it that I was fed and clean, but saved her love for Edie. Today, that was good: I was aiming for late afternoon, when my sister had her bath and when Mrs. Rollins, the mother of two grown sons, fussed with Edie's curly hair with the infinitely patient attention that mothers of men lavish on little girls' coiffures.

Vicky, Randi and I skated over to Thrifty Drugs for nickel Creamsicles. After, we played jacks on the sidewalk between the dichondra—a peculiar, flowerless, low- to no-maintenance clover, planted in lieu of authentic grass—on my front "lawn" and the narrow green strip that divided the sidewalk from the curb and gutter.

"Going to the library?" Randi asked.

"Nah," I said, collecting my jacks. "Not today." I went up my front steps, through the living room and past the bathroom, into my room.

"That you?" called Mrs. Rollins, from the bathroom. "Don't be tracking your dirt in here, keep outside! Not through the kitchen neither, the floor's wet. Go through the garage." She returned her attention to my slippery, splashing sister. Stealthily, I took my pillow and slipped outside.

Our fenced-in yard had three elements: patio, driveway, and more dichondra, here a spongy, lima-bean-shaped green expanse, punctuated by the sprinkler heads that regularly kept it lush. I sat on the dichondra with my pillow, then stripped the pillow of its case. The tag tore off easily enough, but I couldn't rip the ticking; the fabric was stronger than me. I got my father's screwdriver from the garage and shoved it into the ticking. Hand clenched around its handle, I dragged the tool downward. A six-inch gash in the fabric began oozing feathers.

I put my hand in, wrist-deep. With a fist full of feathers, scouting fast for the babysitter, I spun around and threw the feathers up over my head. Feather-snow fell all around me. I took another fistful, then another, then two at a time, flinging each upward, turning face-up to receive the snow. Pretty soon, Randi and Vicky came by—they had seen the "snow" billow over our backyard fence. They stuck their hands in the pillow and started throwing snow, too, and then all the kids came, all scooping up snow in handfuls from where it settled on the dichondra, throwing feather snowballs and wadding great piles of down into soft, hand-packed snow bombs. The aquamarine sky turned white with clouds of feathers, and we raised a racket, screeching and shouting and hollering in wild delight, because before too long, Mrs. Rollins came to the sliding-glass door in the den and stopped dead at the sight of us. "I don't know what to do with you wild ones," she scolded. To me, "Wait til your mother gets home."

When the big Buick lumbered into the driveway, we were still playing in the dichondra, twirling in the flurries. My immaculate mother emerged from her car to see us, and her yard, covered in feathers, and seemed to stumble on the air. She regained her physical balance but went a little crazy, there on the hot drive-way. Muttering through gritted teeth, half-Polish, half-English, she took me by the shoulders, shook me hard, shamed me in front of my friends.

"How could you do this?" she demanded. "Get rid of them"—my friends—"and clean this up." Then, she wept. My rock-solid, impermeable mother cried, there on her driveway in July 1963, ensconced in a perfect suburban world of her own devise, and her shoulders shook like mine had, only no one was shaking them.

"Clean this up," she said again, then lit a cigarette, and went inside.

Cleaning up the feathers was more of a challenge than making the snow had been. Scooping them back into the pillowcase was slow going. I tried the rake; all it did was kick up little eddies of feathers, which settled into the dichondra again. Meanwhile, my father came home.

"What are you doing?" he asked.

"Ask Mom," I said, sullen, on my hands and knees in the dichondra. He went into the house, then came out again, and said, stiffly, "Clean it up. All of it. You'll work until it's clean, you understand me?" I had violated something inviolable. What? And why didn't someone help me? All I wanted was snow ...

I found the garden hose and soaked the dichondra, thinking it would make it easier to get all the feathers out. I felt alone. And the wet feathers just stuck worse. I had to crawl every inch of that green mass, my soggy Capri pants bag-ging at the knees and butt, raking my fingertips underneath the dichondra's clover-tops down to the muddy stems, where the wet down seemed to wrap itself, intractable. It got dark. My father snapped on the yard light for me; no one spoke. I finished after 10 p.m.; my sister was asleep and my mother had a headache. My father sent me to bed. No one spoke of it ever again, until 18

Julys later, when my parents returned to Poland, and to Warsaw, where my mother was born and lived her youth. After a lifetime of imagining, I went, too.

The Umschlagplatz, where transports of Jews were shipped East decades earlier, still received trains, including mine. Disembarking into the early morning haze, I realized I was stepping out of a station where others only stepped in. Better to find a taxi than dwell on that darkness, I thought, and headed out to look for a cab.

We settled into our rooms at the Hotel Warsawa and began to tour the capital once known as Paris of the East. The elegant "Cosmopolitan" restaurant in the hotel lobby was open for business but hadn't any meat; grocery stores were open, too, but bare, with long shelves standing empty or lined with limp cabbages and cauliflower.

A horse-drawn droshky drew us through the serpentine paths of Ogruzaski Park and the cobbled city streets until we reached a low, broken brick wall, the perimeter of what once was the Warsaw Ghetto, where my mother's family were moved when the war devoured Poland.

"We will walk now," announced my mother, aloud and to no one. My father paid the driver a fistful of zlotys as my mother strode off, down Mila Street, past Pawiak, the prison building where underground school was held, "only for boys." She looked around as if she could see through the Soviet-issue cinderblock apartments that stood on the old streets. Abruptly, she back-tracked to the block where she had left the burning Ghetto, through the sewers. She thought she found the manhole cover in the street, but couldn't be sure. It had been the middle of the night, she reasoned, and everything was up in flames. She couldn't be sure.

We traced bullet-grooved bricks with our fingertips as we wandered the alleys, looking for remnants of buildings that had burned in the Uprising.

"Here," she said to me, grabbing my wrist in her hand, pointing up to an empty slice of yellow-grey sky between buildings. "Here was the bridge where they shook the feathers."

"Ma," I said, pulling my arm back, "let go."

"When they took people out from the Ghetto, see, it was all very official, with the yellow papers and the official stamps, you needed the Nazi permission to go to the east. It will be for the best, they said, we will give you food, two loaves of bread and a kilo of margarine, and you will settle in a new place. People believed them—they wanted to believe, and what did we know?"

"But the women did not want to leave everything behind; they took pots and pans, beds, quilts, pillows. This took too much room. You could always get goose feathers on a farm—they thought that's where they were going, see?—

so they shook out all the feathers on the street, up from on top of the little bridge, and packed everything else away. So everything was under feathers the days the transports left." She looked at me again. A shudder rose through her, until she touched the hollow of her throat and pushed back a wavy lock of hair. Then, she stopped talking.

JENNIFER DEMERITT
NOW THAT IT'S OVER
what was the sensation really about at the brooklyn museum?

All that publicity worked, and on a Sunday in December I went out to Brooklyn for the Sensation show. Immediately, I wanted to start smelling the paintings to see which of them were made with elephant dung. I didn't have to wait long—in the second or third room of the exhibit, the notorious Virgin Mary painting stood behind a protective layer of Plexiglas. The dung is shellacked over so it doesn't smell, but you can see little pieces of straw mixed in with the brown stuff. Would I be able to tell that it was elephant dung without all the hype? Would I care? Apparently this guy does a lot of work with dung. One of his paintings in the later part of the exhibit was a pretty-enough psychedelic job with brown lumps on it. One of the dung lumps had the name Miles Davis written on it, I guess the implication being that Miles Davis was some good shit. It was pretty, I liked it, and since I'm no art critic (or I wasn't until I started writing this) my analysis normally wouldn't go deeper than that.

Of course it was impossible to have any kind of unmediated gut reaction to the Virgin Mary painting because there was so much information, hype about it—and don't forget the layer of plexiglass coming between me and the painting when I finally did see it. Like the other painting, it was nicely composed, with a lovely pastel palette and a flock of butterflies in the background. The brown mound of exposed breast didn't look particularly offensive. A casual viewer might not find anything remarkable in the painting, but the generous captioning guarantees that you will have a reaction. The handy card on the wall tells you plainly that the left tit of the mother of Jesus is made out of poop, and it tells you why. It's like getting a free copy of the Cliff's notes along with the book. The card also helpfully explains that the butterflies in the background were actually cut-out pictures of butts. It saves you (the viewer) the embarrassment of trying to get too lofty and pretentious about it, so you're not stuck there making an art-face—you staring at asses and shit and trying to figure out what the hell it means.

According to the Cliff's notes on the wall, the painting is basically about faith and regeneration. In short, it's about the value of fertilizer. But beyond that, it's about its own shock value. In that regard, it reminds me of a lot of performance art. The main difference is that instead of doing it in a seedy low-rent art-hole like Surf Reality in New York City with all the dollar beer you can carry upstairs from the deli, the artists in the Sensation show are doing it in the pristine booze-free environment of a museum. I think modern art might be better understood if every museum gallery had a Budweiser keg right in it, or if they piped in reefer through the air vents. It would help get the typical viewer on the same wavelength as the typical modern artist. The Whitney Museum especially would benefit from an open bar policy. This occurred to me a few years ago at the Biennial, when I saw the exhibit-and-viewer combination that summed up the modern art scene for me. About half-way through the exhibit was a huge installation hanging from the ceiling, made out of a very large array of soft flesh-colored tubing, with tinting in various shades of pink, purple, red and grey. In most places it looked like strings of sausages, with various out-croppings and ends that resembled penises, or pieces of poop, and a few pinched-off nipply nubs. It was gigantic and totally grotesque, but so over-the-top that it was actually pretty damn funny. I stared at it and just laughed that some crafty mutherfucker got this monstrosity into one of America's premier museums—a strange victory in our screwed-up world. Standing right under the painting was a very earnest museum patron, gazing up at the fake sausage fiesta with his chin resting twixt his index finger and thumb. I could almost hear him going Hmmmmmm... Very interesting. No smirk on his face, no siree, he was there to see art with a capital A, dammit. After all it was the Whitney, and the Biennial purports to showcase some of the most important contemporary art on the scene. I felt bad for the guy. With a slight attitude adjustment he could have actually enjoyed the show.

The Virgin Mary painting reminds me in particular of the original poster-child for performance art, Karen Finley. For those of you who don't remember or didn't care, in the late 1980's Karen Finley got a reputation in the experimental theater world for talking about the oppression of women and sticking yams up her ass. I can't judge whether the yam-ramming did a good job of representing the oppression of women, but the important thing is that she said it did, and it is the prerogative of the artist—in fact the job of the artist—to create meaning any damn way that she wants. On another level, however, I think the real message of her act was that she just liked sticking yams up her ass. Likewise, I think the guy who did the Virgin Mary painting just likes playing with a certain organic molding compound. He is entitled to his obsession (in fact he might not be an artist without it) and, as I said, I appreciate the captioning so I didn't have to stand around and wonder what he was really doing.

The other big to-do artist at Sensation was Damien Hirst, who did the dead animal installations. These included an intact shark suspended in a tank of formaldehyde, a dead sheep in a similar rig, and the piece de resistance, a cow sliced into cross-sections, with each section mounted in its own clear formaldehyde-filled tank. I can't remember how many individual tanks of cow there were, but there were a lot of them, and each one was cleverly configured so that it's slice (which was more like a hunk, actually, but a transverse hunk) was pressed smack up against the clear side of the tank, giving the viewer an unobstructed close-up of grey but still very graphic innards. In case you were wondering, one cow contains an awful lot of innards. Each hunk of cow-in-a-tank was so jam packed with squiggles, slabs and tubes of cow-flesh that the formaldehyde had blanched a sick pinkish-grey, and the tanks went on and on and on. One of the guards was extremely effusive in her praise of Damien Hirst: he makes us look at parts of ourselves that we usually ignore because those parts are conveniently stashed inside our opaque skins. For a minute, the guard's words conjured the image of a necrophilic but earnest artist-slash-philosopher-slash-butcher hauling slabs of beef around a dank, under-heated London studio, up to his elbows in intestines because he REALLY CARES about making us understand. But my romantic image of The Artist Who Cares was way off base. Hirst used to mount dead animals in formaldehyde himself, but now he has money and a flock of assistants who do the dirty work for him. This means that his craft basically consists of telling his minions where to find the chainsaw, which makes him more of an art director than an artist, but these days there is less and less of a difference between the two. It's about the concept, baby.

And it's about making us look. In that regard, the Sensation show was a success in the same way as local performance artist Michael Portnoy's notorious stunt at the Grammys a few years ago, when he ripped off his costume during a production number and exposed his naked torso to America with the words soy bomb written across himself. It was a good pun: soy bomb—I am a bomb—and yes he was, exploding in front of us on national TV. But the content of his message didn't matter nearly as much as the fact that it was being broadcast. For a stunt, the definition of success is simply being able to bring it off. So his performance worked as a statement because the words on his chest vividly and succinctly described his action as he was doing it; and as a stunt it succeeded simply because he did it in front of millions of people. In a similar vein (as it were) Damien Hirst's dead animal installations were a success, regardless of my opinion of the pieces or the man responsible for them. In spite of (or perhaps because of) being grossed out and irritated by his installations, here I am pondering the nature of art, mortality, etc. And, first and last, he got me to look. He got me to say eeeeww, gross and schlepp out to Brooklyn to do it.

So cheers to him. Is his work interesting beyond its obvious shock value? Does it have to be? There was a time when I would have said yes, absolutely. I was interested in art with a capital A, and I believed that to be considered art a work must uplift or instruct, otherwise it's a cheap trick, no more valuable to society than the newest Schwarzenegger flick. (And at ten dollars, the price of admission is about the same). Of course this begs the question of why I think art has to be valuable to society, and I no longer believe that it does. Art is something to do. It's a past-time, and if you play your cards right you can get paid for it.

STEPHANIE HART
A LETTER TO MY FATHER
a journey into her past reveals the present

Dear Dad,

You visited my dream last night looking dapper in a navy blue suit with shiny, brass buttons. I wondered at the ease of your gestures as you helped two young women in chiffon dresses into a taxi. Your thick, dark hair moved gently in the autumn wind. The smile on your face was jaunty, confident, and almost ebullient. You were not the man I had known.

Today, I conjure you up through photographs. I discover you at age six in a black sailor's suit, red and black striped socks and high-button shoes. You are standing on the cushion of a tall wooden chair looking proper and prominent. Your right arm falls easily at your side while your left, bent at the elbow, rests gently against the spokes of the chair; in your small left hand you are holding a wilted bouquet of roses. Your hair has been sculpted into the shape of a cap. Your cheeks appear full and achingly soft. Your lips are parted slightly. There is a far away look in your dark eyes as if the physical reality of the moment were inconsequential to you. I feel your thoughts waft into dreams of imagined greatness, a journey you will make again and again over the next three-quarters of a century.

For you Dad, fact and desire often intermingled. You told me you were born on Staten Island; my birth certificate reveals it was Russia. With the help of your relatives, I reconstructed your early life. You were born in Odessa in the spring of 1904. This picture was taken in 1911, only a year before both you and your father, a builder of patrician stock and sensibilities, crossed an ocean to take refuge in the lap of America from the Russian pogroms. I can envision you on that journey standing on the planks of the ship, your chin pitched upwards, a dauntless little admiral doing battle with the waves.

Once on land, your father's status spared you both the trials of Ellis Island; however, like other Russian Jewish immigrants, you headed directly for the airless tenements of Manhattan's Lower East Side. Your flamboyant redheaded mother and dark-haired taciturn sister soon joined you. A year later the four of you found sanctuary on Staten Island where your father made a respectable living constructing and renting multiple dwellings. Four years later your brother Phil was born, a stocky pragmatist, who worshipped his big brother. You loved him too for his devout simplicity. He seemed to lack the infrastructure of dreams that formed your ambition. You wanted to distinguish yourself from your silent father and effusive mother who let loose a witty hodgepodge of talk in Yiddish and broken English. You wanted to escape the haunted landscape of your sister's face. Like Gatsby you would use the hot clay of desire to reshape your history.

At twenty, after two rejections, the doors of Harvard University swung open. It was the Fall of 1924 and you were Louie Greenberg, an amiable American boy who knew Whitman and Shakespeare, who could ride horseback and play baseball and who cultivated a small compassionate smile that inspired trust and confidence. Majoring in languages and literature, you quickly mastered the written and spoken terrain of French, Italian and Spanish. Captivated by Cervantes and Lope de Vega, your passion for the drama of the Golden Age became synonymous with your love of the Harvard campus. Mental and physical agility characterizes the young man I see in animated discourse with professors and classmates. Your prize winning senior thesis won the praise of visiting scholars and the prospect of a professorship at Oxford where you would complete your doctorate. A warm light would come into your eyes whenever you recalled this period forty, fifty, sixty years later as, "The happiest time in my life."

The Golden Age was not flourishing in America when you graduated in 1928. As we fell precipitously into a depression, neither you nor your father would be able to finance your doctoral work. Your life at Oxford, with its green lawns and lofty spires and ideas became a deferred dream, all the more poignant because it was never realized. You applied your intellect to a volatile economy, discovering in yourself a shrewd business acumen which served you well over the next decade. You worked as actuary, stockbroker, and finally chief executive officer of your own credit bureau. You bought a home on Staten Island and tenderly administered to your garden. The natural world infused you with a lightness of mind. You spent weekends planting and riding horseback. In 1932 a feature article appeared in a local newspaper profiling you as an outstanding young citizen who had read Thoreau and Whitman, attended the Metropolitan opera, practiced vegetarianism and was intimately acquainted with the stock market. I discover a picture taken of you at this time seated on a horse with a pretty, young woman: you are holding the reins while she smiles sweetly behind you. You appear round and stout and unsmiling. Your gaze wanders far from the camera.

As you chafed in the skin of an American businessman, you would cast about for another persona. In 1939 you joined the army, rising quickly from lieutenant to major. Stationed in Washington D.C., you planned battle strategies. You were never called to the front. I have a snapshot of you grinning under your major's cap, balancing a bulky parcel in one hand beneath a sign that reads Post Exchange Main Store. You seem to be showing off your territory. After the war, you returned to the business sector, but maintained your affiliation with the National Guard. Your love of all things French, engendered at Harvard, led you to visit Paris in the fall of 1948. Wandering down Rue de Grenelle, admiring the delicate iron latticework and pristine pavement, you decided to take the street for your surname. Once back in the States, you scrapped Louis Greenberg to become Louis Jerome Grennell. A year later, standing proudly in your major's uniform, you met my mother, a woman eighteen years your junior. She had haunting green eyes and a sure, yet trembling smile that made you vow to protect her. A year later, you married her. My birth would fill you both with a heady sense of joy.

In my earliest memory of you, I was age three or four. You were lifting me gently by the arms and swinging me back and forth in front of a wide picture window. We were living in a house by the sea on the southern tip of New Jersey. "Swing me," I shouted, "Daddy, swing me." Later in the day, you planted rows of tomatoes in our garden. As you lay on your stomach, your solid frame seemed to become one with the earth. In the evening, you filled the house with operatic music. You taught me the libretto of Madam Butterfly. Wrapped in my mother's kimono, I scouted for signs of Lieutenant Pinkerton. Only once in these early years do I remember your fierceness. You stormed at me because I had scrawled squiggly yellow lines on the wall above my bed. You wanted me to be your perfect little girl. You and mother never really fought, yet a furtive silence hung between you. At age six, I dreamed we were living in a paper house.

In the summer of 1956, Mother left you. While the two of you lived separately in Manhattan, I was sent to a boarding school above the Hudson river, a safe haven of pine trees, grape harbors and gentle hills where I came to dread your sporadic Sunday visits. Your labored steps and solemn brooding expression did not belong to the father I had known. Mother remarried four years later. Her new husband was a State Supreme Court judge who was alternately imposing and jolly. When you lost your job and had to seek his help your bitterness reached a Wagnerian crescendo. Making out lists of people who had maltreated you, you asked God to perform acts of retribution. You regarded my mother as a heathen and me as a newly anointed member of the privileged class.

An angry tremble crept in your voice, a tremble I had come to anticipate and dread. When I was twelve on a cold day in February, I remember you taking me to see the Mona Lisa, which was on display outside the Metropolitan museum. As I stood shivering in the icy wind, you said harshly. "You're not Princess Margaret, Stephanie. You have to stand on line like everybody else." Surprising tenderness could cut through your resentment. Driving me back to boarding school on a snowy winter night, I recall your gentility and eloquence as you helped me prepare for a history test. The Puritans and Ann Hutchinson were your intimate friends. I was sure there wasn't anything you didn't know.

When I was fourteen, at my mother and stepfather's insistence, I entered a private high school in Brooklyn. While you agreed to pay the tuition, the burden proved too great. My stepfather shouldered this responsibility, decimating your pride and exacerbating your anger at me. Your comments seemed designed to wheedle away at my self-esteem. "You are not a smart girl, Stephanie. You'll never attend an Ivy League college." Congratulating yourself on your Harvard education, you would speak in a tone laced with regret, "I don't know how a daughter of mine could be so slow- minded." My character was also the target of your reproach. You were appalled by my selfishness; I neglected to comfort you when you were alone and unemployed. My sympathy for you lay in a complex matrix of emotions. I had come to regard you as the Enemy. In a picture of us taken at my high school graduation, you fill the dark folds of your suit with an embittered stoutness. Cynicism contorts your features and your eyes look haunted. I stand next to you in a short, white A-line dress and white patterned stockings. My long dark hair casts a shadow across my face. My gaze darts nervously away from you.

Your remarriage in 1967 allowed you a modicum of happiness. You could bask in your new wife's admiration for your youthful accomplishments. At sixty-three, you were teaching history to preteens in a Queen's middle school. While you professed interest and stimulation in your work, I suspect that sweet breath of Oxford spring never ceased to taunt you.

After my stepfather's death in 1969, the chasm between us deepened. You warned me not to use this event to solicit pity, taking pains to remind me that he had never been my relative. Out of deference to my mother your former friends and business associates came to his funeral; I was stung by their whispers of your questionable financial dealings, dealings which catapulted Mother out of the marriage. Confronting you in righteous indignation, I caused the thread of contact between us to become even more tenuous. Your voice came as a lament through the phone in my college dorm, as I stood in a smoke-filled hallway, "Even my own daughter has turned on me."

In the summer of 1970 you lay bleeding internally in a Boston hospital. You were suffering from exhaustion and the sound of an erratic heart was beating in your ear. Manhattan doctors couldn't find a cure. Your wife, Annette, was angelic in her concern. I visited you dutifully on weekends. When your physician assured me that you were in no imminent danger, I announced my plans to go to Europe. It was then that your wife charged at me physically, exhibiting the wrath that you had taught her to believe was coming to me. I held her thin white wrists, shouting, "I am never coming back here." You made a full recovery later that summer. But the knowledge of your contempt crystallized into a cold hatred; I determined never to see you again. Casting off the shackle of the name Grennell, I took my stepfather's name, Hart.

In the five years we were apart, your shadow hovered ominously around me. I wrote papers dissecting Hawthorne's concept of the power of blackness. Both an intellectual affinity and the discomfort of holding a grudge led me to initiate reconciliation. I discovered you had aged. The lines in your face had become deep crevices, but your anger had diminished. After our initial recriminations, we never again discussed our differences. You were working in the check signing division of a Manhattan department store. Over the next decade, we would meet for lunch in your cheerless office, balancing paper plates on a gray metal desk. It was here that you would rhapsodize about your years at Harvard and the senior thesis that had so engaged you. I came to see you as a tragic figure, a character Hawthorne might have written about and discarded. In your mid-seventies, you had a final vision of forming a financial conglomerate in India. At eighty-four, two years after you retired, you died quietly in your sleep.

I felt an unexpected depth of sadness when you were gone. The following summer, I visited the Harvard campus, that fertile patch of Massachusetts's ground where you had sprung so fully to life. I discovered your prize-winning thesis in the library, the only document to remain on the shelves from the class of 1928. Reading the manuscript at a long mahogany table in a sun-filled room, I marveled at the intellectual ardor and flow of your language. Words were clay we both used with sincerity and awe.

Love and understanding were never gifts I intended to extend to you; instead, they have grown imperceptibly over the years since your death. Along with joy and accomplishment, my life has been rocked by disappointment, both personal and professional. I know how elusive love can be. I have experienced the pain of trying to create. I know the dungeon of self-doubt and self-loathing, the storm of envy that can overtake me when I see others hold what I may never have. I have known the pit of loss and longing where hatred is born. We are not alien to one another after all.

On a recent trip to Paris, I walked down Rue de Grenelle as if in your footsteps. Approaching the Cathedral of Notre Dame at dusk, I watched lights pull at the roots of the sky and wondered which of your dreams still lingered there. Once back in New York, I experienced you as a friendly presence at my side, an adumbration of lightness. And then you entered my dream last night looking gallant and self-assured in a navy blue suit, not masquerading as some bitter old man, but again as my father sans the bitterness that distorted his perceptions for so many years.

I would like to believe in the existence of spirit beyond flesh, which would mean that you are truly listening. I am finding that love has curative powers. By accepting others with their foibles, I am beginning to find compassion for myself. I think you would like the apartment I am living in now. My window reveals a wide breadth of sky above the Hudson River, the sun as a great white ball before it bleeds into a fiery orange. I have abundant green plants and classical music is always playing.

My cousin Judy recently gave me a restored photograph of you and your parents which hangs in my hallway in a gold frame under a soft white light. I see you at three months old in a little white smock, propped up comfortably on your mother's lap. There is a dewy expression on your face. Your toes are pointed outward. Dressed in a proper black suit behind you and your mother, your father looks handsome and aristocratic. Both your parents are shaded in sable-brown tones. You are the bright spot between them.

I can remember when we lived in the house by the sea—you, Mother and me before the divorce. You were such a good dancer then, so light on your feet. Weightless, defying the laws of gravity, you would dart around me in my room with the spotted linoleum floor and my toys strewn everywhere: my Daddy. I have difficulty mastering steps, but I have your sense of rhythm. I feel like dancing tonight in celebration of my love for you, and the peace and good wishes I am sending you across eternity. I hope we meet again someday.

Your daughter, Stephanie

HARILYN ROUSSO
BUYING THE WEDDING DRESS
an affair remembered

It was a traditional Jewish family ritual—the married women in the family going shopping with the bride-to-be to buy her wedding dress. I had been sheltered from knowing about this ritual, perhaps because no one ever expected me to get married. I was born with a disability, cerebral palsy, so that my body moved in ways far removed from traditional standards of feminine beauty. I consistently got the message that no man would ever want me. It became a self-fulfilling prophecy until at age 37, I met Daniel, who convinced me I was the most beautiful, desirable, sexy woman in the world, and that my strange movements were exotic, not weird.

So there I was, one early July Saturday, surrounded by my mother and married sister, going from bridal shop to bridal shop in one of those wedding malls in Long Island, seeking the dress that would transform me into a "real" woman, Daniel's wife, on September 8th. There were only two months to go, so I couldn't afford to be too choosy. I had to pick something off the rack that maybe needed minor alterations. I didn't realize that I had a picture of the ideal wedding dress lying dormant in my brain, but the image emerged full blown as soon as I started trying on dresses. As a woman who favored jeans and simple styles, I was shocked to discover my own preferences for lace and frills, tight waists and wide skirts. The five-year-old who had played with bride dolls before she discovered there would be no groom was at last in charge, unhampered by the restrained tastes of her grown up self. My mother, sister and I let the little girl rule, and she decided upon an off-white satin gown with lace covered with pearls throughout the broad skirt, and deliciously smooth-to-the-touch satin at the waist and sleeves. My reflection in the mirror did not exactly match the one in that five-year-old's head—my body was still less than perfectly coordinated—but I felt more beautiful and womanly than I ever had. I had my first dress fitting, and tried on different crowns of flowers that helped complete that image of myself as a princess.

We went out for a bite after my mother gave the sizable down payment. I felt totally satiated despite the slim pickings at the dingy coffee shop around the corner from the bridal store, so delicious was that image of myself in that long white dress.

I called my groom-to-be from the restaurant, and although he tried to show happiness about my purchase, I couldn't help note some distance in his voice. I attributed this to pre-nuptial anxiety, but I had a visceral feeling of loss, as though the Polaroid picture of myself in the wedding dress was starting to fade.

When I saw Daniel that night, he suggested that we not go anywhere special for dinner, an odd request given the events of the day. I found myself in yet another bleak coffee shop. I don't recall how the conversation started, but fairly soon after we got to the restaurant and had ordered our cheeseburgers, he came out with a litany of complaints. "You don't read *The New Yorker*. That magazine is such an important part of my life. It makes me feel lonely to think of marrying someone who doesn't like *The New Yorker*." And "You don't understand poetry. My mother and I have always read poetry to each other. I am afraid that when she dies, I won't have anyone to read poetry to." Unprepared, I was unable to defend myself or to question the legitimacy of his complaints. In my state of disorientation, I was falling back on old truths about myself. Perhaps they were myths but they felt like truths. In my mind, what he was saying was that there was something deeply and basically wrong with me, a defect in myself, my character, my humanity. This was the feeling I had developed as a little girl, the result of people repeatedly pointing, staring, asking what was wrong, expecting the least, praising the most mundane acts in a patronizing way. It had always been hard to feel all right about myself, disability and all, when the world treated me as though something was gravely wrong. It was the world's reflection of me as defective that made me assume I would never marry. And it was Daniel's supposed love for me that made me question that image for perhaps the first time.

In hindsight, it is absurd to think that my not reading *The New Yorker* could transform me back into a freak, but it had that effect, at least temporarily.

"Are you sure he really asked you to marry him?" my dad inquired when I told him the wedding was off. "That bastard!" was the immediate response of my mother, always my supporter. "Thank God!" is what the three of us might have said had we known then what I learned later about Daniel's history of near-marriages before and after his encounter with me. Many wedding dresses had been bought and abandoned after early fittings at bridal shops, even by some women who read *The New Yorker*, I suspect.

That image of myself in the wedding gown has lived on, although it has lost some of its sharpness after fifteen years. I did see a reflection of a real woman, not a freak, when I gazed into the mirror that day, and that woman was in me, not in the looking glass. She goes in and out of my awareness now, but I know she is there. She has a disability and she is whole.

ELLIOT RAVETZ
OF PHILOLOGY, PENTIMENTO AND PRECISION
an elliptical view of words and usage as they relate to thinking, feeling, comprehending, and writing

How does *Moby Dick* begin? Put the question to 100 people and it's likely that 99 will respond, "Call me Ishmael." Ninety-nine mistaken responses, 99 important oversights, 99 deflected readings yielding incomplete appreciations of a great novel.

The novel begins with the word "Etymology," followed by a mock-scholarly etymology of "whale" along with numerous illustrative sentences taken from world literature in which the word or a synonym for it is used. This alters our reading of what follows. *Moby Dick* is, finally, a book largely about perceiving, *naming*, and understanding.* Melville offers an extensive inventory of whaling terminology: names for whales and whale parts, for whaling instrumentalities and procedures. Clearly, though, *Moby Dick* is rather more about perceiving and comprehending (relationships primarily: man/nature, man/man, man/God, man/himself) than whaling. The true vessel for the undertaking is the English language, not the Pequod.

* * *

What follows is an elliptical view of words and usage as they relate to thinking, feeling, comprehending, and writing.

* * *

Words are the medium of thought. *Logos*, reports the *OED*,

"A term used by Greek philosophers...developed from...its ordinary senses 'reason' and 'word'...." And J. Mitchell Morse observes in *The Irrelevant English Teacher*, "to the extent that we recognize our feelings we even feel in words...." People whose command of language is weak "have little command of their thoughts or even of their feelings." "The thought is born with the sentence that constitutes it, or not at all; the sentence *is* the thought...thinking is a process of composition." Cf., Wittgenstein: "The limits of my language means the limits of my world." Boswell: "Johnson's comprehension of mind was the mould for his language. Had his conceptions been narrower, his expression would have been easier." And Hugh Kenner: "One senses that Hegel was possible only in German, and finds it natural that Locke in a language where *large* and *red* precede *apple* would have arrived at the thing after sorting out its sensory qualities, whereas Descartes in a language where *grosse et rouge* follows *pomme* should have come to the attributes after the distinct idea." [I necessarily prescind here from the mental processes that enable Paul Morphy to excel in chess, Einstein to grasp and elucidate physical laws, Bach to compose music, and Balanchine to discover art in the controlled patterns of bodies moving in space. All involve mental discipline, a well-developed critical faculty, and other properties of thinking, which, though perhaps co-extensive with the kind that concerns me, differ from *logos* in ways that are both subtle and obvious.]

* * *

English was reinvented for us in the mid-18th century (see Hugh Kenner's *The Pound Era* and his brilliantly alembicated *The Stoic Comedians*). This was primarily a consequence of the birth of lexicography, itself a byproduct of the Gutenberg Revolution. The new widespread availability of print hastened the transformation of literature from a primarily oral medium to a medium that is primarily visual, and it precipitated the sense of need for standardization of the way the spoken word would be rendered in print.

With his 1755 *Dictionary of the English Language*, Samuel Johnson (the first modern lexicographer) aimed to stabilize language, which was "exposed to the corruptions of ignorance, and caprices of innovation." He sought to bring discipline to "the boundless chaos of a living speech," to "catch [words] on the brink of utter inanity, to circumscribe them by any limitations, or interpret them by any words of distinct and settled meaning...." He recognized that "Words are seldom synonimous (sic); a new term was not introduced, but because the former was thought inadequate...."; and "Most men think indistinctly, and therefore cannot speak with exactness...."

Johnson's dictionary, seeking to create stability and order, seeking to differentiate and disambiguate words, provided 40,000-plus definitions, along with approximately 114,000 illustrative quotations to demonstrate the shades and hues of individual words as employed by the best English writers known to Johnson, which, together with the etymologies Johnson deduced, also helped to trace the permutations the words had undergone in their histories. Why the labor-intensive bother with historical illustrations and etymologies that often, and sometimes anfractuously, travel through foreign tongues? Johnson: "Such is the exuberance of signification which many words have obtained, that it was scarcely possible to collect all their senses; sometimes the meaning of derivatives must be sought in the mother term."

Because Johnson also knew that language is a living organism, he sought judicious stability (presciently fearing that willy-nilly change risked the loss of Milton and Shakespeare's English to future generations), not intractability. Thus, before definition and illustration, we find etymology, the "mother term(s)," the roots of verbal life: an organism, notes Kenner, "that can maintain its identity as it grows and evolves in time...that can remember ...anticipate...mutate...."

James Joyce also knew this: "The cords of all link back, strandentwining cable of all flesh"—Joyce's form also illustrating different possibilities of the oral and written language. Beyond performing visual operations ("strandentwining," many puns lost to the ear are disclosed to the eye, etc.), we usually expect

serious writers to be more conscious of discrete word-values, to be discriminating and more accurate (from *ad* + *curare*, taking care).
C.S. Lewis put the matter this way:

> ...words constantly take on new meanings. Since these do not necessarily, nor even usually, obliterate the old ones, we should picture this process not on the analogy of an insect undergoing metamorphoses but rather on that of a tree throwing out new branches, which themselves throw out subordinate branches; in fact, as ramification. The new branches sometimes overshadow and kill the old ones but by no means always. We shall again and again find the earliest senses of a word flourishing for centuries despite a vast overgrowth of later senses which might have been expected to kill them.

Etymology, then: the morphology of logos, the word, the necessary, irreducible constituent of thought, reason, and comprehension. To understand the nature of something—its quiddity—perhaps a whale, perhaps good and evil, or perhaps the particular meaning when we say it of "I love you," for any of us wishing to individualize and particularize the sentiment in order to give it personal value, we will have to come to terms with the nature and singularity of the words we select to define it. Only by means of the painstaking choices and ordering of words, by careful amplification and specification, can we retrieve and recrudesce the words "I love you"—words as talismanically potent as they are vague—from what Beatrice Webb called "the dustbin of emotions."

We are indebted to Lillian Hellman for calling her memoir *Pentimento* and thereby introducing (or reintroducing) us to that word: "Old paint on canvas, as it ages, sometimes becomes transparent. When that happens it is possible, in some pictures, to see the original lines: a tree will show through a woman's dress, a child makes way for a dog, a large boat is no longer on an open sea. That is called pentimento because the painter 'repented,' changed his mind. Perhaps it would be as well to say that the old conception, replaced by a later choice, is a way of seeing and then seeing again."

Gore Vidal took a similarly evocative path in calling his own memoir Palimpsest. The American Heritage Dictionary defines palimpsest as a "manuscript, typically of papyrusor parchment, that has been written on more than once, with the earlier writing incompletely erased and often legible."

Streets that followed like a tedious argument
Of insidious intent
To lead you to an overwhelming question...

When T.S. Eliot composed these lines for the first stanza of "Prufrock," his fastidious choice of the word "overwhelming" adumbrated the poem's denouement for readers with some knowledge of etymology and a willingness to credit certain writers with precise, accurate usage. *Webster's* Second cites these as the first two meanings for "overwhelm": 1. To overturn, upset, or overthrow. 2. To cover over completely, as by a great wave; ...submerge...; ...immerse....

We have lingered in the chambers of the sea
By sea-girls wreathed with seaweed red and brown
Till human voices wake us, and we drown.

As Eliot says in the "Four Quartets," *The end is where we start from and In my beginning is my end.* In this way, careful writers may create a pentimento effect—the *drowning* being perhaps partially discernible in the *overwhelming*—and thereby enrich the text. To the eye of the attentive reader, words can suggest histories that enrich the present, adumbrate the future, and even superimpose meanings.

Richard Chenevix Trench, a philologist and an instigator of the *New English Dictionary* (which became the *OED*), noted that "Many a single word...is itself a concentrated poem, having stores of poetical thought and imagery laid up in it." We know that James Joyce spent many hours reading Walter Skeat's *Etymological Dictionary* (1882), a habit (Joyce ever reluctant to waste experience) he imparted to Stephen Hero, who, like his creator and model, "was often hypnotized by the most commonplace conversation." "People seemed to him strangely ignorant of the value of the words they used so glibly." Like Flaubert, who struggled to find *le seul mot juste* ("the exactly right word"), "When literature attains the precision of an exact science, that's something!" and like that ironic genius and formidable lepidopterist Vladimir Nabokov, who often referred to "the precision of art and the passion of science," Joyce was a verbal retentive, a compulsive logophiliac, continually looking up words, learning their roots and their histories and their *proper* meanings; and having registered the sense in which they occurred, then stripping away layers of obnubilationand distortion with which marketplace negligence has encrusted them, he would enlist them to his purposes.

Again like Flaubert, who wrote the *Dictionary of Accepted Ideas*—a compendium of overheard clichés and platitudes, the unconsidered ideas polluting people's minds—and others who are discriminating in the application of words, An acquaintance had trouble accepting the fact that Joyce, the greatest master of the English language after Shakespeare, had spent two days working on two sentences. "Yes,"Joyce responded, "I had the words. What I was working at was the order of the fifteen words in the sentences. There is an order in every way exact. I think I have found it." That is, usage. Grammar and syntax. Rules and traditions that were designed to serve clarity and precision.

There's a significant difference, for instance, between "I can say only that it's brilliant" and "I can only say that it's brilliant." Ambiguities may have serious consequences: to wit, "People who eat this often get sick," wherein the two-way adverb invites confusion, misinterpretation, and potential health problems. And just as misplaced modifiers invite confusion: "There are many reasons why lawyers lie, some better than others," so too do the ill-considered proximity of relative pronouns to the nouns they modify: "She's the mother of an infant daughter who works twelve hours a day."

* * *

Though language is itself a congeries of arbitrary conventions and rules (to an extent, historical accidents) whose purpose is intelligibility, we may speak of the "natural" use of words in two senses. There is, first, the way in which a word is used—the norm, the standard, the ideal—that reflects back on its nature (its origins, its history, including accretions of meaning that have altered without deracinating it) and, alternatively, descriptive linguists argue that the use of words is natural whenever people use them, irrespective of how, so long as the intended meaning is conveyed. Presupposing sufficient numbers of people adopting a new usage, however coarse or ultimately damaging to clarity, modern lexicographers are there—too eagerly it sometimes seems—to codify and legitimize that usage as they update dictionaries.

Words *do* accrue new meanings in time, and change is natural when the new meanings are cognates of earlier ones or are metaphorically related to them. We have seen this in Eliot's use of "overwhelming," whose present sense is clearly derived from previous senses. Perusing (which is not skimming or scanning) the *OED* or [Merriam-] *Webster's New international Dictionary*, Second Edition evinces the point. What descriptivists fail to appreciate, it seems, is that word-growth resembles and is part of human-growth: it should be guided by caring adults who wish, by precept and practice, to help shape healthy, responsive and responsible lives (word or human). Too readily to condone or approve verbal corruption and irresponsibility is to invite correspondingly dissolute or diminished thinking, feeling and behaving.

As standards have steadily loosened, instances of verbal sloppiness, catachreses and solecisms seem to be proliferating at a geometric rate. They appear not only in casual speech, where it is somewhat more pardonable, but also in the formal address of lawyers in courtrooms and elected officials in Congress, in newspapers, magazines, books, and in the copy read by television newscasters—alas, the source on which a majority of Americans most depend for their knowledge of current events. Among the common abuses are: Between you and I. Ten items or less. The reason is because. My family and myself. Ironic for coincidental or paradoxical. Merge together. Self-confessed. Mingle or mix together. Future plans. Free gift. Surrounded on all sides. Throughout the entire. Misrepresent for lie. At this point in time. Fulsome for robust or generous. Visible to the eye. Data as singular, media as singular, phenomena and graffiti as singular. Tragedy or tragic for something that may be exceedingly sad or unfortunate. Postmodern. To impact. To critique. To mentor. To e-mail. Prioritize. Notorious for celebrated, well-known or famous. Fortuitous for fortunate. Disinterested/uninterested. Imply/infer. Anxious/eager. Masterly/masterful. Further/farther. Quote/quotation. Nauseous/nauseated. Transpire for occur. From whence. Indicated for said. Precise estimate.

English is rich in near-synonyms, and the ability to chose intelligently from among, say, *inextirpable, inexpungable, inextinguishable, ineradicable, impregnable, indestructible,* and *inviolable* or, say, *skinny, emaciated, cadaverous, skeletal, slender, spindly,* and *wizened* allows us to clarify and refine what we say, think and feel—that is, our identities—to give them and us greater value, nuance, subtlety and individuality.

* * *

Forty or more years ago, when academic standards were consistently higher, reflecting a less heterogeneous culture for which something resembling a classical education was still a common goal of unquestioned importance, it was possible to speak of a language war between descriptivists and prescriptivists.

The publication of the Third Edition of *Webster's New International Dictionary (Unabridged)* in 1961 marks a cultural watershed: its appearance revealed a great deal about the changes in our culture since the publication in 1934 of the great Second Edition of *Webster's.* The salient difference between the editions is that *Webster's* Third accepts as standard English most of the words to which *Webster's* Second attached warning labels: *slang, colloquial, erroneous, incorrect, illiterate.*

The differences between the editions reflected the philosophies of their editors. Dr. William A. Neilson, the editor of *Webster's* Second, followed the lexical practice that had governed since Samuel Johnson's time. He assumed that there was such a thing as correct English and that it was his and his colleagues' responsibility as lexicographers to decide what it was. He included substandard words, of course, because of their common use, but these words came with warning and usage labels. His approach was normative: it assumed an ideal standard that he sought to clarify for anyone consulting his dictionary; it also assumed that people often consulted a dictionary for expert guidance.

Dr. Philip Gore, the editor of *Webster's* Third, was, like Neilson, a dedicated scholar, but he was also a Structural Linguist who sought to apply scientific methodology to his editorial task. A dictionary, he wrote, "should have no traffic with...artificial notions of correctness or superiority. It was to be descriptive and not prescriptive." Consequently, *Webster's* Third described ain't as "used orally in most parts of the U.S. by many cultivated speakers [sic]" and it included such terms as heighth and irregardless without any monitory labels on them.

About descriptivists in general and Gore's dictionary in particular, Dwight Macdonald wrote, "They seem imperfectly aware of the fact that the past of a language is part of its present, that tradition is as much a fact as the violation of tradition."

The descriptivists have probably won the war. Even the great Samuel Johnson had to concede: "Pronunciation will be varied by levity or ignorance...illiterate writers will at one time or another, by publick infatuation, rise into renown, who, not knowing the original import of words, will use them with colloquial licentiousness, confound distinction, and forget propriety...."

But some lost wars are still worth fighting. With his concession, Johnson also issued a rallying cry: "But if the changes that we fear be thus irresistible...it remains that we retard what we cannot repel, that we palliate what we cannot cure."

* * *

H.W. Fowler's *A Dictionary of Modern English Usage* (1926) and Eric Partridge's *Usage & Abusage: A Guide to Good English* (1942) are still invaluable—and brimming with wit, elegance and lively intelligence, they are also fun to use and even to browse through. Fowler's *Dictionary* was gracefully updated by Sir Ernest Gowers in 1965, and this second edition is the one to get. But take pains to avoid Robert W. Burchfield's *The New Fowler's Modern English Usage*, 1996. It is unseemly for Burchfield to have appropriated Fowler's name and for Oxford, Fowler's publisher, to have permitted it. For though Burchfield is a serious student of language and for a time edited the OED , he is, unlike Fowler and Partridge, permissive about usage; he is unwilling much of the time to make important discriminations or to issue those informed warnings and judgments that can help us to elevate the quality—the strength, clarity and grace—of our writing.

Bryan A. Garner has inherited the mantle of Fowler and Partridge. Garner is already one of the most important figures in Anglo-American linguistics and dictionary-making, and his *Dictionary of Modern American Usage* (1998; second edition 2003) is indispensable for anyone who is passionate about the language. He manages, somewhat miraculously, to wield his unsurpassable knowledge of the language with natural grace, to be firm and agile (he's a non-rigid prescriptivist), wise and reasonable, confident and confidence-inspiring, as he guides us through even the thorniest issues of usage.

William Gass's inspired title, *The World Within The Word*, succinctly captures what I have been trying to say. Ponder that title. Savor it. Words are valuable and they are powerful. As the breadth and versatility of our vocabularies expand, so does our ability to understand ourselves and others. Yet there are some who are put off, even antagonized, by the use of unfamiliar words; to these people, I suspect, such words seem pretentious or pedantic, and dictionaries are an inconvenience rather than sources of potential wonder and revelation. Charles Harrington Elster shared such an experience.

> It is almost a truism to say that words have the power to transform us and crystallize our vision of the world. I say almost because, though the statement may seem trite, it is unassailable. Every literate one of us has experienced its truth.

> My crowning moment in word serendipity is seared into my brain. I was thumbing through Paul Hellweg's "Insomniac's Dictionary" when I stumbled

upon the word resistentialism, which Hellweg defines as "seemingly spiteful behavior manifested by inanimate objects."

Reading that definition, I had what can only be described as a revelation. I felt that an entire category of my experience had been uplifted from the Cimmerian realm of the Inexpressible into the clear, comforting light of the Known.

* * *

I admire Nabokov's response to Edmund Wilson who, of all unlikely people, attacked Nabokov for an "addiction to rare and unfamiliar words." Nabokov: "It does not occur to [Wilson] that I may have rare and unfamiliar things to convey.... Mr. Wilson can hardly be unaware that once a writer chooses to youthen or resurrect a word, it lives again...and will keep annoying stodgy grave-diggers as long as that writer's book endures." (Cf., Samuel Johnson: "Obsolete words are admitted"—into his dictionary—"when they are found in authours not obsolete, or when they have force or beauty that may deserve revival.")

Wilson may be taken as a representative for all who would circumscribe language (the range of expression) to a breadth approximating their own; those who abstractly preconize the abundance of English vocabulary but are vexed when comfortable theory is occasionally put into challenging practice. This, like a laissez faire toleration of sloppy usage, can be self-perpetuating: those editors and writers who fear taxing and perhaps losing readers may simultaneously impose vitiating constraints on less demotic, more rarefied language and tolerate slovenly formulations because they are growing commonplace. The practice truncates the living language and impoverishes for all the extent to which we can be more precisely and imaginatively expressive, and more fully realized human beings. To lose a word is to lose part of ourselves (or potential selves), our heritage, and our abilities to understand our connections to the past and to grow. When departing from or seeking to alter the traditional stock of words, we're better off in the direction of neologism.

Civilized mankind defines reality and itself primarily through language, and we are obliged to ourselves and to civilization (past, present, and future) to preserve and extend the health and vitality of the language, our most important living legacy.

----

*Since *Moby Dick* is no longer protected by copyright laws, it is available from many publishers. Some editions omit Melville's dedication of the novel to Nathaniel Hawthorne and its proper opening. I suspect that most of the publishers who delete Melville's opening have glanced at it just fleetingly and have mistaken it for someone else's appended material.

KATRINA MARKEL
THE BILL RILEY TALENT COMPETITION
hordes of marauding tap dancers descend on iowa

Like Medieval Mongolians, hordes of marauding tap dancers descended on the state of Iowa each summer. Their aim was to plunder first place talent show trophies that rightfully belonged to some deserving local kid who only wanted a shot at performing on the Mainstage of the Iowa State Fair.

I was one of these local kids and no matter how loud I may have belted out, "Don't Rain on My Parade," those tap dancing attention hogs always seemed to get in my way.

Each of Iowa's 99 counties could sponsor a local "Bill Riley Talent Competition." The first place winner in each age group would then advance to the State Fair competition where there were quarterfinals, semi-finals and, of course, finals, which were televised statewide. Oh sure, Omaha had *Show Wagon*, but winning that was a decidedly minor honor when compared to the prestige of being the Bill Riley Iowa State Champion. Bill Riley was the Oscars and Show Wagon was the Cable Ace Awards.

Bill Riley was only a name on the franchise until you advanced to the State Fair. The first time I made it to the Mainstage I was only 10 years old and shocked to discover just how small in stature this legend was. He was a leprechaun of a man. At 4 feet 11 inches, Riley presided over his self-titled talent show with the kind of flair and showmanship not seen since Robert Preston starred in *The Music Man*.

By 14, I had made it to the State Fair a couple of times, but had never advanced past the first round. I learned not to expect to beat those flashy tap dancers and, instead, to look at performing as "practice" for my larger ambitions as an actress-performer. Nevertheless, I harbored secret ambitions of being the Bill Riley State Champ. As a competitive, over-achiever, it was difficult to accept the idea that I couldn't win The Bill Riley Talent Competition. After all, I had won state and national oratory titles. In fact, I was used to winning at most things. Why couldn't I win this?

Every time I qualified for the State Fair, it gave me hope that it was finally *my* year. So, at 14 I decided to try something new. I figured if I picked the right routine, I was certain it would be my year. No show tunes, patriotic medleys or interpretations of Whitney Houston hits – this time I would charm them with jazz. I planned to wear a royal blue, satin gown complete with a tea-length bubble skirt and matching gloves. I would perform a jazzed up version of "Blue Moon" because when I heard it on an Ella Fitzgerald cassette it seemed much classier than the doo-wop version that I always heard when my dad played the oldies radio station.

The best and worst thing about The Bill Riley Talent Competition was that you weren't confined to your home county. If you lost in Montgomery County, you could travel to Pottowattamie County the following weekend and have a shot at winning there. If the first place winner already won somewhere else, the second place winner would advance to the State Fair. Normally, I would hit two or three county shows before earning my ticket to advance. Inevitably though, my chances of placing first at the state or local level were crushed. If I advanced, it was because the kids who won first place had already qualified somewhere else and were simply racking up trophies and experience by going from competition to competition. I almost never placed first—not because I wasn't doing the best damn *Annie* medley around—but simply because I wasn't a tap dancer.

My career as an amateur child performer began with a little record player from Sears and the album from the movie version of *Annie*. On summer afternoons, when I was 7 years old, I climbed the stairs to my attic bedroom, Dad's tape recorder in one hand and the Annie soundtrack in the other. Originally, I requested that the entire attic be painted orange, but was forced to compromise with my mom who felt that it would be better to only paint the molding orange. I relented only when she agreed to paint a giant rainbow across the wall. I had the whole attic of our tiny old house to myself. I could even touch the ceiling where it met the walls! My favorite spot was a little nook in the back of the room. It was a balcony of sorts that overlooked the staircase and seemed to float above the stairs.

I shared the room with my little sister, but that was okay since she always did what I said. I would scale the long staircase (perfect for Slinkies by the way), pass the giant rainbow and the orange shelves filled with books and toys and crawl into my floating nook, gingerly placing my beloved Annie record on the denim covered, Sears record player. I'd press the record button on Dad's old tape recorder and set the needle down on the vinyl. Bubbling with the anticipation of recording my own version of "Tomorrow," I spoke to myself as the record began to crackle, "Oh boy, this is gonna be great." As Aileen Quinn, the movie *Annie*, belted away, I wailed along with her. I expected to sound like I was on the album when I played the tape back. Of course, when I did, the results were startlingly amateurish. My excited gurgles at the top of the song were audible on the tape and I didn't really know the words that well. I was constantly a beat or two behind Annie and this was deeply disappointing to me. However, one thing was impressive. I was loud. Really loud.

My mother must have heard me belting away from downstairs. She decided that anyone with a set of "big lungs" like mine must be a talented singer and so I was volunteered to perform songs from the musical *Annie* at the upcoming

Silver City Ice Cream Social. Not just songs, but a medley of songs—and thus began my career as an amateur child star of the American Heartland.

Silver City, Iowa (population 287) was my first home and it was here that I would begin my performing career. It was the kind of town where my mom could send me to the grocery store when I was four years old to pick up an order, which the owner would then put on a tab for Mom to pay later. I could ride my bike anywhere. We would find fossils in the limestone along the railroad tracks, have imaginative adventures along the creek, play in the streets and leave the doors unlocked.

The first annual Silver City Ice Cream Social was held during the sweltering Iowa August. Temperatures would easily reach 90 degrees, if not higher. The humidity was often unbearable and yet the old German farmers had all learned to bear it. The makeshift stage was a lowboy—a flatbed wagon used for hauling things like hay. There were dozens of folding chairs and tables covered with plastic tablecloths. Mr. Roenfeldt (don't ask me which Mr. Roenfeldt, the county was full of them) had his giant grill and was serving everyone roast pork sandwiches from a big hog he butchered himself. The ice cream was homemade—soft and sweet and drippy. Entertainment was local. There was a square dance group with a female caller (apparently it's very unusual to have a female caller), performances by Sunday school groups, guys with guitars in cowboy hats, kids who took piano lessons and me.

Mom bought me a red curly wig at the costume shop in Omaha. I didn't have a full orphan costume or the famous Annie dress, so I wore a red sailor shirt with a red "skort" (half skirt/half short). I sang a few verses of the melancholy song "Maybe" to a rag doll, swung a mop across the stage for "It's a Hard Knock Life" and capped off my performance with a belted (and most likely flat) version of "Tomorrow." Some of the key elements to performing that last song well include: Pointing to the sun when singing, "The sun will come out" and remembering to gradually raise your arms to the sky on the finale. For instance, "You're only a daaaaaaaaay," arms extended down, "aaaaaaaaaa," lift arms to shoulder height, "waaaaaaaaaaaay," arms to the sky! Also, hold "waaaaaaaaaay" until you run out of breath. Folks will be impressed by your "big lungs."

I continued to perform at local events and the Annie costume got more authentic and my singing more on pitch. I took my routine to nursing homes, church dinners, a talent show at McDonald's and, eventually, the Bill Riley Talent Competition. Singing at competitions was excruciatingly nerve-wracking. I loved singing and performing. I loved winning awards and getting my name in the paper. Unfortunately, the perfectionist in me was unbearably nervous at competitions. Even so, I felt driven to compete. Who wouldn't want another trophy on their shelf or another newspaper clipping in their scrapbook?

As I got older the routines became more sophisticated and Annie gave way to vintage Julie Andrews and Barbra Streisand tunes. I did more community and dinner theatre and my performance skills were more refined, my acting was more subtle, my voice more trained, my routines less cheesy. By 14, when I was singing "Blue Moon," I was almost classy. You have to keep in mind that royal blue dresses with bubble skirts passed for classy in the late '80s. In the summers I chased after that elusive Bill Riley title. I made it to the state fair two or three times, but never passed the first round. Each State Fair experience was identical. Bill Riley was short, it was brutally hot and I could always count on some tap dancer with big hair to knock me out of contention.

It took a few years to figure out the fastest way to win a slot in the State Fair line up. By 14 I learned that if I wanted a first place trophy from a county fair, the town to compete in was Missouri Valley, Iowa. The stage for that competition was a very slick, very non-tap dancer friendly, tile floor. Slick floors are like kryptonite to hoofers. One shuffle-off-to-Buffalo and they're flat on their frilly bottoms. Other dancer repellent surfaces include: Low-boys made of splintering wood, concrete that ruins knees and holds the potential for cracking heads open (even with the padding from extra big hair), and muddy parade grounds. That was the year I performed "Blue Moon" and the first year I won at "Mo" Valley.

The following year, at 15, I scored again with a knock 'em dead rendition of "Don't Rain on My Parade." According to my mom, Bill Riley took notice when I belted out the Streisand tune at the State Fair and maybe she's right. You could always tell if Riley liked someone. He wasn't officially a judge, but he could "signal" to the judges that they should consider letting someone through to the next level. "Wow, that was really swell. Let's have another round of applause for the little lady with the big voice from Mills County..." and so on.

Among his favorites was a young woman named Alexis from Denison. Alexis would later do me the favor of moving to my hometown, but the first time I encountered her was long before she ever moved to my turf. I was 11 and it was the first time Mills County had sponsored a Bill Riley competition. Our state of the art amphitheater was one of the more desirable places in Iowa to perform, except maybe the State Fair. Yes, my patriotic medley was a tad trite and uninspired, but that never stopped anyone in those parts before. It wasn't as bad as the girl who sang the national anthem and the whole audience had to stand through her entire piece, seed corn caps over their hearts. Performing, "You're a Grand Old Flag" and "Yankee Doodle Dandy" wasn't milking it as much as the kid who had his dad accompany him on guitar while he rallied the audience around that God-awful Lee Greenwood, cheese-fest, "God Bless the USA." In later years the raincoat and umbrella costume for "Don't Rain on My Parade" would be more charming, but I was still pretty good for a 6th grader from a small Iowa town.

Nevertheless, the tap dancers invaded with their snazzy costumes full of poofs and sequins, their creepy Jon-Benet Ramsey hair and make-up, their throngs of parents and supporters who hooted and hollered through performances as if they were watching a sporting event. Imagine people screaming, cheering and shouting out, "Way to go! Woo-hoo!" at the ballet. Worse, they would talk all the way through the performances of other kids. Audience reaction was supposed to be a criterion for judges. Unfortunately, not all the judges were familiar with the Iowa tap dancing juggernaut. I was intimidated, but also ticked off. This was my town. "They can't take the trophy away from me in my town," I thought. Of course, they did. I think that I took 3rd place.

The young tap dancing pair who won in my home territory was Alexis and her partner Bobby. They were my age and I had already seen them perform on Star Search. I remember the pangs of jealousy that I felt watching these Iowa youngsters get a shot at what seemed like the big time. Bobby was a 12-year-old Gene Kelly, but with a little more make-up than Mr. Kelly would have tolerated. Alexis was a pre-teen Barbie. She had the big, blond '80s hair and the long dancer legs. Years of extraordinary physical activity would keep her underdeveloped and thin as a swizzle stick into her teens. I, on the other hand, had been struggling with the early maturation of my body and the inevitable weight gain that comes along with it since I was 9 years old. I looked awkward and dumpy next to Alexis's beauty pageant perfection. Their routine was so flashy and polished that I knew there was no way I could ever compete. Even Barbra Streisand herself would have been given a run for her money by this razzle-dazzle, I thought.

They practiced year round and lived for talent competitions. In between softball games and plays and speech contests and swim team and hunting with Dad and piano lessons and band and voice lessons and 4-H, I tried to come up with winning Bill Riley ideas. I also tried to be a tap dancer. Since I was doing a lot of theatre my mom insisted that I should take dance lessons if I wanted to be a "triple threat." I reluctantly agreed because I knew she had a point. I liked modern and jazz, was frustrated with ballet and loathed tap. I was good at so many things that whenever I was bad at something, such as tap dancing or math, it was easy to decide that I hated it rather than work to get better at it. My one attempt to work tap into a Bill Riley routine was when I performed the patriotic medley and that was my least successful routine. The fact that these kids were beating me with an art form that I hated (if you can call what they were doing art) probably fueled my dislike for them.

A local legend from my neck of the woods was Kathy Stuart. In the late '60s Kathy was only 14 and the toast of the Bill Riley Talent Show. I think that I felt some pressure to accomplish a similar feat. She won a Mustang — that she wasn't old enough to drive — at the State Fair by balancing a cup of water on her forehead as she did the splits across two metal folding chairs. Twenty years later they were still telling that story and Cathy was still performing the same routine and wearing the same outfit. Everyone was touched by the part of the story where she turned down a job offer to tour with Gene Kelly in order to marry her high school sweetheart. I wanted people to still be telling the same stories about me decades later. Well, except for the marrying my high school sweetheart part. My story was going to end Paul Harvey style, "... and that little girl grew up to be Oscar winning actress, Katrina Markel. And now you know, the rest of the story."

At 14, performing "Blue Moon," I did go to the State Fair and, as usual, made it no further than the first round. Knowing that some singers had placed at the finals, I vowed that the next year I would come back with a belty, in your face, show-stopping number. The judges seemed to be impressed with volume and, after all, loudness was my original talent. Sometimes a college student who was studying opera would make it into the finals. Even if it wasn't good opera, the general assumption was that it was hard to do opera (and opera was loud), and therefore took more talent. Volume was also the primary weapon of Tracey Spencer, a teenage sensation from Waterloo. She placed on Star Search and was awarded a Columbia recording contract. I haven't heard anything else about her for a dozen years now. Alexis was constantly making it to the finals, both with her dance partner and later as a solo dancer. Another flashy pair of hoofers from Denison, Jason and Megan, were forever winning as well. Jason's much older sisters were the dance teachers who had created a dynasty in Denison. They were famous for bullying judges and trying to get contestants disqualified on technicalities so that their students would win. They favored Jason and Megan so heavily, that Alexis and Bobby were forced to drive several hundred miles every week to study with another set of superstar tap teachers in Mason City.

My final year performing at the State Fair I sang "Don't Rain on My Parade" from the musical Funny Girl. This time I really believed I had a shot. I was 16 and no longer an awkward pre-teen. I had good control over my voice and the routine had audience appeal. There was every reason to believe that this year I was a contender. My grandparents and my great aunt and uncle all drove up from Missouri to check out the latest farm implements, see the famous State Fair butter sculptures and watch me perform. That day my performance was solid and the audience response was strong. Riley "signaled" to the judges that he approved. I was in. I had to be in. I knew I was in.

I didn't make it in. Some piano prodigy edged me out. I couldn't even blame the tap dancing juggernaut this time. I got beat. Plain and simple.

As I sat under a tent eating pulled pork sandwiches with my family, the loss stung. In a couple more years I would be leaving Iowa, of that I was certain. I was also pretty sure that I would move on to bigger things and a more interesting life. At 27 I'm no longer performing, although I am still telling stories. Oh – and they are still talking about me back home. The Omaha World Herald theatre reviewer recently compared a young woman, performing in "Meet Me in St. Louis," favorably to me as a teenager. Nevertheless, I still feel a sense of unfinished business since The Bill Riley Talent Competition had to remain unconquered.

PATRICIA KINNEY
BLOOD AND WATER
she meets her birth mother

I am sitting in this miniature windowless room with my new mental health case manager. Her name is Maria. I thought there might be a problem when I first spoke to Maria over the phone because I could not understand her. She sounded as if she'd downed a fifth of vodka and put marbles in her mouth. She is foreign—Spain, Italy, Portugal, or maybe that French part of Canada.

Sometimes they say if you go just go toward the pain it helps. So I went there. I turned myself inside out like a sock and I went there from the top of my head to my toes. I went there. I dove into the pain from a high dive. I licked its icing and stuffed its cake in my mouth. I lay the pain on a platter and served it to guests. I inhaled its perfume as if smelling a red rose warmed by the sun. The fragrance was heady.

I am the product of a backseat date, a one-night stand in a used car. My birth mother traveled to New York City by train to attend *Carmen* at the MET. She got sick on the trip. That's when she discovered she was pregnant. She was six months along.

She worked as a salesgirl and went into labor on the fifth floor of Frederick and Nelson, an upscale department store in Seattle. She gave me up for adoption after glancing at me—once.

It's Friday. Tony smiles when he sees me. I notice dimples set deep in his cheeks and wonder to myself why I had never made note of them before. We enter his office and sit opposite one another. We both start to laugh.

"What's so funny?" I ask.

"I read that piece. The one about your family," he said.

"Which family?" I ask as I put my feet up on the edge of one of the other chairs in the small, dimly lit room.

"The adoptive tribe," he said.

Nurture—Fourth of July

It is six days since my fractured ankle and broken tibia and I am zombied out on pain killers. They brought me home from the hospital

early so that I would not miss the family Fourth of July celebration and my Uncle Don's wake. Everybody hated Uncle Don, and I wondered why we were giving him a wake. But none of us wanted to go to hell. So, Uncle Don's wake was celebrated on the Fourth of July since we were all together anyway.

My kids propped me up in a lawn chair with some of my mom's couch pillows. My Uncle George, who has a volume ten voice, was in the yard next to the neighbor's fence complaining that they only make lawn hairs for people the "size of Japs."

"Goddamn clothes too. Everything is made for Japs. Cars, furniture, silverware. It's all made for them," Uncle George said.

He walked toward the driveway where his new Dodge Ram truck was parked and returned a minute later with a red, white and blue canvas camp couch.

"This is what you call a chair," he said, as he unfolded his all-American settee.

"I got this down in Yuma at a real store. A real American store. A True Value hardware store. Owned by an American. Left the label on too. Made in the U S of A. Made for the working man. Not for no Oriental."

I want to tell Uncle George that if he is talking to me I cannot make sense of what he is saying because I am on good American painkillers. I stop myself when I realize, even as high as I am, that he is talking, just talking. He doesn't need an audience to rant. But, apparently, my mom is listening.

"I don't think all Orientals are that bad. Just the ones who are buying up all our stores. There are some nice ones at church and they bring good food to the Altar Society meetings. There are four of them in our guild," she tells my Uncle George. "I don't know what it is that they cook, but it all tastes good."

"Probably cat," Uncle George said.

"That's not very nice, Uncle George," I manage. He, like the rest of them, ignores me.

"Well, they better not touch my cat," my mom replies and leaves to look for beloved Rowdy-Do, her spoiled orange kitty. I watch my mom waddle away in her navy blue stretch pants complimented by a silk-screened t-shirt decorated with a red, white and blue birdhouse. Uncle George looks at me.

Unfortunately, my mom's next-door neighbors, the Chungs, are also hosting a picnic in their backyard. The Chungs are from South Korea. They know about my uncle. Last year, I told them to blast one of their Korean CDs loud and turn the speakers in the direction of our backyard when they saw Uncle George pulling in.

In the garage, my brother Tim and my cousin Jeff (staying at my mom's house after being busted last night for spraying perfume in his wife's face) have set up a little mini bar in the icebox. My mom thought it would be a good idea when we were kids to purchase a second refrigerator to put in the garage and then fill it with pop so that we were not running in and out of the house all day long. From that point on, we pretty much supplied all the neighborhood kids with Shasta cola and Hires root beer. In high school, our special "kid fridge" was filled with Rainier beer. We kept plastic Wonder bread bags full of hallucinogenic mushrooms in the tiny freezer on top.

Today, Tim and cousin Jeff are mixing Crown Royal with Coke in the red plastic cups my mom has earmarked for raspberry party punch. Jeff walks over to me to ask if I have any extra painkillers. He has a bad, bad headache

A car pulls up. We hear a door slam. Cousin in-law Donna, the red headed wannabe country singer is here. She heads for our nice little picnic city under the pie cherry tree. Of course, she selects the empty blue and white lawn chair next to me. Everyone gets quiet. My mom announces in her singsong voice that it is time to eat.

Around the picnic table, Donna says that I sure don't look like the rest of the family. I tell her that I am adopted.

"Have you ever looked up your mama?" she asks. This is something my adoptive mom, who is in charge of the picnic, is not too wild about. It is the closest any discussion in this family has ever come to sex. To talk about my beginnings conjures images of fornication, fucking. I was never a baby like other babies. I was a product of a sex act. They all know that's my history. Why talk about it? My sister-in-law, Janet, the one who has worked at K-mart for 27 years, changes the subject to baked salmon. Meanwhile, my brother and cousin are getting wasted on Crown Royal and trying to fire up my dad's old generator so we can listen to some Irish tavern songs while my mom is complaining about the cache of illegal fireworks from the local Indian reservation that she has just found on the bench in the garage. Uncle George is leaning over the fence separating my mother's yard from the Chung's. When he begins to growl at their German shepherd, Johnny, Mr. Chung begins to scream loudly in his native Korean. In any language it sounds like, "Bite me, you fat fuck."

Mom is doing this thing where she reaches into her pocket and wiggles her fingers as if she is looking for her rosary. She says she thinks she is going to jail because she can hear sirens and that Cousin Jeff and his wife Donna should not be within 100 feet or is that 100 yards of one another because of the restraining order.

By this time, Mom needs to sit in a lawn chair under the pie cherry tree because she is feeling light-headed. Brother Tim, topped off with Crown Royal, drives Mom to the hospital in his vintage Cadillac. Over watermelon and cake, the rest of us talk about my mom and what could possibly be wrong. We think she's had a heart attack. It turns out she ate a plate of cookies and about half the American flag frosting off the Fourth of July cake. She's diabetic.

Nature—Labor Day

On Labor Day I visited my birth family in Seattle. My 83 year-old Memphis born birth mother and I discuss the poetry of Alexander Pope. Wagner's Opera, The Flying Dutchman, makes scratchy pirouettes on the record player. My aunt Agnes, former Director of the University of Washington's drama department and founder of the Seattle Children's Theater, is in the kitchen preparing ham and cheese sandwiches on rye. She uses margarine and mayonnaise. I don't like my sandwiches with margarine and mayonnaise, but I never tell her this. We pull antique Hitchcock chairs up to the dining room table and pour our Diet Cokes into my grandmother's Waterford crystal goblets. It's a tea party. A tea party just for me. I am 43 years old. After we say grace, we eat our sandwiches.

My mother says she remembers looking at me once. I was blond and small. She says she was pretty drugged up so she didn't hold me. So, on August 2, 1959 in the labor and delivery ward at King County Hospital in Seattle, a nurse wrapped me up and took me down the hall. I wonder now. Did I know what the hell was going on? I mean I'd been in the woman's belly for nine months. Forty weeks of riding downtown on the bus, walking the sales floor at the downtown Frederick and Nelson. There was even a trip by train to New York City at 24 weeks. We went to the MET. To the Goddamn MET. We slept in a sleeper car. A sleeper car like Jack Lemon and Tony Curtis in "Some Like It Hot". I loved the opera when I was a child. Because I was a flutist in the school band, from the fifth grade on I was able to travel to Seattle three or four times a year to attend the Opera. Of course, this is before I knew I'd been to the Met. Before I knew my mother. Before I knew she lived for the opera. It is one of many connections. Unexplainable connections they call them.

Most days my childhood was like Monet's garden—colorful but a blur. I survived by keeping one step ahead of the unfocused lens of my family. At age six, I wanted to have pointy pink tits like Barbie, eat Tollhouse cookies for breakfast and marry Father Kevin, the young priest at church. I also called myself Mrs. Hogan. I became Mrs. Hogan when I wore my white church hat with the poofy pink bow. Mrs. Hogan was a reporter. I thought that I worked at a big city newspaper and that I wore the hat. I made my mom a little crazy. She still treated me like a kid. Whenever my mom gets the chance she reminds me of how childish I was.

"You embarrassed us. You insisted we call you Mrs. Hogan. You wouldn't take the damn hat off. Acted like you were writing a book, always taking notes on us, following us around the house—like you were somebody, a regular Jackie Kennedy or Mrs. Astor. You even used a snotty little voice and pretended that a box of my pencils was a pack of cigarettes. That's when I put a kibosh on things. You were a little to smart for your own britches, Mrs. H-O-G-A-N."

Barricaded behind a wall of dust-covered Reader's Digest Condensed Books, I sat at my mother's metal typing table on New Year's Day, pretending to type on her black Royal Typewriter. My chair was a musty pile of *National Geographic* magazines waiting for September's rummage sale at Sacred Heart of Jesus, our church.

One afternoon, I showed my mom a poem I'd written at school. At age six, I wrote poems about Mount Rainer almost daily. I don't know why I showed her. She always got mad.

Challenging ramparts
Rule the Sky
Made by God
They are mountains high
With their icy arms
They pray
Protecting us
Every day

I did use two words in my poem that I had found written under a color photo of a snowy mountain peak in one of those *National Geographic* magazines.

"Challenging Ramparts? What Goddamn kid says that? You can't write poems. You just steal words. You're in the first grade, you're not smart enough to write a poem and nobody wants to be bothered reading this crap on these stupid little pieces of paper. Now take that hat off and get out of here. If I hear another poem, Mrs. Hogan is going to get a stick over her ass."

When I found my birth mother in 1992, she told me that my grandmother's name was Johanna Hogan. Miss Hogan was society's child, a writer for Catholic Digests and other periodicals. She resided in the affluent Hyde Park area north of Chicago. And, she always wore a hat.

Nic Darling | **the day my grandpa didn't die** *Poem*

inside he was gathering
on the floor
into a pile of inanimate flesh,
a body i could not handle
alone, it was too big.
outside i chipped ice away,
to clear the steps for the paramedics,
and it gathered in tiny crystal shards
around my feet
until i brushed them aside,
they were not the issue.
i thought that he should die
in bed,
a selfish wish for the slow dissipation
of life allowed by cotton sheets
like an iv drip,
drip, drip...
i used to feel
in some youthful understanding
of morality/mortality,
that my goodness (promised)
could be exchanged for a life,
so i screamed into the night
and my screams solidified
into tiny ice crystals
and floated (i am told)
toward god.

TOM FAST
NAKED MAN
volume 3: sports days, culture festivals and drinking parties

Sports Day

What a day. In September most Japanese junior highs have 2 special days that ALL students take part in: Sports Day and Culture Day. When I explain that we do not have these days in U.S. schools, Japanese people are stunned and amazed. They can't fathom life without them. I learned later, that it is not just an event that takes place in school. Japanese people engage in Sports Day events from kindergarten through college and beyond. Many Japanese companies hold a Sports Day for their employees as well.

Our Sports Day began with the opening ceremonies. Everything begins with at least one opening ceremony in Japan. Sometimes there's even a ceremony for the opening ceremony. The students marched out onto the dirt playing field in the same manner that they've been practicing for at least 2 weeks, carrying their class flags and hand-painted paper banners. The school principal stands on a makeshift platform in front of the students and delivers a rousing speech, through a bullhorn, on the virtues of group participation, how it makes everyone feel good and makes the Nation stronger.

This is followed with calisthenics, which is to this day, one of the most hilarious things I've seen in Japan—or anywhere else for that matter. The whole school population stands at military attention in really "gay" looking uniforms: White shoes, white socks (pulled up to the knee), blue shorts (pulled up to the armpits) a tight, white shirt that accenting girly arms—and to top it off—a cotton white cap with an elastic strap that goes around the chin. Yes, the students are required to look like total dweebs so that no one in particular will stand out as "cool."

Then the music starts. Like an army of robots, they engage in some of the most awkward exercises invented by Man. The music is a nostalgic, patriotic anthem on a scratchy record, boomed over the loudspeaker. *"Ich-Ni-San!"* (1,2,3). Who invented these exercises?! What good do they do?! Who wrote that music?!! Why the Hell do they play it?!! Have they no idea how ridiculous the whole thing looks?!!

Masahiro (one of my favorite students) knew. He was constantly a half step behind, exaggerating every move like a Japanese Gomer Pile. It was comic genius, but I was the only one laughing. Everyone else looked so rigid and serious that you'd have sworn WWII was about to happen all over again. Isn't this supposed to be fun?

Finally all the pomp and circumstance was over. The races began: Relay after relay: 100m, 200m, 400m, 800m, 3 legged race, 5 legged race, team jump-rope

(30 kids jumping together with one huge rope! Now that's Japan teamwork at its best), and other inexplicable events. Mine was yet to come.

After a bento lunch (complete with a whole octopus! It was a little one but yes it was fully in tact and I ate it), it was time for my first event: "American Folk Dancing." That's actually what they call it and apparently it's a sport in Japan. Everyone in this country is instructed how to "Oklahoma 2-Step" by the age of 13. (At first I thought this strange, but now that I think about it, learning the "Glow Worm," square dance and "The Hustle" were mandatory in my junior high days.)

You really need to have been there to fully grasp this. There we were: The teachers, the students, the PTA moms and me, all dancing to the music of "Oklahoma!" on a hot September afternoon. The Japanese were precise and calculating as they executed their steps. Me, I must have looked like a rodeo clown. Most of the girls and moms recoiled in fear when I reached out for them with my hand and yelled, "Howdy!"

After the dancing, it was finally time for me to prove just how fast I really am. The 100 meter relay was next and I'd been elected anchor for the teacher's team. I stretched with the PE teacher (whose English nickname is "Mr. Big Moon"—a translation of his Japanese name), and put on my green headband. All participants had them in various colors, tied around their heads *kamikaze* style.

Our team got off to an awful start. By the time I was up, we were a full 100m behind everyone else. When I strutted out onto the track the students roared my name. You could have sworn that Carl Lewis himself had just taken the field. It made me recall the all-Russian audience cheering for Rocky in *Rocky IV*.

I basked in the glory of the moment, raising my arms like Sylvester Stallone on the steps of the Philadelphia Art Museum. But it was all for not. Huffing and puffing her way toward me was our short, out of shape and uncoordinated, little old librarian. When she saw me, she got a little too excited and—in the process of trying to speed up—fell flat on her face. I ran to her and checked her pulse. Still alive. I ripped the baton out of her hand and sped away like a purse-snatcher. I felt bad about leaving her there in the dust (literally), but my primary duty was to win the race for our team.

You see, many Japanese have an inferiority complex. They thought because I'm a tall, white male, that I'm some sort of physically superior being. I was sorry to disappoint them. The kids had a hell of a lead—and a sprinter I am not. There was no way I could catch up despite the ecstatic cheers.

I felt pretty good about my performance all the same. After all, it was the first time I'd run a relay in at least 10 years. Everyone seemed to be impressed—at least they acted like they were anyway. What they really think is always a mystery in Japan. Of course I came in dead last, but everyone liked the fact that I "did my best." That's what counts here most.

Culture Day

For some reason, I was more worried about how I would perform today than last week's Sports Day. To add to my concerns, I had no clean shirts and was out of deodorant. It would be very important not to sweat.

Note: Being out of deodorant would be small problem in the US but for a foreigner in Japan, it's a perfect example of something minor getting way out of hand. What do you do when you don't know how to read or speak and you've got B.O.? After an hour of staring at various illegible cans and bottles, you end up buying hair spray for your armpits.

The festival started again with the usual preliminary pomp and circumstance. During the previous week, the classrooms had transformed into exhibition spaces and art installations. Meanwhile a series of original short plays (15 - 30 minutes) were to be performed by each of the 3rd year classes. There were also some musical interludes thrown in. My rendition of "Yesterday" by the Beatles was to be one of them. (FYI: Yesterday is a karaoke anthem for foreigners in Japan. Did you know that Okayama is the birthplace of the karaoke machine?)

I was surprised by how creative and theatrical the students were on stage considering how in my classroom they can be so completely comatose! Most of the time I had no idea what I was watching (it was kind of similar to opera in that regard) but it was still highly entertaining.

After an hour or so, my moment in the sun arrived and I walked out onto the stage. The music teacher started playing the intro. I began to sweat. The smell wasn't good. Then a solar flare of a spotlight momentarily blinded me. I sweated more. Needless to say, I didn't get off to a good start. I could hear my voice quivering as I stood there in front of the entire student body singing, "Why she had to go I don't know, she wouldn't say..." By the time I finished (probably a half note below where I should have been), I had repeated the 2nd verse twice by accident, and was standing in a pool of my own perspiration. I stunk in more ways than one—but I looked good in my tux.

My performance was loved by all but me. Once again I had done my best and completely failed, which is what they really love here. During the afternoon I sang again. This time the song was a Japanese tune ironically entitled, "Tomorrow." Musically it was a piece of cake—a typical gum droppy sweet Japanese pop song. But the hard part was reading the lyrics. They were entirely in hiragana! It was the closing number of the culture festival, so I was joined by the heads of the student body, who helped me a little, but they barely opened their mouths. Booming out over the speakers, I was the only person you could hear. I was singing away but not knowing what I was saying. I must have sounded like Arnold Schwartzenegger trying to sing "Puff the Magic Dragon."

Drinking Party

The lousy singing didn't stop there. The best part of Culture Day was the teacher's "drinking" party that same night. I like the fact that they aren't ashamed to call it what it is. On these occasions Japanese get together with the sole purpose of releasing stress by drinking themselves into oblivion. We had a great dinner, all sitting on the tatami floor of a typical restaurant, pouring each other beer and sake, eating sushi, tempura, etc. The quiet, controlled people I'd been working with for the last month were quickly unraveling. Faces were turning red and behavior becoming boisterous.

A strapping young PE teacher challenged Inoe-sensei to demonstrate some of her Aikido skills. Inoe-sensei was a young, "fresh" teacher, only about 6 months out of college, where she was rumored to be one of the top members of her Aikido club. Being a very sweet, traditional country girl, she demurely declined his challenge. Much like a scene from a kung fu movie, the PE teacher turned to the rest of teachers and mocked her, then continued bullying and poking her, trying to get a reaction. Inoe-sensei, who had been seated on the tatami, was forced into a standing position against the wall. She was at least a foot smaller than the PE teacher and maybe half his body weight. She continued to apologize and explain how she really knows "very little" about martial arts. To which the PE teacher replied, "She's lying! Watch this!" And he actually threw a punch at her!

I'm not exactly sure what happened next because it was all so fast. She must have dodged the blow, grabbed his arm and then used it to flip him over her back. In less than a second after his attack, he was slammed to the floor with a heavy "THUD!" He was left staring up at the ceiling with Inoe-sensei bowing over him and apologizing profusely for having defended herself so successfully.

On that note, dinner was finished. Next, it is customary for the party to move to a smaller, more private establishment, such as a karaoke bar. A few of the hard-core partiers invited me to continue on with them to a hostess club. I felt it important that I keep up and establish myself as one of the group. Besides, I'd heard a lot about these "hostess" establishments and was curious to go where not many gaijin have been before...

Back at the restaurant, I noticed that our esteemed English teacher, Mr. Fuji, was drinking pretty hard and fast. Before I continue, let me describe Mr. Fuji for you: He is a man in is early 50's who truly deserves the Japanese title of *sensei* ("teacher"—but the word seems to carry a lot more weight here in Asia). He speaks very good English (which isn't really a requirement for the job) and he is highly respected (feared?) by his peers and students alike. Mr. Fuji can be seen most days in a bright purple warm-up suit and tennis shoes. His thin, wispy, white hair is usually standing on end—wind-blown by the brisk bike ride to school. It stays in that position for the rest of the day.

Mr. Fuji does not take kindly to teenage rebellion. I have seen him literally yell at a student (in English) for a full 30 minutes in class. I asked him about his disciplinary approach once, and he replied proudly that he'd never once had to "hit" a student. (FYI: Up until about 10 years ago, corporal punishment was still OK in Japan, if for example a student's hair was too long).

At our school there are small number of hoodlums (who are oddly referred to as "Yankee Boys") who for the most part have the run of the school. Most teachers fear them, despite the fact that they are just skinny little 13 year old boys. Mr. Fuji on the other hand, takes them to task. The other day, we had a class together. I couldn't locate Mr. Fuji at first, but ultimately found him in the photo copy room with two blue haired punks. They were sulking with defeated looks on their faces. Mr. Fuji had one by the scruff of the neck in one hand and was shaking a bottle of black hair spray in the other. "You go on ahead of me, Tom. I'm going to be a little late" he said, sounding a lot like Clint Eastwood.

Mr..Fuji likes to engage me in conversation from time to time. Sometimes he is mundane and other times, very profound. He always uses his hands when he speaks English (not Japanese though). He's got a low, clear, booming, baritone voice and sounds like he's either perpetually teaching or slightly hearing impaired. He also has a cadence to his speech that's sort of a cross between Captain Kirk and Mr. Rourke from *Fantasy Island*.

"Hello Thomas!...And HOW are YOU today?"

"Aahhh... You say you ARE FINE? Hmm... And WHY are you FINE today Thomas?"

"Aahhhhha....Hmmm... YES!... Mmmmm...VERY GOOD... I see." etc.

Now that you know Mr. Fuji, try to imagine him drunk out of his mind. We went to the karaoke bar. Mr. Fuji was already displaying signs of heavy intoxication. The drama teacher right away got a bottle of brandy for our table and 2 somewhat sleazy hostess girls to serve. They sat with us and gingerly dropped ice into our tumblers. They were pretty I suppose, behind the make-up, the tinted hair and tight dresses. They both had low, sultry voices (the exact opposite of the ideal, cute, cherpy Japanese female voice), probably the result of way too much cigarettes, alcohol and karaoke. The drama teacher held the bottle of brandy up for me to see. "You rike blandy?" He asked and grinned? (He had strategically positioned himself between the hostess girls) "Yes," I lied. He immediately patted one of the girls on the knee and she poured me a glass straight! Everyone else had theirs on the rocks and diluted with water. Shit. At that point, I had already drunk more than any night since my college days in Seville, Spain. I was in way over my head but I fought on. I had no other choice.

As expected, I soon found a microphone being waved in my face. The karaoke torture was about to begin. They had selected an English song for me: "How Deep is Your Love?" by the BeeGees, a personal favorite of our grey-haired, slight of build, school Vice Principal (I wonder was he a fan of the movie "Saturday Night Fever" as well?) I was in trouble. They didn't seem to grasp the fact that I am a baritone and that the Brothers Gibb are sopranos. I looked at the karaoke video screen: "Haaaaaaaaaaaaaaa, Ahhhhh, uhhh, ahhhh...Is your love how deeeep is your love. I really need to know..."

I am glad that I was in a foreign country and in a place where everyone else (except the hostess girls) was too drunk to remember. Before the night was to end, I would submit to singing not only the BeeGees but also: 1) Simon and Garfunkel's "Bridge Over Troubled Water" (also out of my range); 2) Richie Valens' "La Bamba!" (I impressed the Hell out of them with my Spanish); 3) and lastly, "Rhinestone Cowboy" by Glen Campbell. Like Goldie Lox, the last one was just right. I had everyone in the bar swaying back and forth and smiling like we were old friends.

At 1:30, it was time to go home. There was just one problem: Mr. Fuji couldn't even stand-up. Each time he did, he'd fall just as fast. But he kept trying—like a drunk Captain Kirk—saying: "I AM FINE. Please do not WORRY about ME!" I was the only one who understood him, as he was addressing the whole room in English.

At last we got him on his feet. The other teachers asked him if he would make it home ok. He laughed a hearty laugh (you know how opera singers laugh? Same thing) and said again, "YOU do NOT have to worry!" He pointed at his chest with his thumb (still swaying in the wind), "I...AM.......FINE!"

Mr. Fuji had ridden his bike that day, just like me. And as fate would have it, he also lives in my neighborhood. The other teachers looked very relieved when they discovered that we were going in the same direction. Thus I was charged with getting the honorable *Fuji sensei* home in one piece. I asked him:

"Do you know where your house is in relation to mine? Perhaps we should take a cab?" Not possible. "Thomas, I AM FINE. You do not need to worry... and YES! I...KNOW....WHERE I live....BUT! I do not KNOW Where I AM! HA! HA! HA! HA! (again the opera laugh)."

So I showed him the way and we rode our bikes—he insisted. You don't deny Fuji-sensei, when he insists on doing something. All I could do was ride out in the middle of traffic and create as much of a buffer as possible, between the cars and the weaving bicycle of Mr. Fuji. He made tremendous S curves all the way home, bumping into me and then careening off toward a wall or curb and back again to me in the middle of the road.

Cars were honking at me but I held my ground and made them pass. I was scared to death as we crossed a bridge, that Mr. Fuji would fall into the Asahi River. Several times his bike brushed up against mine and almost killed us both. Finally we reached the point where our paths diverged. I asked him one last time if he was ok. I don't have to tell you his response. We said good-bye and he sped away... sort of. I could see him now taking up the entire road still swerving back and forth. I decided to follow him at a distance—just to make sure he made it home alive.

I was about 20 feet behind him when he suddenly veered to the left and out of sight. I thought for sure he had crashed. I caught up to see what had happened. There was his bike, laying on its side with the front wheel still spinning. Remarkably, Mr. Fuji was still standing and apparently unharmed. He had his back to me and stood there staring into the sky, entranced by the harvest moon. Then I noticed that he was releasing a cascade of pee into the gutter. At that moment I knew that he would make it home in one piece. I turned around and headed home.

On Monday I saw Mr. Fuji again and it was business as usual as if nothing had ever happened: "Aahhh THOMAS! And HOW are YOU today?"

DOMENICK ANGIELLO
THE STORE
the son learns about life amid used typewriters,
calculators and checkwriters.

"If you're not going to work at being a college student, then you might as well help me at the store," my father announced after examining my spring semester report, which revealed an F in Calculus II and no grade over C. My father's dream that I would be a doctor had died when I was dropped from Fordham's premed program at the end of my first semester. That and my continued poor grades in the spring convinced him that I wasn't willing to make the investment in study that he thought would guarantee a lucrative, independent career. Unaccountably, I would not stand on the broad shoulders of his hard work, self-deprivation and shrewd investing to reach above the world in which he struggled with wits and will to make his family safe from material hardship. Maybe I would stand shoulder to shoulder with him in that world.

Not that my father wasn't proud of his accomplishment in establishing his business; he had told me more than once that it had turned a profit from the very first month he opened it in 1955.

The store, as we always called it, located first on Church Street near City Hall in Manhattan, was the sort of business machines establishment that is almost extinct now. We sold and serviced new and used typewriters, adding machines, calculators and checkwriters. The word store doesn't do the place justice, really. It was a storefront, perhaps thirty feet wide and fifty deep, but the rear third was walled off as a repair shop with a long workbench, at which four mechanics could work simultaneously. On the back wall of the shop were chemical baths and a compressor for washing office machines in preparation for overhauling them, and a powerful, noisy exhaust system to remove the fumes and clouds of spray from the solvents used for this purpose. Still, the smells of Fedron cleaner, carbon tetrachloride, alcohol and lubricating oil were always present.

A partition of "frost green" sheet metal topped by glass panels formed the otherwise open office which occupied a corner of the showroom and contained two heavy steel desks: my father's, where he gleefully typed his invoices with two fingers on an ancient Royal model XS; and the one where I would eventually sit, earnestly doing the bookkeeping that always revealed a comfortable profit. Along both walls of the showroom, in the same green as the office-partition, were steel racks on which were displayed new Olympia and Smith Corona typewriters and reconditioned Royals, Remingtons, and Underwoods. Occasionally, an Oliver, L. C. Smith or Woodstock, relics of another era, would squat there in the stolid meditation of old age. IBM Electrics, mostly model As early on and some older 01s, so heavy that they could easily anchor a small craft in a storm, patiently awaited the fingers that would set their motors humming and their keys clacking. Other shelves held adding machines and various brands of calculators: Monroes, Marchants and Fridens. By the standards of our microchip era, these mechanical miracles of that time were noisy and slow. The stock was rounded out with checkwriters and occasional Comptometers, time stamps, check signers, Stenographs and stock cancellers. From the store, my father also ran a wholesale business in used checkwriters and parts for them, shipping them to dealers all over the States and in a few foreign countries.

Before I arrived, he ran the whole enterprise alone, riding the subway from the Bronx to open on weekdays at 8:30 a.m. and closing as late as 9:00 p.m. on the nights when the various mechanics would come in to work on the machines he couldn't fix himself. On Saturdays, he opened at the usual time, but he allowed himself the luxury of driving in and of leaving work by 3:00.

When my father expressed his desire that I help him in his business, I couldn't deny that it would be only fair. I began to go in with him on Saturdays, often suffering with a hangover and lack of sleep, and occasionally did a business errand or two during the week. Summer work at the store became part of my routine, too. As Dad expected, none of this had any effect on my studies because they consisted only of going to class and cramming before tests. We continued in this way through the rest of my college years, and when I graduated without much sense of direction and without attracting the attention of corporate recruiters, I made the transition to full time work at the store, an inauspicious beginning, as I saw it, under a penumbra of failure.

If I wasn't so young, twenty-two, and just starting a family, I might have surrendered to despair. As a pragmatic solution having to do with curriculum requirements, I had become an English major when I was no longer welcome in premed, and in spite of my poor grades, I had been touched by the world of ideas as they are expressed in writings of philosophy, history and literature. I hadn't accumulated much knowledge, but I had, between bouts of drinking at the Web and marathon sessions of poker in the student union, developed a sense of the world and of myself that made my heart unquiet at sharing my father's success at the store. Although it immediately provided me with an adequate living and promised me affluence in the future, the store also was the place to which I had been sentenced for crimes the nature of which I couldn't fully articulate but which had to do with a waste of promise.

My talents, if they weren't illusory, lay in some other direction—although exactly what direction that was I couldn't say. Nevertheless, I resolved to do the best I could because, apparently, the store would define my life's work.

The work and the surroundings were dirty and my daily tasks boring. Malaise hung over me like the fumes from the washing tank in the rear, and I breathed in ancient dust that seemed like the ashes of the mercenary Dutch from centuries ago. The basement was the turf of rival gangs of quick roaches and bloated water bugs that embodied the revulsion I had to suppress to come to work each day. My father advised me to adopt the way he used to deal with his disgust over the bugs: turning on the light a while before going down to the basement. That would drive these denizens of the dark into hiding so that I wouldn't have to see them. But the bugs were so large that I could hear them scuttling over the dry and dusty cardboard boxes stained with their filth. When packing anything in a carton retrieved from down there, I would have to knock the box against a wall several times to avoid sending a stowaway cockroach as an accidental immigrant to Seattle or St. Paul.

Right from the start I was thrown into every kind of work we did. Dad gave me little training or instruction. For example, he might say, "See what you can do with that Royal HHP. The backspace isn't working." More often than not I was able to troubleshoot the problem. Or I'd be sent by subway on a delivery in the Empire State Building, shifting from time to time a heavy Friden calculator from one hip to the other to counterbalance its weight, and lurching like a drunken seaman, first to one side—then the other. I shipped Speedrite matrices to Denver and F & E inkrolls to Savannah, Paymaster model 900s to Hamilton, Ontario. I kept the books, set up the window display, demonstrated equipment to customers, and designed mail order brochures.

In spite of my disappointment with myself for not making more of my education, there was pleasure for a while in learning new things. In those days before great economic shifts rearranged the geography of commerce in the city, before Hunts Point market and the World Trade Center, before Tribeca, Soho and all the acronymically-named places, I learned my way around the city in general but especially lower Manhattan: Vesey and Varick Streets, Nassau, Water, Mott, Houston, Lafayette, Greenwich, and West Broadway; the financial district, radio row, the wholesale shoe section along Reade and Duane and the produce markets.

I learned to correct a typewriter's uneven line spacing by rubbing down a platen with emery cloth soaked in carbon tet or alcohol, and how to use bending tools to bring skewed letters back into line; how to renew a Royal keyboard, using a special tool to fasten the nickel-plated rings that would secure the shiny new letters under clear plastic; I learned how to adjust a Paymaster checkwriter matrix to achieve a uniform imprint; I learned why the German-made Olympia typewriter we sold, with its spring-steel keys and precision engineering, was better than the new Royals, Remingtons and Smith-Coronas.

I never did learn not to make that one last turn on the screwdriver in an effort to bring nearer to perfection something that was already satisfactory. Ping! The overstressed assembly would fly apart, screws and springs scattering across the bench and dribbling onto the floor, the tiny parts bouncing and rolling invisibly into crevices and under immovable objects to lurk there forever lost in the dust. "Dom!" My father would call from the office. "Didn't I tell you it was good enough?" I learned how to break expenses and income into their appropriate categories in maintaining the books. But I never learned to be comfortable offering five dollars for a used checkwriter I would eventually sell for ninety. I learned a whole new language of brand names and machine parts. I learned the prices of all the things we sold. But it took me a long time to learn the value of my experience in the store.

My main interest was always in the people.

In the relaxed atmosphere of the evening, I chatted with the mechanics who came in to do piecework, moonlighting after their day jobs.

Bill Pond was a handsome and engaging young man with a permanent tan and a carefully maintained pompadour of full, black hair. He would wrestle with one of the Friden calculators he stopped by to repair, his face an ever tightening knot of frustration. Clearly not a student of Zen, he would finally lift the heavy machine six inches off the bench and let it drop with a slam—after which, usually, the stubborn opponent finally submitted. Bill would sometimes drive Dad home. They became friends, and my parents had Bill and his girlfriend, Karen, to dinner a few times. When I first met Karen, she was a pretty and self-possessed girl. I always remember her with a prim smile on her lips and a pink chiffon kerchief around her neck. But she seemed more and more forlorn as the years passed, delaying the culmination of her expectations. She was middle-aged by the time she and Bill married. By then Bill's careful coiffure was streaked with gray along his temples. Their long courtship seemed strange and wasteful to me as one who had married straight out of college.

Vinnie Randazzo didn't look like a mechanic with his carefully trimmed mustache, immaculate white shirts and fashionable gray suits, their slacks pressed to a dangerous edge and his left hand adorned with a gold ring in which was set a large, sparkling stone. His hair was pure white from the first day I saw him when he was, perhaps, forty. Having a wife and children didn't prevent him from a carnivorous inspection of any attractive woman—defined as anyone in a skirt or dress who was not wearing surgical stockings. There was an opening over the bench that would allow us to see the sales floor from the repair shop in the rear. When he was back there working on a Remington adding machine, Vinnie's head was sure to appear in that opening whenever the click of high heels signaled the entrance of a pretender to his surreptitious attention. If I happened to be back there with him, he'd turn to me momentarily, pointing the screwdriver in his hand to the subject of his appreciation and say, "I'd bite that!"

Salesmen stopped by for the gab and the rest it gave their feet.

Andy, a neat, diminutive Royal salesman with curly blond hair, a snap brim hat and a gray suit with narrow lapels, complained of the company cutting his territory in half just when he was starting to make some money. Whenever I asked him how he was doing, he would answer in his distinctive southern accent, "Well, Dom, it's a great life—if you don't weaken."

Jerry Feit, the short, plump salesman from the Italian company, Olivetti, had dark, thinning hair which rolled back in tight waves along his scalp. He was a forty-something Jewish guy who had seen action in Italy during World War II and knew more Italian language and geography than I did. When I had occasion to tell him that my paternal grandfather came from Santa Maria, he responded with a perfect accent, "Ah, vicina di Napoli!" Jerry had the salesman's tendency to tell the same stories or make the same observations over and over, forgetting where in his many stops he had already delivered them. Consistent with that habit, he must have told me a dozen times that there were many Jewish Italians. Fellow Jews addressing him in Italian was an experience he hadn't anticipated, so he found it remarkable and amusing. He was very fond of the Italy in spite of the war.

Gregarious and cheerful, Jerry seemed a person married to his habits but, in all other respects, committed to lifelong bachelorhood. He only became miserable when, after a brief period of bliss, he ruined his relationship with a woman by marrying her. In his visits to the store soon afterwards, he would tell us of his wife's recriminations and tears in perfect innocence as to their cause. Within weeks, he reported, with the puzzled wistfulness of a child who couldn't understand how one of his favorite toys had gotten broken, that she had packed her things and returned to her mother. He, in turn, was freed to resume his whimsical good humor.

A lifetime city dweller, for a year he repeated the story of finally buying his first new car, a Chrysler New Yorker, only to have Olivetti provide him with a company car two weeks later. In a combination of regret at his unnecessary expense and appreciation of the irony, he would tell over and over of the Chrysler New Yorker that never came out of the parking garage. One day he said, "When I die, I'm not going to be buried in a coffin. I'm going to have them make a ramp into my grave, and I'll be buried in the Chrysler New Yorker—you know, so I can drive to the candy store to pick up the newspaper." In the spirit of these comments, I replied, "I just wish everyone could be so sensible about such arrangements. I can't tell you the number of people I know who haven't given a moment's thought to how they would follow the Knicks once they're dead."

Dealing with customers exposed me to a variety of experiences, not all of them pleasant.

Two late middle-aged ladies came in once, sisters who looked like twin knock-offs of Aunt Bee on the old Andy Griffith Show and exclaiming in the same musical voices. Dad sold them the heaviest electric typewriter in the store, and I was to have the pleasure of delivering it to their home in Brooklyn. By the time I got to the address on the receipt, both my hips were sore from shifting the machine from one to the other to ease my fatigue. Theirs was an ill-kept house near the end of a street of modest single-family houses in Coney Island, the edge of nowhere from my perspective. I knocked on the door several times, but no one responded, and it seemed dark inside. I was about to leave, puzzled and dreading the punishing trip back to the store with my burden, when a neighbor caught my eye. "They're in there," he called from the front stoop next door. "Just keep knocking." Thanking him, and wondering at the tone of disdain in his manner, I did so.

After several minutes, one of the sisters did come to the door, and as she opened it, a stench rose from behind her and surrounded me. I took one last breath outdoors and held it as I stepped over the threshold into a nightmare. The interior was dark and gloomy. I must have visibly shuddered as I realized that indistinct shapes oozed along the floors. The woman asked, "Are you cold, dear?" and without waiting for an answer, slipped into the next room for her checkbook. As my eyes adjusted, I saw that the walls and floors of the place were riddled with holes and that the oozing shapes were cats, which were emerging from some of them and disappearing into others. Judging from the stench that assaulted me again when I had to take a breath, there must also have been many rats, which the cats killed and left within the walls, the headless bodies gradually changing to liquid and gas and leaving behind a maggot-ridden pelt.

What business the cat ladies had with an electric typewriter I couldn't guess, nor did I pause to ask. I hoped its weight wouldn't send me crashing through a hole in the floor to a snake pit in the cellar.

Another time, a woman in a neatly tailored suit and a pillbox hat with a veil came into the store. Her look was familiar to me from the many films I had seen with my mother twenty years ago in the late forties. She glanced at some reconditioned IBM electrics then approached the office cubicle. As I rose to meet her, she peered at me through the veil which gave her eyes a hint of intrigue, but her tone was matter-of-fact when she said, "I wonder if you could assist me."

"Certainly, madam" I said, unintentionally falling into the obliging tone of the eager shopkeeper from those same films, and she walked back to the IBMs with me in tow.

"Maybe you are the people to help me," she whispered in what seemed a mock-confidential tone suggesting facetiously that she and I were, after all, on the same side.

"If we can't, no one can."

"I have one of these at home," the woman said, pointing at a model A. I thought whimsically that her voice and look suggested both fascination and fear, as if she were playing Barbara Stanwyck in Double Indemnity.

"Are you looking for a later model?"

"Do you do repairs as well?"

"We do expert repairs on the IBM. What's the problem?" Her manner had begun to shake my initial view that, although we were playing a scene from a B movie, we might ultimately come to terms on the purchase or repair of an IBM electric.

"My typewriter is bugged," she said in a conspiratorial tone. She didn't wait for a response, adding that she had recently discovered that the FBI and the CIA had wire-tapped her phone. She'd avoided using it, but then she discovered that they had cleverly placed a listening device in her typewriter. Perhaps I broke the spell or undermined her confidence in me when I said that I didn't see how a typewriter could be bugged. Anyway, she never returned. For all I know, she had cast me as a double agent.

When Paul Muni walked into the store I recognized him immediately. It was 1966. The character actor, famous for his portrayal of Al Capone in Scarface, was seventy at the time and looked his age. He was tall and gaunt with a ready smile and spoke with the resonant voice of a stage actor. Dad smiled with pleasure as he chatted with him, and called me over to meet the famous man. It was the only time I ever saw my father star-struck. But Dad never lost focus. He still sold him a Marchant calculator. When I went to deliver it to Mr. Muni on East End Avenue, I brought along a cousin, who was a Marchant mechanic, under the pretense that he could better demonstrate the machine's features, but really to meet him. The aging star, who was to die the following year, told my cousin he could be typecast as the good kid in a film about inner city youth.

When I went on a delivery in City Island, I expected to find that my destination was a conventional place of business since the delivery receipt read, "Lynch's Tugboat Service." Instead, the place on piers lapped by the waters of Long Island Sound seemed to be a residence, though only a little more than a shack. Its siding shakes were gray and cracked, the asphalt shingles of its roof curled and the paint on the boards of its door raised in flakes. Every thing on the pier which was the bungalow's roofless porch was cracked from many cycles of dousing and drying. As I knocked, the high sun of late morning shone on the door, which, after a minute's delay, Captain Lynch opened. Since he stood inside the doorway in nothing but his boxers and a ruddy beard with matching curly hair, it was easy to see that he was trim and well put together. His eyes revealed that he had been sleeping off the night before. He apologized and invited me into the modest sized room which was his home, as I could see from the daybed with its rumpled sheets—and the terra firma part of his business, which he apparently ran from a desk by the window.

"Thanks for lugging this thing all the way out here," he said with a sleepy smile as he handed me the signed receipt.

"That's what I get paid for," I responded, and then added, "Oh, thanks, but this isn't necessary," as I realized he had also slipped me a five dollar tip. As the owner's son, I always felt that I should reject tips as offered under a misapprehension of my position.

"Not to worry," he said. "I've done worse with my money."

We parted on a laugh. His seemed to affirm that he had, indeed, done worse and didn't entirely regret it. Mine was meant to indicate that I had done the same and had adopted pretty much the same attitude about it. In my case, this was a lie, the kind of thing that I said to put a stranger, and myself, more at ease.

Being with Dad at the store was, in part, the reprise of a familiar experience that had receded into the past.

A dozen years before, during the time he was employed by Checkwriter Company, Dad would put in a long day downtown and then do piecework at home. After dinner, he'd overhaul checkwriters on the sturdy bench Grandpa had built for him in the basement. I was allowed to keep Dad company, doing my homework down there, as he worked at the bench. I paced back and forth, a textbook in hand, reading or working at some task of memorization. When I had finished, we tuned the radio to Boston Blackie, Gangbusters, The Shadow or Inner Sanctum. As we listened, I clasped with one hand a lally column, one of the central supports of the house, circling it with the cool, rough steel pulling at my palm and fingers, and seeing in turn, my father's back as he bent over his work, the wall that separated this room from Grandpa's wine cellar, some washed garments Mom had hung to dry by the old steam boiler and the windows to the world outside.

When Dad went on his own and opened the store, he put in the same long days, but now they were spent entirely away from home, and I saw him less. High school and college, along with a maturing social identity of my own, took me away from home more, too.

Although starting to work at the store was not what I had envisioned for myself, it was, in a way, a return to some of the pleasures of that earlier time. In fact, I saw Dad more now, and talked with him more than I had at any other time in my life. In the process, I discovered more about my father and formed a closer bond with him than I would have if I had become a doctor as he had hoped.

I had already realized he was generous in the large matters affecting his family: the provision of a good place to live and a high quality of education; but I was aware also that he was careful about money to the degree one might expect of a person who came from a relatively poor family and who had arrived at working age just at the moment the Great Depression began. One of my aunts, who had lived with us in the two-family house on Giles Place, complained in a letter to Uncle Robbie when he was away in the Navy during World War II: "Don't tell Joey [Dad], but he won't let us turn the heat on, and I'm freezing." A story, which was supposed to be about my mother's naivete when she was newly married, sheds just as much light on my father's relation to money. At the end of the week, Dad would ask Mom if she had any money left, and if she did, he would take that remainder in return for what he called "fresh money." By becoming his right-hand man, I got a more intimate look at how close he was in his spending—mostly in his expenditures on himself—and at his determined pursuit of money, but I also saw his remarkable generosity.

Some of this was the ostentatious kind. If someone who was driving him wouldn't accept his offer of the toll, he would throw the money out the window of the car. Whether he went out to dinner with four people or twelve, he would insist on paying the check. But much more of his generosity was unostentatious. Dad was by no means wealthy, but I saw him lend $5000 to a friend without a shred of paper to record the transaction or any real expectation of being repaid. On the way home with him in the car once, he asked me to stop by the home of one of his sisters, who was having financial problems. Shy about going in himself, he handed me a thick envelope to bring in to her.

Not all his business practices agreed with what I had learned from my mother or from the institutions in which I was educated. Still, I couldn't help admiring his cleverness, his charm and the intensity of his focus on the task at hand in the store: making a buck. Among his family and friends, he was generous, forgiving and loyal; at the store he could be tough, skeptical and opportunistic. One instance stands out as typical.

Richard

Richard Bolton was one of our regulars. Usually he came in with something to sell. One day he tumbled into the store, the compressed features under his ragged curls eerily lit by a smile. His Hawaiian shirt, its tails sprung from the waist of his slacks, was in kaleidoscopic combat with the tie that hung loosely around his neck like a noose. He wrestled to keep four heavy F&E checkwriters under control as he glanced around for a place to set them down. Coincidentally, back in the glass-partitioned office, Dad was, at that moment, on the phone with Richard's boss, the manager of a Safe-Write branch. He covered the mouthpiece just as Richard called out a greeting in his distinctive voice that suggested a tightening of the noose and a corresponding constriction of the vocal cords.

"Hey, Joe, where can I put these beauties down?"

"Hi, Richard," I answered, "How are you?"

"Hi, Dom; give me a hand with these, willya."

I hurried forward as Richard hobbled toward a crowded display table, and I quickly made a space for him to let down his burden. The machines were the recent Premier model and looked to be in almost mint condition. Behind me, Dad was getting off the phone as quickly as possible, and I winced when I realized I had used Richard's name while his boss was on the phone. As Dad approached, he glanced at me with compressed lips and a tilt to his head that communicated his exasperation with me. It was the policy of the Safe-Write Corporation to destroy trade-ins to reduce competition from used checkwriter dealers like us, but some salesmen sold them to make some extra money. If Richard's manager found out he was doing this, Richard could be fired, and we could lose a source of highly profitable merchandise. We could also lose the business of the Safe-Write branches all over the country that bought checkwriter parts from us.

"Howya doin', Joe? Look at these babies! Just like new."

Dad said, "Hi, Richard," and pursed his lips as he looked at the merchandise.

"You're the first one I thought of when I got these, Joe. I hadda come all the way from Bensonhurst, but I figured I'd give you the first shot at them."

Dad looked into Richard's eyes and smiled. "Richard, you have to stop doing me all these favors."

"What're ya talkin' about? All you have to do is maybe ink them and run a rag over them and you couldn't tell them from new—perfect finish and everything. Not a scratch on them. Joe, you should've seen me. Last time I went through this place I put my repair stickers on all the machines and I rigged the sum bars so they wouldn't slide all the way over. It's an insurance outfit—fuckin' crooks. So this time I go to do an inspection, and I show the office manager, a woman, that it would be simple for someone to put another number on their checks ahead of what they already wrote, make a thousand dollar check into eleven thousand. The hag's mouth fell open like a fish." Richard laughed, maybe at his deception, maybe at the memory of the woman's alarmed expression. "I sold four new electrics, $425.00 each and gave her a loaner and got these babies out of there real quick. Told her she better not use them. If somebody altered a check, they could be out thousands."

Dad let Richard run down, and let his own smile shift to a wince as he continued to look the machines over. "Where's the door for this one, Richard, and the electric cords? That's twenty-five dollars worth."

"Oh, Jeez, let me have a look in my car." As Richard turned, to look, he spotted a meter maid eyeing his double-parked station wagon and leapt out the door, shouting, "Hey, whoa, wait a minute, hold on, I'm just finishing up here." The door closed giving the rest of the scene the quality of a silent movie. Through the plate glass I watched the exaggerated flailing of Richard's arms and the impassive stare of the meter maid. His arms stopped flailing, and he held them spread slightly from his thighs with his palms forward as much as to say, Now, isn't that reasonable? Finally, the meter maid addressed him, wagging a finger in his face, and Richard nodded his head vigorously at her, but when she turned away, he raised a finger of his own at her retreating back. As he entered the store, he said, "Give them a little power and they want to run the world, for Christ's sake."

At the display table, Dad was taking imprints from the checkwriters with an air of expertise, sliding a sample check into each machine and punching in whole rows of buttons with two hands and hitting the operating bar with the side of his hand.

"Have you got the electric cords?"

"I just remembered I didn't take the cords. The broad said she wanted them."

"How about the door? And did you see the scratched check table on this one? I'm going to have to disassemble it and have it nickel plated. That's another twenty-five dollars worth in itself."

Richard was beginning to lose air; he seemed smaller, his muscular chest deflating. "It may be in the car, but I'm gonna get myself a ticket if I try to find it. What do you say I get it for you later?"

"Richard, what do you want for these things, anyway?"

"I was thinking maybe fifty each? They go for much more in your catalogue."

"Would you like to pay my rent and insurance, my electric bill, overhaul each of these, wait thirty days for payment, guarantee them? They've got custom nameplates, too, which means I have to install regular sum bars in them as well as get the door and the cords."

"O.K., give me forty each," Richard conceded. All the while he had been frequently turning to see if the meter maid was returning.

Dad said, "Look at these two imprints. These have to be adjusted or may need new matrices or matrix supports. This one here has an earlier serial number that won't bring as much. The best I can do is eighty for all four—cash."

Richard was edging toward the window—looking like a pummeled fighter back-pedaling into the ropes—so that he could see down the street. Just then, he spotted the meter maid making her way back on the other side. "O.K., Joe," he said, torn in two directions at once like one of those carnival figures suspended on a string, the ones that spin when you squeeze the sticks. Dad reached into his pocket and snapped four crisp twenties from his wad, and Richard stuffed them in his pocket.

"Thanks, Joe," he said, as he plunged for the door. "I gotta get out there before that bitch starts writing."

He met the meter maid at his car just as she flipped open her pad. She looked up at the flurry of limbs that was Richard. He spread his arms in a gesture that said, Why me? She was clearly exasperated as she moved her considerable bulk aside to let him get into his car. His mouth never stopped moving until he glanced back to the store. With his full jack-o-lantern smile and a wave of his hand, he pulled out, cutting off a beat up delivery van whose tires screeched against the pavement as its front dipped in arthritic pain. The driver leaned on his horn. Richard, apparently not realizing where the sound had come from, braked hard in instinctive response, then lurched forward, his left arm raised out the window in the waddaya-want-from-me gesture, and blasted his own horn three times in response.

"God," I thought, "What ever will become of him?"

"How about coffee," Dad said, handing me a twenty when I turned back to the office.

"Sure, Dad. What would you like with it?"

"Get me a bowtie."

We sat at our desks which were laden with papers, my father's in neat piles, mine awash. Our coffee was on their pull-out writing tables, the pastries next to the paper cups on the spread deli paper. I was alternating sips of coffee and bites of cheese Danish, saving the thickest part of the cheese filling for last. Dad was eating his bowtie neatly, so that every stray crumb fell on the paper. He mused, "That was not a bad buy. I have what amounts to a standing order for those Premier models from Checkwriter Sales and Service out in Boulder."

Between then and noon, Dad removed a door and a perfect check table from one of a batch of damaged machines he had been cannibalizing for saleable parts and took four sum bars from a bank of parts drawers. He inspected the type and found it clean. The inkrolls of two of the machines were slightly worn, so he changed them expertly and quickly. He inked the inkrolls of the other two machines and took imprints of all four. Before lunch, he was balling newspaper to pack the checkwriters for shipment, and soon I heard him on the phone with Ted Martin in Boulder. "They're cream puffs, Ted. You can't tell them from new." As I worked on the books, Dad sat at his ancient Royal manual and clacked out—hunt-and-peck style—mailing labels and an invoice for $780.00, plus shipping, and filled out the C.O.D. form. The net cost was under $100.00. Dad was illumined with satisfaction. Lunch from the Greek deli was a celebration.

As I munched ravenously on my roast beef hero, the lopsided victory gnawed at me even though I rationalized that Richard was an unscrupulous roughneck and Dad had treated him accordingly.

Students

I wouldn't have believed one incident if I hadn't witnessed it. Two young men dressed in the style of Hassidic Jews came into the store and identified themselves as students at a yeshiva over in Brooklyn. They rented a typewriter and paid for the first month, saying they expected to use the machine for several months. Dad took an address from their identification and, when the first month had almost passed, he sent them the usual document offering the options of renewal or return of the typewriter. Weeks passed without payment, typewriter or response of any kind. Finally, Dad called the "yeshiva," if that's what it was. The person who took the call said that he had never heard of the men and that he didn't know of any rented typewriter on the premises. Dad, apparently at a loss, put down the phone. But in a few minutes he redialed the same number and got the same voice on the line. Then my gentle father, who had never struck any of his four sometimes unruly sons—or anyone else, as far as I know—made the following concise statement very much as if he meant it: "This is Mr. Angiello again. Tell those boys you've never heard of to have that typewriter you've never seen back in my store in two hours. Otherwise, I'll pick up the phone and call a man I know who will find them and break their legs."

Then, without waiting for a response, he promptly hung up the phone.

The "yeshiva students" walked through the door with our machine forty-five minutes later, faces as ashen as those of real and honorable scholars who spent most of their time indoors studying the Talmud. Dad inspected the typewriter, saying sternly, "It better not be damaged." The "yeshiva students" stood by anxiously until it passed muster. Then they apologized for their "error."

Dad didn't forget to charge them for the extra month either.

Eddie

Dad's relationship with Eddie was a different story. Dad identified with him to a certain extent, perhaps because they were about the same age, in their early fifties when Eddie first started with us. Their association was close, and as with all of those in his small inner circle, Dad did his best to treat him equitably.

"Oo, Joe, oo, Joe, oo, Joe," Eddie would cry as he strode through the door at lunch time. The first oo was drawn out and all of them were intoned like an indefinite article. The name was stressed, and the whole series accelerated in a ritual crescendo of bonhomie. Eddie was a salesman of business machine maintenance and repairs. He had come to us from Downtown Business Machines, where the owner, Jake Graberman, had a reputation for being hard-nosed and ruthless. The Grabber, Eddie called him, his sandy eyebrows raised and his chin dropped in disdain. I had occasion to visit Graberman's premises from time to time to deliver or pick up various items for Dad. Errands to that place always depressed me. Graberman was a humorless man with a post office slot for a mouth, and when I entered his place, he looked at me as if I were just another check or bill. His business was conducted from the ground floor of a stolid building on a desolate corner of Canal Street. It wasn't a bad neighborhood; it was a non-neighborhood, isolated between bridges and tunnels and jammed among cars honking vehicular expletives day and night.

I suppose Graberman was not sharing with him what Eddie would have considered adequate compensation for the revenue he brought in because, after a few weeks of negotiation, Eddie wound up with us on the basis that we would split profits fifty-fifty. He would hawk the work and the maintenance contracts, and we would do the actual service and repairs.

The checkwriter business, from which Eddie's methods derived, was a tough one. Its salesman faced many closed doors, hostile rejections and flat-eyed resistance. The competition in Manhattan was especially fierce because the concentration of money was like blood in the water. Cold canvassing there must have felt like being in a tank with slippery sides and lots of sharks. As I saw it, these denizens were a reflection of the whole evolutionary enterprise, full of the most ingenious adaptations in the name of survival. Some cultivated a veneer of integrity; others practiced fraud and a few committed outright theft.

Eddie had generalized methods common in the checkwriter business, to the whole array of other office machines such as typewriters, adding machines and calculators. He would make his way into an office by any means he could think of. He was a tall, gangly man with Buster Keaton hands and a large and formidable nose, which was a prow he used to barge into the various places he hoped to do business. He could be charming or businesslike, navigating fluidly the environment in which he found himself. He would use the front entrance or a side door, if he could find one. To him, a PRIVATE sign was just a convenient indication that there would be no receptionist inside to challenge his entry. Rejection could never drive its teeth through his tough skin. As long as he was doing well, being ordered out of an office by an indignant manager was just a sign that he had, in fact, pushed hard enough to determine that no business was to be had there. "Ock 'em!," he might say, his euphemism for fuck them, an expression he would never use in its undisguised form.

One office manager called to complain that he had encountered Eddie in his office under what he considered bizarre circumstances. Passing a secretary's desk a number of times, he had noticed a tall, gangly man, whom he assumed was an employee of the company, chatting with her as they ate their lunches, which were spread on the desk in front of them. When he finally discovered that Eddie was not an employee, he ordered him out of the office and forbid him ever to return. That afternoon, we told Eddie of the complaint. "Shkee," he said, with a ping-pong slap at an invisible butt. This expression had several meanings, pretty much in line with skedaddle. In this case, it seemed addressed to the absent office manager, advising him to piss-off. What did Eddie care? Business was good, Manhattan was a big place, and for that matter, office managers came and went.

Eddie's main tool was his supply of stickers. These were, in effect, small business cards with his name and telephone number. They were made up on a roll and backed with a permanent adhesive. When he got into an office, he'd slap his stickers on dozens of machines in a few minutes, wandering at will from one office to another taking care to cover anyone else's sticker. Sometimes he did this by permission of the office manager; sometimes he just did it. Often he was covering the stickers of companies that already had the machines under contract—machines that some other company was responsible to repair free of additional charge. He especially liked large, busy offices that had many machines and a staff too busy to be fastidious in researching the most economical sources for service and repairs. Sometimes in such places, personnel who had the authority to order repairs didn't have detailed knowledge of service arrangements. When the secretary or the receptionist heard a strange noise from her typewriter, or her calculator jammed, he or she would follow management's instructions to call the number on the machine. Only it was Eddie's number. He was energetic and relentless. He would pick a large office building on Madison Avenue or Fifth Avenue, say, and, starting at the top, he would work his way from office to office, floor to floor, putting his sticker on every machine he could find. I used to say that he'd put his sticker on your butt, if you bent over at the wrong moment, probably one on each cheek.

When Eddie sold a service contract, we had to check the machine out initially, clean it once a year and respond to repair calls—if there were any. If he decided the machine needed to be overhauled, there was a hefty additional charge, often depending more on what he guessed the office manager would go for than what the typewriter or calculator actually needed. Although Eddie had been in the business for a good many years, he knew next to nothing about the operation of the machines or how to repair them. Sometimes we would get a desperate call for help from him because he had tried to do the simple task of replacing a ribbon and couldn't get the machine to work right. Still, he often ordered a machine pulled (brought into the shop) with the price of the work already established, based on the extent of the repairs he judged necessary. He might quote the customer $225 for "extensive repairs" which turned out to be releasing a cam that was stuck, something that would have taken five minutes to detect and fix in their office.

When he quoted the price of the work, it was always some squarish number, from his grab-bag of prices that were usually in multiples of $25. The price would be $175, or $225, or $325. Seldom did the actual cost to us amount to more than $25 to $50.

Eddie would come in around noon after a morning's canvassing. "Oo, Joe, oo, Joe, oo, Joe," he would cry, "Oo, Dom, oo, Dom." If he thought both Dad and I weren't noticing, he might run a cold hand down our middle-aged bookkeeper's back under her blouse. Ronnie would give out a little yelp, but like many, she didn't quite know how to cope with someone who crossed lines of propriety with apparent immunity from embarrassment. He loped up the stairs, two at a time, to the small mezzanine space a section of which contained the small desk that was his office. On the desk was a telephone and a 3x5 card file. That was it.

Sitting alone with his long legs crammed under his little desk, he opened the brown-bag lunch he had brought from home or that he had just picked up at one of the many nearby delis. He stared vacantly as he ate. Dad, who always pressed lunch or coffee and a Danish on any regular who was present when he sent me out, often spoke with disdain of Eddie's near-perfect record of avoiding his generosity, which Dad attributed to Eddie's reluctance to reciprocate. As Dad used to say, "Eddie wouldn't go for spit."

When Eddie was finished with lunch, he began the series of phone calls to quote on the pulls he had ordered. Later, he would come down and sit with Dad to set up the next day's pulls, to give him information on new contracts and to give him OKs on his quotes for repairs and overhauls, all scribbled on scrap paper. Dad encouraged or commiserated. For him it was a win-win situation. He got highly profitable additional business with no aging receivables and no increase of overhead, the only added cost the direct expense of doing the actual service work. Eddie did OK, too, churning out hundreds of dollars a day in OKs—substantial money in the sixties and early seventies when a dollar was worth five or six times what it is now.

Like many a salesman, Eddie was usually upbeat. Then he would chatter ebulliently about "darling Millie," his wife, whom he never mentioned without her fixed epithet. But when an extended dry spell got him down in the dumps, Dad would walk him out of the store and across the street, and there give him a pep talk. When Dad was finished, Eddie was ready for another swim in the shark tank. He'd walk back into the store exclaiming, "Ock 'em, Joe; ock 'em all."

When Eddie left for the day at around four, Dad was usually brimming over with satisfaction. Everything Eddie brought in was over and above what Dad needed to consider his business successful. He would outline each deal for me in terms of revenue versus the actual cost of the repairs. I think he could hardly believe how fat the deal was. Things went along this way for several years.

Enter entropy.

One afternoon, Eddie handed Dad a couple of routine cleanings under a service contract for a company whose name my father didn't recognize. He had a good memory and the confidence to rely on it. He told Eddie the machines weren't under contract, but Eddie said he was sure they were. When Dad asked him to show him the record, he couldn't produce it. In time, these incidents grew in frequency. When Eddie was forced to produce records, it might turn out, that he had concealed a contract for as much as three years. As long as the machine didn't need any real service work, he could keep the whole contract amount for himself. Nice work, if you can get it! When Dad confronted him, Eddie agreed to reveal all the hidden contracts and promised not to withhold any in the future. Although Eddie hadn't lived up to his end of the deal, Dad knew that he couldn't push him to recover all the back payments to which we were entitled. Eddie would "squeal like a stuffed pig," as he used to say. So Dad settled for what was due him for the current year when these hidden contracts came to light. The bottom line is that Dad didn't want to drive Eddie away, and even with the cheating, having him was very profitable. So whenever he caught him cheating again, something which happened many times, Dad recovered what he could and maintained the relationship. He had no illusion that Eddie could be replaced. Whenever Eddie said, "Do this service call the first of the new batch," it was a pretty reliable sign that the machine involved was another of those on which he had secretly had a contract for a long time but had never serviced. The urgency arose because the customer had suddenly realized that the machine had never gotten the maintenance the contract promised.

When Eddie announced his decision to retire, he had been speaking for a long time about moving to a rural area upstate, where, by his description, he would live an idyllic life with his "darling Millie." I doubted an idyll was her style. He had been involved with the Boy Scouts for many years. Now he planned to make this volunteer work his life, he said.

For a while after he left, Eddie continued his telephone service, and though the business his stickers generated declined precipitously, his phone rang occasionally, and Dad continued to send him his share of the revenue that came from that source.

When Eddie's phone went completely silent, Dad's suspicions were aroused. He got a dial tone on Eddie's phone, then dialed his own number from it and got through. The phone hadn't been turned off. How could it be that, with the tens of thousands of stickers Eddie had slapped on machines, not one call had come through in weeks? Not one person had called the number—even by mistake—in all that time? Then he tried a call to Eddie's line from his. He got a recorded announcement directing him to a different and instantly familiar number with the old CANAL 7 exchange. Eddie had abandoned the scouting Eden in the Adirondacks to return to the shark tank.

He was back with the Grabber.

Heroes

Well rewarded financially, I was a partner in effect, and soon would be in fact. I had begun to enjoy a modest affluence. I bought my first home overlooking a pretty lake in a rural area an hour north of the city. As my family had grown with the birth of my first two sons in 1963 and 1964, the chance of doing anything other than continue at the store seemed to fade.

My father's sheer weight of authority as the source of my life, livelihood, and education was enormous, and although he was kind and generous, other elements of his personality only added to this weight, which I carried all day and all night—even in my sleep, wearying my bones. He was sure he was right when he wouldn't let me purchase an Addressograph for a few hundred dollars, a machine which would have made easier and more frequent the direct mail advertising which reminded lucrative wholesale clients around the country of our existence. He was sure that it wasn't necessary to stock many of the new Smith-Corona electric portables in various colors and typestyles when I wanted to make a splash to attract new retail business. In his opinion, we would be better served by purchasing the machines on receipt of customer orders. He probably saved me from many mistakes. But his protectiveness did not allow me to develop an adequate sense of my value to the business, so I regarded my substantial annual bonus more or less as a gift.

Getting smothered with love was still getting smothered. I could have fought back against meanness and hostility, but I felt helpless in the face of Dad's generosity. I came to understand that, if I didn't do something on my own, I would always stand in his shadow. I longed for my own achievement, something I could be proud of doing for its own sake, but that would also allow me to support my family.

Eventually, I became tormented with my sense of missed opportunity and failure. This grew more and more profound, and early in 1965, I was crying myself to sleep at night over it. When I finally became desperate enough, I forced myself to realize that I would have to leave my father's business, but I knew that I couldn't do it quickly. I would have to prepare. Whatever path I might be interested in taking would require graduate school. Where would I get the time?

Phil Garfield had been my father's accountant from the time the store opened. Warm-hearted and absolutely loyal to his clients, Phil seemed to me a Damon Runyon character that had somehow escaped into real life as that humorist attempted to type him into fictional existence on a page in the world of Nathan Detroit. I always enjoyed seeing him. He'd come in with a big smile and a witticism which he, at least, always found amusing. When I tried to comment in kind, he'd raise his hand to my arm to forestall my response, saying, "Wait, wait, wait a minute!" And then he would launch into a follow-up that he thought was even more amusing. He wore a trademark fedora that seemed a size too small for his head. Even back then, when he was in his mid-thirties, he had begun to develop bags under his eyes that would eventually turn literal, becoming almost big enough for a squirrel to hide nuts in.

He was dead-sure of all his business and accounting advice. And there was good reason. He was, in all my experience, right. When Phil said, "I want you to do it this way," any uncertainty I'd had disappeared, and I forged ahead with confidence. His own practice was the best evidence of his business acumen and his character. He built it from a one man show to a Madison Avenue accounting firm with several partners and over a dozen employees. He chose good people, trained them well and rewarded generously those who could step up and take on the responsibility that went along with the opportunities he offered them.

When Phil saw the numbers arrange themselves in a certain way on our financial statements, he would come into the store with his smile, his fedora and a cigar. He would hand down his pronouncements about the appropriate future course of the business as if he were the descendant of Moses and had inherited the tablets containing the business commandments. At one point he suggested getting into photocopiers; another time he advised us to expand into stationery; another to devise a regular marketing program. He might have been Cassandra as far as Dad was concerned. He seldom took Phil's recommendations, any of which would have achieved good results, preferring his own time-tested method, which boiled down to: Buy as cheaply as you possibly can and sell as expensively as you can.

When I decided that I wanted to go to graduate school and eventually leave the business, I had difficulty approaching Dad to tell him. I felt guilty. I sought Phil's advice, and he offered to come in and talk to Dad about it. I'll never forget it. He called ahead but wouldn't say what it was about. When my father asked me, I simply shook my head in silence. I couldn't say the words. No matter how I put it, I would be leaving Dad to carry the whole load of the store again, after he had rescued me from aimlessly drifting into some dead-end job. Any words would have been hypocritical euphemisms for: ingratitude, selfishness, abandonment and betrayal.

Phil came in with his usual smile and his usual fedora. He found my father and me in the showroom and said, in his most commanding tone, "Come into the office, Joe, we have something to discuss."

"What's this all about," my father asked, "Dom won't tell me a thing."

"Let's talk inside."

"So serious?"

"Sit."

"O.K. What is it?" Dad asked, not sure whether to be irritated or apprehensive as he sat down and looked back and forth between Phil and me. Phil stood over him next to his desk, and I hovered at the entrance to the office as if poised to make a break for the door if things didn't go well.

"Dom wants to go back to school to get his masters so he can teach. Can you let him leave early, say two P.M. each day, so he can go to class and study?"

"Is that all?" my father replied, "Of course."

In some ways, Mitchell Goodman was as different from Phil as another human being could be. He was a regular customer in a small way, buying typewriter ribbons and bringing his portable in occasionally for repair. From the first time he found the store, which was within ten blocks of his home, we began to talk.

Mitch was a tall and large-boned man, in his early forties, balding but with long iron-gray hair sticking out from under a knit cap. His eyes were soulful, and his smile warm and genuine. When I helped him, his attention made me feel I was being regarded as an individual rather than a type (shopkeeper) or someone who functioned occasionally as a tool (the guy who fixes my typewriter).

My favorable impression of him was ratified as a relationship developed between us. I was very ill-informed, had never developed the habit of reading the newspapers, and was very focused on myself and my family. I was nesting, I guess. I had two children by then, the spring of 1965. Over time, Mitch and I shared our stories.

He had been in the army during World War II, and had written and published a novel, The End of It, based on this experience. He was married to a poet, Denise Levertov. I didn't know who she was really, but I was impressed anyway. I showed him some poetry I had been writing for a while, and he said he liked it. He shared it with his wife, who had been a friend of William Carlos Williams. I'd never even heard of Williams, who had recently died, much less read his poetry, so I was surprised to hear from Mitch that he and Denise thought that my stuff sounded a lot like his. I had lunch with them once at their home over a meat packing plant down on Greenwich Street, and they encouraged me in my poetry, Denise saying she thought it pretty good: "Better, in fact, than lots of the stuff that is being published in the little magazines," is how she expressed her judgment.

Mitch was a person of conscience and commitment, who was growing ever more concerned about American involvement in Vietnam. During the time we saw each other frequently in the middle to late sixties, he wrote and edited a book called The Movement Toward a New America, which amounted to a manifesto of all the high-minded ideas that surged into the public consciousness then, some of which have survived as permanent changes in our culture: women's liberation, the anti-war movement and racial equality, to name a few.

When I was admitted to Fordham with the help of an old professor of mine at the college, a Jesuit, to pursue a graduate degree in English, Mitch and I saw each other less but still kept in touch. That was the summer of 1965.

In the next few years, his anti-war activities, became more consuming and put him in league with such people as Noam Chomsky, the Berrigans, Marc Raskin, Rev. William Sloan Coffin and Dr. Spock, the famous baby doctor turned peace activist, and Mitch was convicted in 1968 along with the rest of the Boston Five for his courageous stand in support of the draft "refusers," as he called those young men who wouldn't serve in Vietnam, some of whom demonstrated against the war by burning their draft cards. The conviction of the Boston Five was overturned in the same year.

In his conversations with me, Mitch never made much of his own peril, sacrifice and hardship, but he did tell me once that the local people in Temple, Maine, where he had a small subsistence farm, people he regarded as decent folks, had warned him that strangers had been in town asking questions about him: the FBI, of course.

Mitch opened my eyes to an idea about life different from those models I had been offered previously. His life was one of courage and conviction but not buttressed by religious faith nor dedicated to the service of family. He served mankind as a pacifist warrior who held himself responsible to do the right thing at all costs. At a time in the Cold War, when it appeared to me that the human race would end in atomic annihilation, a fear Mitch seemed to share then, I asked him why he bothered to struggle at great cost to himself against the inevitable. He answered, "When the end comes, I want to know that I've been on the right side." Just as I never had the vocation or faith to emulate the Jesuits, whom I admired, I did not have the courage or vision to follow his path. But I have been grateful ever since that he saw something in me worth his time to encourage.

When I finally left the store to begin my teaching career at Mercy College in 1970 and to raise my family, I left, too, the common ground on which we met, where I used to fix his typewriter and he used to read my poetry. I still heard from him from time to time and had his wife to the college for a reading of her poetry. Then we fell out of touch as people often do when the practical business of life carries them in different directions. When I learned that he had passed away in 1998 up in Temple, Maine, I hoped that he did so with the conviction to which he had earned the right: that he had been "on the right side."

During my interview for the professorial position at Mercy, Sister Joannes was impressed with my business experience, which she felt would eventually be of practical value in the conduct of the English Department's affairs. The truth is that I had learned very little of business methods or principles that could be transferred to my work at the college. But when I first met Ophelia gone mad in Hamlet, she was not the first case of insanity I had ever known. Troubled people, heroes, thieves, lechers and opportunists in the plays of Shakespeare and in Chaucer's Canterbury Tales had counterparts in my experience at the store. When, I read in the General Prologue of the "verray parfit gentil knyght," his moral qualities were reminiscent of people of courage and virtue to whom the store had introduced me. Much of what I had learned at the store came from my insights about the people I encountered there, especially Phil Garfield and Mitch Goodman, and about my father, my knowledge of whom deepened as we worked together.

When I had occasion to encounter dishonesty and hypocrisy in my later life, especially in academic life where it abounded, I had the examples of these people to guide me. They helped me, too, in recognizing those flaws in myself. When I could help someone else by listening or by intervening in their behalf with authorities they found intimidating, I did so. When I had the platform to speak against unfairness for friends and faculty colleagues, I spoke with directness and passion. Often it didn't count for much—but I was aware, at least on those occasions, of being "on the right side." I know that the heroes, whom I met at the store and whose beliefs were so different, were part of that. Mysteriously blended with my father's strength and unwavering dedication to family, they have been my models.

HILLERY N. BORTON
ABSOLUTELY, TOTALLY, AND IN ALL WAYS, INCONCEIVABLE!
how one girl waits for the love of iñigo montoya.
courtesy of The Simon

I was a preteen in the illustrious 1980s and as much as I loved *Family Ties* and *Remington Steele*, I watched a lot of movies. Many of them I watched over and over again. In fact, I made my father rent *Real Genius* so many times that he finally saved himself some money and bought the damn tape. Sadly, I had the dialogue completely memorized shortly thereafter. (It was a moral imperative.) In the years since, I have logged countless hours hawking fake butter on popcorn in movie theaters, renting porn to PTA members at my local video store, indulging my imagination and bankrupting myself in film school, and amassing a respectably large—though often questionably broad—video collection. (Yes, *Shanghai Surprise* is there on purpose.) These days, when I consider my desert island list, I feel I have matured into a first stringer in the biased and zealous sport that is watching movies in America.

And then I spot a holdover from my innocent youth. In the gruff and glamorous group that constitutes my favorite films, *The Princess Bride* sticks out like a virgin at the breakfast table the morning after prom. Faced with this incongruity, I immediately remember why it has remained on top all this time: "We are men of action, lies do not become us." On this lean scrap of dialogue rests the indubitable value of the film as a whole, but I'm getting ahead of myself, as usual.

First, let me prime you. This is not a typical review, as in a critique, but a review in the sense of re-experience from a particular perspective. So, if you haven't seen this movie...Do It Now! There are many good reasons to check it out: "Fencing, fighting, torture, revenge, giants, monsters, chases, escapes, true love, miracles!" In short, it is the perfect fairytale, low-sap and high-satire with just as much character as charm and a self-awareness that defies mockery. Throw in an albino and André the Giant in a speaking role and you've got a damn near perfect flick.

Now that you have seen it (and love it, natch!), imagine what these characters represented for a twelve-year-old girl watching awestruck in the dark in 1987. You see, despite its title, this is a movie about men, and that is a subject to which I was paying attention early on.

Westley and Buttercup, our two in true love, were admittedly somewhat empty ideals, easily molded to fit the contents of our individual hearts and minds. Everyone envied Westley's dashing, daring charm. All of us believed that, like Buttercup, we too were intrinsically lovable—complete with a perfect pair of breasts, or the beginnings of them. It was in their friends and foes that we found the qualities to seek or steer clear of in searching out our beloved.

Vizzini, the ultimate example of those who talk tall and walk small, showed us the danger of false pride. When challenged in the slightest, he denounced his compatriots, "When I found you, you were so slobbering drunk you couldn't buy brandy!" When faced with the fact that his flawless plans are foiled on the boat, the Cliffs of Insanity, and again on the road to Gilder, he consistently spouts, "Inconceivable!" Besides bungling a kidnapping, an escape, and the starting of a war, in one final display of his true wit he drops dead.

Prince Humperdinck, the yellowest rat bastard of the bunch, displayed the downsides to dating a killjoy and a coward. He managed to get the lay of the land—literally, if not by consent—and all he wanted to do was kill her so he could send his legions to war. You just know this kid was looking for a fixed fight from the day he was born. When Buttercup refused to marry him he killed Westley in a fit of rage, "You truly love each other, so you might have been truly happy. Not one couple in a century has that chance, no matter what the story-books say!" Not that he wanted her for himself, mind you, he just couldn't stand the thought that no one would ever feel that way for him. Which is why Westley, of course, never killed him but challenged him to a duel To The Pain—an ordeal of amputation and disfigurement meant to leave the loser with the lifelong anguish of being obviously lesser.

Count Rugen, the six-fingered man, was simply a bully and an antiseptic bore. After his first session torturing Westley in his dungeon/study, the Pit of Dispair, he explained that he was compiling a definitive study on pain and said, "I want you to be totally honest with me about how the machine makes you feel...And remember, this is for posterity." Then there is the fact that he battled and scarred an eleven-year-old Iñigo Montoya, for which I could never forgive him—ever. This reprehensible sin was compounded in the finale when Rugen told Iñigo that his was the most pathetic story he had ever heard. Well, apart from his requisite moment of contrition, these are the last words he speaks.

Fezzik, the strong but not so silent type, shows the importance of being a good sport and a good friend. What can I say here that isn't glaringly obvious? He was a poet and a walking wall ("It's not my fault that I'm the biggest and the strongest, I don't even exercise!"), and without his thoughtfulness our gang would never have gotten to ride off into the sunrise. "There they were, four white horses, and I thought, there are four of us if we ever find the lady—hello lady—so I took them with me in case we ever bumped into each other, and I guess we just did."

Which brings us to Iñigo Montoya. Though he was not technically prince charming, he was the realistically flawed version—a man whom we may hope to meet and one day beguile. How, you might wonder, could a drunk with revenge in his heart be the ideal man?

If you look, you'll see that flourishing in his imperfect humanity are a sense of duty to his family, honesty, chivalry, loyalty, dedication, determination, faith, self confidence coupled with humility, and quixotic optimism. Need I remind you that once the six-fingered man killed his father and beat him in a duel, Iñigo did nothing but study swordplay and pursue Rugen—and for twenty years? Or, that even though he meant to "do him left handed" when he first met Westley ("You seem a decent fellow, I hate to kill you.") he ended up admitting that only the man in black could help him? Or, that he relied on the spirit of his dead father for guidance in his most desperate moment? Or, that he rushed Westley's "mostly dead" body to Miracle Max for a cure? Or, that no matter how many times Rugen seemed to kill him he rallied again and said, "My name is Iñigo Montoya, you killed my father, prepare to die!" He was the embodiment of Westley's great words—he was a man of action.

Like Peter Falk, you might say that I am taking this all very seriously, but to even the most worldly-wise twelve-year-old girl Westley and Buttercup were a sort of promise. It was as if someone was telling us, if you are good and you are patient you will find someone wonderful. Not for a minute did we expect this to be easy, I mean, we were ready for the modern day equivalent of the shrieking eels. But listen, William Goldman and Rob Reiner, now that we are older, we know: you mislead us! The ratio of men of action to faithful women is cruelly skewed. Men today are afraid of calling us, much less pledging devotion. They won't give us a seat on the subway, much less their word of honor. They are loyal to bands. They are devoted to PS2. They are determined to get laid. Men, in this day and age, are boys.

This outlook is bleak and cynical, I know, but it's not just mine. Most women I know, save for the few fortunate and the fools, echo these complaints. Here's my attempt at quixotic optimism: maybe this consistent disappointment IS the faithfulness part. Maybe we have to wait diligently for our dearest loves to come for us before we have even met them. Maybe they won't be quite as cool as Iñigo Montoya (horrors), but hopefully they won't be drunks or killers either. Maybe they won't always say, "As you wish," but hopefully they won't make us say, "I'm not a witch, I'm your wife—but after what you just said, I'm not sure I want to be that anymore!" Massively disappointing alternatives notwithstanding, I am holding out for the ilk of Iñigo. I hope you will too.

CHAPTER 3: FICTION

MARGARET HUNDLEY PARKER
I AIN'T PROUD
a search for love in a world of married men,
best friends and professional wrestlers

I been trying to get rid of Married Man Boyfriend for months. I am sick to death of that shit. If playing second fiddle wasn't enough, now they're threatening to take my baby away. If anyone tried to take Sarah Sue, I don't know what I'd do. Guess I'd have to become an outlaw. It's The Wife—we have been going at it. We got into a fist fight at our daughters' basketball game a few months ago, and ever since then she's been showing up at my house, yelling for her husband. Whenever I see that frizzy perm outside my window, I know it's time to pull the shades down and turn the TV up. She's been talking all this mess about going to court to help my ex-husband get custody if I don't watch my ass. I don't care if Married Man finally moved into a motel; I am sick sick sick of it. But out here in Denver, North Carolina, who else is there? That's why it's taken me so long to get rid of him—we keep fucking. But after all this business with The Wife, I have finally had enough.

My best friend Lea is sick of it, too. She's been telling me the only way to get rid of Married Man Boyfriend is for me to go get me some Strange. Like I'm gonna go and screw that one-armed man who pumps my gas, get real. There ain't nobody I don't know in this pea-niney town. She's tired of my

antsy pants anyway. We had a little episode a few weeks ago. We were at her house drinking and I got too drunk to drive so Lea told me to go get in her bed. I was sleeping when Lea and her husband got in next to me and started fooling around. I thought, yum, some sex! So I took off all my clothes. Lea jumped outta that bed like I had thrown a curling iron in her bathtub. I put my clothes back on and left. I felt awful; Lea is my best friend and I didn't mean to fuck that up. The next night we sat in the car and talked. She knows I have a crush on her, have since we met five years ago. She admitted that she thinks about me that way too, but she doesn't know if we could love on each other and then get up and be friends again.

Anyway, one night a couple weeks ago I was at home watching a movie with my daughter when the phone rang.

"Hey girl, get your ass over here to the Beer Joint." It was Lea. She sounded drunk and I could hear the tinny harmonies of Lynyrd Skynyrd in the background. Gimme three steps towards the door.

"Girl, I'm sitting here watching a video with Sarah Sue," I said.

"Damn. Well, there's somebody here you outta meet." Then she put her hand on the phone and yelled, "Hey, Boogie Man, come here."

"Hello?" A high pitched male voice asked. I didn't say anything yet because I was trying to figure out who the hell the Boogie Man was.

"This is Clay, maybe you know me as the Boogie Man. You ever watch wrastling?"

I had to admit that I did not watch wrastling.

"You ought to! Oh Shit! My song's on! You wanna meet me for lunch tomorrow at The Open Kitchen?" His voice actually squeaked when he said this. Lea must've told him that was my favorite restaurant.

"Umm," I looked at Sarah Sue; she was concentrating hard on Men In Black.

"Okay," I said. "How about noon?"

He said fine and we hung up.

Sarah Sue paused the movie. "Who was that, Mom?"

"You ever heard of the Boogie Man?"

"The wrestler?"

"Yeah, that's what he said."

"That was the Boogie Man on the phone? How do you know him?" Sarah Sue was clearly excited.

"Lea knows him. I'm gonna have lunch with him tomorrow."

Sarah Sue jumped up on the couch with me. "Can I come?"

"No honey, you have school," I said and ran my fingers through her sandy hair.

"But Mom! He smashed up the Undertaker! Will you at least get his autograph for me?"

"I'll try, sweetie. Let's finish this movie so we can go to bed."

"Is it a date?" she asked.

"No," I said but I could feel a smile creeping through. "Come on, now, let's watch this movie."

"It's a date," she said and turned the movie back on. I could tell she was glad; she hated Married Man Boyfriend.

"I ain't got time for that mess," I told him and hung up the phone, quick. I couldn't risk softening up.

I work at a magazine corporation in Charlotte. My job involves calling businesses and telling them to pay their magazine bills, which means I have to deal with stacks of paperwork and people who do not want to talk to me. The lies they tell! Sometimes that can put a person in an ugly mood.

When I got off work Friday, I felt like I had spent all day slamming my head in a door, so I went to Lea's house. She gave me a Xanax and that helped the hairs on my back lay down. I picked Sarah Sue up from after school care and dropped her off at her Dad's. It was his night to have her. We finally got all that visiting shit straightened out, got us an every other weekend pattern. It seems easier on Sarah Sue to know when she's going to that Jesus-infested house. I can talk to his new wife, but he can't even look me in the eye much less discuss something. He discovered The Lord after I left, and he can't bare to face a sinner. My daddy was into that Jesus shit but I left all that when I was 16 and never looked back.

I know Sarah Sue's Dad's house must seem like a more stable home in the eyes of The Law, but Sarah Sue belongs to me. We're like toes in a sock. Her dad just doesn't get her. When she was a baby, he didn't even know how to change her diapers; he'd hold her legs up and crane his head back and try not to look. He was embarrassed by his own child! And now he gets mad at me because I don't make her wear dresses like some kind of priss-pot. The other day he even told her, my beautiful 10 year old, that she was getting chubby. Hello eating disorder! Lord, don't get me started on that man and his poisonous ways.

I went home and put on my snake-skin cowboy boots that Married Man Boyfriend gave me for Christmas (he does have taste), and squeezed into my tight black jeans. I knew Clay had a flair for the exotic, so I went ahead and wore my off-one-shoulder leopard print lycra top. Mee-ow. I slapped on a little lipstick and let me tell you what, I looked good. I was all that and a bag of chips. Clay picked me up in his truck and we went to Club Diamond. He was looking pretty damn fine his own self.

Club Diamond is the new karaoke bar near by. We got there around nine and

the place was already filling up, but we found a couple seats at the bar.
We hadn't finished our first beer when some scrawny guy in a Budweiser tee-shirt came up and yelled, "Boogie Man! Hell yeah! What's going on, buddy? Who's your friend?" He looked me up and down.

Clay grabbed the guy's head and gave him a fake head butt. The guy let out a yelp and scurried off, rubbing his forehead.

Turns out, Clay's like me; he likes to drink beer. I forgot to go to the bank machine so he bought us beers all night. More and more people came up to talk to the Boogie Man, and after awhile, I couldn't help but call him by his professional title, also.

Somebody put on "Funky Cold Medina" so me and Boogie Man cleared a little space and started dancing. We danced pretty good together, close without stepping on each other's toes.

After that song about six people got up there and howled out "Sweet Home Alabama" so we sat down.

"You wanna sing something?" Boogie Man nudged me. "I bet you could break some hearts!"

"I might could sing something funky," I said.

Boogie Man put our names on the list.

Once my name was on there, I got nervous. I'm usually the heckler in the crowd. A few beers later, when I heard my name called I almost ran out, but once I got the microphone in my hand, I was ready to get it. I sang that George Clinton & the P-Funk All-Stars song that goes, "If you ain't gonna get it on, then get your dead ass home." I worked my shit like a drag queen. I sounded good, too. When the song was over I took a big bow and everybody clapped and hollered.

Boogie Man was up next, and then the crowd started chanting for him, "Boo-gie, Boo-gie, Boo-gie." On his way to the stage he gave me a big kiss and told me I did good.

He sang his theme song, "I'm your boogie man, that's what I am." He shook his butt and flexed his biceps. He pulled his shirt up and moved each tittie individually to the beat of the song. Good lord I never laughed so hard.

It was loud.

I was happy.

I didn't think about Married Man once.

118

Later, when he was driving me home, we turned up the radio in his car and yelled out all the words to a Led Zeppelin rock block. The funniest was him singing "Black Dog" in that high voice. I invited him in to teach me some wrestling moves. My neighbors were out of town so I cranked up the stereo and cracked open a couple cold beers.

"Boogie Man, what's your favorite move?" I asked him.

"Girl! I'll teach you the Boogie Hold! Nobody on this earth can mess with you after that."

He got behind me and grabbed my arms, then he jammed his knee in my back. "Now I ain't gonna do it to you, you sweet thing, but you get somebody like this and then WHAM you slam 'em on top of you with yer knee all jammed up in the small of their back."

Normally I would've killed anyone who grabbed me like that but the Boogie Man was gentle and I really did want to learn the Boogie Hold. A girl never knows when she's going to need a pro-wrestling maneuver. I took a self-defense class for gym credit at the community college where all we got to do was yell NO! to some man with an oversized head. Fuck that pussy shit; mess with me and I'll put you in the Boogie Hold!

"Now you try it," he said and let go.

I got behind him and started to mash his arms together but he felt so good I started rubbing my hands all over that giant barrel chest. It felt like he was made of solid rubber, all muscle and not a stick of body hair. After a little more of that I heard myself saying things I never, ever thought I'd say: "Fuck me, Boogie Man! Fuck me!"

It was good, too. I hadn't done it with anyone but Married Man Boyfriend in three years. I slept in Clay's (I went back to calling him that) arms all night and we did it again in the morning, then we dozed off. About that time, I heard a motorcycle pull into my driveway. Married Man Boyfriend still had a key so he walked right into my house! I know he knew I had company because Clay's truck was there. I jumped out of bed and met him at my bedroom door and backed him up into the kitchen. Even though he deserved it, I did not want him to come into that bedroom and get his ass kicked by the Boogie Man.

"What the fuck are you doing here?" I was naked and mad. "Get out of here, you married truck full of dog shit!" was all I could say.

He just stood there like I had goosed him with a knitting needle, all hurt and surprised looking.

"Don't look at me like that!" I said.

"But Suzel, baby..." he whined and held his fat paw out.

He looked so pitiful it started to make my heart hurt so I opened up the front door and told him once more to Get Out. I gave him a little shove on his back, and shut and locked the door. Then I went into my room and curled up with Clay. Finally, I heard Married Man Boyfriend's Harley spin a hole in the driveway and tear on down the road. Clay acted like he was asleep, and I had been yelling in whispers, but I knew he heard what happened. I was afraid my chances with him were shot to hell.

On his way out, though, he asked me if we were still on for pizza on Tuesday before he had to go back on tour. He still wanted to meet Sarah Sue. I wanted to beg him to take us with him, but I didn't. Married Man was an addiction and I never have been much of a quitter. If you want me to quit smoking, you better hide all the cigarettes in North Carolina. I wanted to grab Sarah Sue and jump in the car with Clay, and get away from Married Man, my job, my ex-husband, everything. Maybe I had found a safe place for me and my daughter. Or maybe it was just lust. Whatever, just keep me away from Married Man Boyfriend and his frizzy headed Wife.

Later that morning the asshole came back over and I told him right away to get off my property.

I said, "You are no longer welcome in my home." I meant it.

He screamed and cried, "Come on, honey, it's me! I'm staying at the Motel 6 now! Let me in! Who the hell was over here this morning?" but I wouldn't let him in. I just cracked the door and yelled at him through that small space. I tore Sarah Sue's sign off the door and threw it at him. He tried to muscle his gorilla body in anyway, but I leaned all my weight on the door and finally he stormed off. He still had my damn key. I called The Law. They said I could put a restraining order on him but I had to file all kinds of papers, so I said, "What else can I do?" I didn't want to file nothing because I was already worried about losing custody of Sarah Sue. They said they'd keep an eye out and if they ever saw his bike in my driveway while they were patrolling, they'd stop by.

Good. That way I can't let him back over. Unless he borrows somebody's car.

Then I went to Lea's house. We drank a few beers. She wanted to know how my date with the Boogie Man went, but I was so pissed off, all I could talk about was Married Man.

Lea said, "Fuck him, he ain't worth losing a daughter over." And then she confessed, "besides, he don't love you. He gave me his beeper number last weekend at the Beer Joint."

Big fucking surprise there. That Married Bastard had a lot of nerve because he knew Lea would tell me anything. He had us lined up like Mormons, but the biggest chump was his wife. She knew all about me, but I was tired of being the bad guy, she needed to hate her husband. I didn't do this all by myself. I wanted her to back off those goddamn custody threats. Married Man cheats on his wife, always has. He had a dang girlfriend when they got married! On one of The Wife's rampages, she asked me to tell her everything but I wouldn't. She begged me, "As a friend, you got to tell me everything you know." I almost did, too. Until I found out she was just gathering information to take to court. That was the night we stepped outside at the basketball game and I lost a fingernail in her arm. I had been ready to fight then, but at this point I needed for this shit to be resolved. I was done with Married Man Boyfriend and ready to get on with my life. The last three years had been like eating a bowl of ice cream with a rock in it; tastes great until you crack a molar. I couldn't do it anymore. I wanted to be clean.

"Let's go tell her," I said.

"Tell her what, exactly, Suzel?"

"Tell her it ain't just me. I ain't the problem, it's her husband. He's the fuck-up. I swear she's going to court with my ex. I do not need her as an enemy." I stood up; I was getting into it. "We gotta tell her what a piece of dog shit, ocean-bottom, scum-sucker her husband is! We owe it to her as a fellow human in this world!"

"Damn, girl. If you put it that way, come on then." Lea said.

"Will you tell her about him hitting on you and all that?"

"Yeah, come on. Let's go before we get too drunk."

We got our cigarettes and piled in Lea's Dodge Caravan.

I went to the front porch by myself and rang the bell. When Married Man's wife opened the door and saw me, her body got so rigid it started to curl up on itself like a drying shrimp. She had asked me to tell it, and I was ready to, but I guess she changed her mind. I must've looked wound up because she called out to her daughter, "Casey call 911! Call 911!" What a fucking wimp. If it were me I'd a just stepped outside and dealt with it. No need to get your damn baby all scared. Anyway, she tried to shut the door on me but I grabbed her arm.

I said in a low voice, "I got something to tell you and you are going to listen."

That's when she went ape shit. She yelled, "I HATE YOU I HATE YOU I HATE YOU!"

I asked her how many times she could say that. "Do you really hate me?" I was cool. Let her have her little shit fit.

She was all squealing trying to wiggle out of my grip, calling me a "BIG FAT FUCKING BITCH. HE EVEN SAYS YOU'RE A BIG FAT FUCKIN' BITCH AND

WOULDN'T BE CAUGHT DEAD WITH A FAT ASS LIKE YOU!"
So I said, "You don't believe me, then hang on a minute." I hollered for Lea to come on out and talk.

Lea wouldn't come to the door.

She yelled from the yard, "Shit girl! The Law's coming. Get back in this van!"

I let go.

As we drove off, I got madder and madder. For some reason I thought about the time I got an abortion when I was a teenager. I had waited for hours at the bus stop for my boyfriend to come to the clinic with me but he never showed up. Never called me back after that, either. People fail, they always have. Lea was supposed to back me up, that was the whole reason we went over there, to tell that bitch that it wasn't just me that her husband was after. It wasn't all my fault.

"Why the hell didn't you say something?" I said.

"She was calling the Law!"

"Your ass is going to get me in trouble," I pouted.

"Your ass is already in trouble. His wife is a dumbass, but it ain't worth going to jail just to tell her off. I heard her yelling, 'call 911, call 911.' Fuck that. I said that man gave me his number. Did I call it? No, I did not. Don't blame this shit on me," she said with so much meanness, I couldn't stand it.

I didn't really intend to, but I reeled back and punched her in the side of the head and made her swerve.

She screeched into a driveway of an abandoned house and we both got out. She jumped over to my side and punched me dead in the eye. I came right back at her and we were nothing but arms and legs and hair tangled up. Finally, I got behind her like I was going to put her in the Boogie Hold but she was wiggling around too much so I chomped down on her neck.

"Ouch, bitch!" she yelled and tore herself out of my grip.

We stopped and faced each other.

I don't know if she kissed me or I kissed her but all the sudden we were leaning up against the van making out.

I had just put my hands under her shirt when she stopped and said, "You hear that? I hear a siren. Get in the van."

I got in and ducked down just before the ugly blue lights of The Law appeared

122

in the rearview mirror.

"I just thought I heard something so I needed to check my tires," Lea said, her voice loud and shaky. "Everything looks okay, but thank you for stopping, Officer." I was feeling bad for her; she's had her share of trouble with the men in blue.

"Tires look fine, Ma'am. I'm looking for a Suzel Suitor."

When I heard Johnny Law say that, I couldn't hold it in. I stepped out and said, "I'm Suzel Suitor. I had an affair with a married man. I ain't proud, but I did it. I went over to come clean with his wife. We thought we should tell her what's been going on, that's all."

The Law just stood there stony-faced and told us to go on home. I don't think he knew what to make of the two women standing in front of him, looking pitiful and wild with hair shooting up out of bobbie pins and shirts all sideways and torn. Maybe he thought we got whatever punishment we needed already. No ticket, no handcuffs, nothing.

When we got back in the car, me and Lea looked at each other and started laughing. We gave each other a big hug and drove off.

"Don't listen to that woman, honey," she said, patting my thigh as we rode along. "You ain't fat, you're voluptuous."

That made me feel good because it's true, that Wife can sure hit me where it hurts.

I wanted to go home with Lea so bad, but her husband would be there, and besides, I needed a night to get myself together before Sarah Sue came home. I couldn't wait to see my daughter, even if I was a big mess. I miss her on her weekends away. She's my anchor, without her to come home to, I could float away.

When I got back, I saw a bird lying in the grass under the window. I leaned down to see if it was breathing, but it was dead. I thought, is that typical or what? Every year seems like we get at least one kamikaze bird flying into our window. Stupid damn bird. I carried it to the back yard and dug a little grave with my garden shovel and threw it in there and covered it up. I stuck my chewing gum between two sticks and made a cross and put it on top.

The phone was ringing when I got inside.

"I just wanted to make sure you got home okay." It was Lea.

"Yeah, I'm here. Hold on, let me go get a cigarette." I ran to my room, I was glad she called. "What are you doing?" I asked.

"Making this family some dinner," she said.

"What are ya'll having?"

"Beer," she said and broke out laughing.

"I miss you," I said.

"I miss you, too. David, quit it! Suzel, honey, I gotta go. I'll call you back."

I sat by the phone and finished my cigarette and looked at my reflection in the microwave. My eye was red and bruised and I had scratches all over my face. My voice was still raspy from whooping at the karaoke club. I was in some sorry shape.

Now, I have a date with Clay and a meeting with the big boss at work this week and I don't know how I'm gonna cover up this eye. I guess I'll wear my tinted glasses; say I was helping Lea paint her house and the ladder fell and hit me in the face. That's what I'll tell Sarah Sue and Clay and everybody at work.

But right now I just want to be myself, put some ice on my eye and watch the sun go down. I want someone to come over and make me some soup. Shit. I swear I learned my lesson. I'm done with Married Man. I'm done with fighting.

Goddamn would you look who just pulled in the driveway, carrying a bunch of flowers.

Mehmed Begic | **IDENTITY (IDENTITET): MB2302977341927**

You ask what I am?

Born as
a wish, a child, a tale, a dream,
black, blue, partisan and yellow,
a fool, a love,
not hatred

I grew and was
permanence, a swimmer, suicide,
an apology, a crime, seven words,
one hundred words, as-many-as-you-need-
words, a gesture, never fast, a lie,
a lie because of the truth, a promise,
the friend who listens. I was music.

Now I am
sea and sky. Cloud and rain.
Two clouds, the wind that drives them.
The dust that forgets the morning.
The berry by the roadside.

I don't know how to hate
or sleep.
Looking for what I can't be
I run from waiting.
I know. I wait.

Every moment I become
name, number, shadow, marijuana,
firewater, winner, mountain,
loser, silence, memory,
a circle, a word,
the end so I stay at the beginning.
I do not hate.

This is what I am
and some more details.

(translation by Jack Richold)

MITCHELL LEVENBERG
THE CAT
a question to the answer: the pen is mightier than the sword

I live in the big city. One night, right outside my building two men began to argue so loudly I could barely hear my TV set. When they finally stopped, the street grew quiet again, but a few seconds later my downstairs buzzer rang. "It must be those men," I thought, so I let them in. They came right up to my door, knocked on it, and when I asked who it was, they said, "Us." That was good enough for me.

When they walked in, I thought I recognized one of them, the one with the tangled hair and thick red eyes like tomato juice. Maybe it was from college that I knew him, I thought. "Can I get you fellows anything?" I asked them as if we had been friends for years and in a way I wanted that, I wanted them to think I cared, that I had no evil intentions towards them.

"We don't want nothin'," Tangled Hair said, eyeing the TV set, the stereo, the VCR, and the CD player. Then the other one, the one whose face looked like a torn envelope stuck his nose into my refrigerator and said, "Jesus Christ, he ain't got no Meisterbrau!" This made me think of my college English teacher, Mr. Bloom. "Beware of men using the double negative," Mr. Bloom used to say. "They're not only out for no good, they're out for double no good."

Then Tangled Hair said, "Got anything else to drink?" so I handed him my last bottle of scotch. I figured it would make them feel at home since I had always noticed men just like these drinking scotch in my doorway. Then Envelope Face looked at me and said, "Are those your real teeth?" I laughed, but he was serious and when he reached out to touch them with his fingers I shut down my mouth real hard like the lid of a piano.

The two men really smelled bad, and this more than anything reminded me of college and the old days of not showering and wearing torn, dirty clothes. Tangled Hair drank down his scotch from the bottle like it was lemonade on a hot day and even Envelope Face shook his head in amazement and when he did things flew out of his hair, some dead some alive. Then Envelope Face went to work. He grabbed the scotch from Tangled Hair, swigged down the rest of it, and wiped his mouth with his sleeve like in the old Westerns. Then he took out his knife, brandished it around the apartment for a while and said, "Now what do

you got around here that I can cut up?" I thought about the cat my neighbor left here for the weekend so he could go upstate and visit his girlfriend. I thought about all those girlfriends who for some reason or other live upstate and how now a cat was going to die for it.

"Put that damn knife away," Tangled Hair told Envelope Face. At last, I thought: A voice of reason. "There's plenty of time for that later," he went on. "We've got to get some pussy first." He really seemed determined to stick to a schedule. This gave me some time so I excused myself to go to the bathroom. They might have stopped me but they seemed to like the idea there was a bathroom. "Bathroom!" Tangled Hair shouted. "Well, don't we live in the lap of luxury." Then I exhorted them to make themselves at home and went looking for the cat.

In the bathroom I noticed the cat was right where I expected it to be, right in the litter box. The cat tried to get away, so I grabbed it and tied a note around its neck. I had a note for every occasion for life in the big city. This one said, "Help! I am being tortured in my own apartment. Please send help. Sincerely, Weinstein, 4A." Perhaps I was getting a bit ahead of myself but I couldn't find my "Help, I'm being threatened" note, or even my "Help, I'm being held hostage note," and there was no time to look for either one of them. But then, suddenly, all the cat wanted to do was play. It licked my face and then rubbed its cheek against it. It looked into my eyes and I became totally consumed by it. Perhaps I would speak to my neighbor about this when he came back.

My neighbor was grossly misinformed about cats. Cats did not sit on window sills all day looking out at cars blurring by but studied human beings in action in order to determine whether or not they were worth being saved. I thought about how they already must be getting tired of us, of that superior "you'll eat when I'm ready to feed you," attitude and how it was just a matter of time before they abandoned us completely. I remembered how I had often trembled when coming upon a cat in some deserted alley when it simply walked past me, not once stopping to stare into the deepest core of my soul. "What have I done?" I had thought to myself. "Whom have I offended? And how do I get back into the good graces of the world?" Questions like these had gone through my mind, which I like to think of as a big sponge soaking up all the doubt and uncertainty in the universe.

But now, fighting off that special attraction between me and the cat, I tossed it out the bathroom window and watched it spread its legs and then land right on top of one of the great garbage heaps of the city.

From the bathroom, I could hear chirping noises, as if small birds had alighted upon the window sills. When I came out I saw it was Tangled Hair and Envelope Face smacking their lips at the whores in the street. When I joined them at the window, I noticed one looking up and around, confused, not knowing where the sounds were coming from. Her arms went out, her palms upward as if pleading for more clues as to our whereabouts. Taxis stopped for her but she kicked their doors in and spat at their tail pipes as they sped down the street. "Fourth floor!"

Tangled Hair yelled out. I was worried. What if the neighbors heard?

I buzzed in the woman without asking. When she came up the boys looked at her like they were starving and she was the Chinese food. As for me she looked very familiar and the first thing I thought of was college; in fact, I wracked my brain going over every class I ever took, but still I couldn't place her. Then again, maybe I didn't know her after all.

"Would you like to wash up?" I asked the woman.

"Why?" she asked. "Do I look dirty? Do I smell? You should have thought of that before you buzzed me in and made me burst my lungs walking up here. My job is a lateral one," she continued. "It is not straight on, it is not up and down, it is lateral."

She seemed to enjoy using that word, and it seemed to turn on the boys too. "That's just what we're looking for," said Tangled Hair. "Some lateral action." But Envelope Face disagreed.

"Up and down!" he shouted. "Up and down!"

"Two hundred bucks up front," she said, "and you boys can go in any direction you want." The boys laughed very hard.

"Since when you been workin' on Park Avenue?" Tangled Hair asked.

"Since I took a look at you two," she said. "And who are you?" she asked looking at me. "Our host?"

"With the most," Tangled Hair said sweeping his arm across the room of TVs, VCRs, CDs, and other stereo equipment like he was showing off prizes on a game show.

"I think I'm the victim," I told her, looking at the boys, hoping they'd laugh, but they just kind of stared right through me and I knew that either there would have to be a sudden and decisive rearrangement of the molecular structure of their brains, that is their total transformation into kind and loving boys, boys just out for a harmless good time, or else I would have to get out of there as fast as possible. But I really couldn't hope for either, so I thought that if this were a movie we'd be just about up to the part where the squeamish start to cover their eyes and everyone else gets ready for the blood and gore.

Then, just like that, Tangled Hair wanted to get started. "The money first," said the woman, closing up her jacket to hide her breasts more. "We don't have no money," Tangled Hair said, grabbing the woman's left arm. "Yeah! We ain't got nothin' but needs," Envelope Face said, grabbing the woman's right arm. And before I could even suggest we all sit down over a strong cup of coffee and talk things over in a civilized and grammatical way, the boys had already dragged her over to the couch and at that moment I wondered what Mr. Bloom would have thought about all this, good old Mr. Bloom who kept telling us how much potential we had to be great in the world and how it was our responsibility to make the world a better place to live in and how you had to start with an appreciation of good literature and a solid foundation of grammar because the power of the English language was the greatest power on Earth and so forth and so on and I looked at Tangled Hair and Envelope Face just giving it to her like that while I stood there helpless, although with a solid foundation of grammar behind me, so first I tried the imperative and said, "Stop it or I'll. . .!" and then the conditional and said, "If you don't stop, I'll . . .!" and finally the subjunctive saying, "If I were you I wouldn't . . .!" but nothing helped and then I looked towards the open window and there stood my neighbor's cat, the note gone from around its neck, just staring at the woman with the boys on her. Funny how at that moment the cat looked so much like Mr. Bloom did back in college, the yellow and bloodshot eyes like an exotic cocktail mix, penetrating our poor souls soaked with alcohol and linguistic indifference. How too, just like the cat now, Mr. Bloom's back would arch, the fur on the back of his neck stand up, his neck thrust outwards, his legs spread wide as if he were about to spring on us for all our grammatical transgressions.

And now the cat stares and the woman screams and Tangled Hair says, "It won't do no good screamin' " and Envelope face says, "No way you ain't gettin' yours today," and I say to the cat, "Attack, Mr. Bloom, attack!" thinking of Mr. Bloom even though I'm looking at the cat. "You heard what he said!" I scream. " 'It won't do you no good, No way you ain't?' Did you hear that? Did you? Are you deaf or something? Attack for God's sake!" But the cat won't move. He just stands there staring at me and then at the boys who are on the woman, and so we wait, standing there in the middle of my living room, in the middle of a world of doubt and uncertainty, for the cat to make up its mind.

It's amazing how many strands go into one hook in a carpet. Lily counts fifty-seven grey fibers and moves on to the next hook. She has already counted the holes in the ceiling: nine white squares above her with one hundred and ninety-two holes, give or take a few—because sometimes, she found, one hole in one square bleeds into a hole in the next square. Eight ceiling squares the width of the room, fourteen squares the length. She swallows the lump in her throat, shifts uncomfortably in the metal folding chair, and begins to count the feet of the other women.

It is deadly quiet but for the low drone of the counselor in the corner; such a change from the previous area where the men are, where Jake would be waiting if he weren't so busy at work, she thinks. She smells the faint aroma of disinfectant but notices the pine doesn't cover the deeper musty odor of something old and unused. The smell is the color grey, like the walls; not a crisp starched grey or even a warm charcoal, but, she realizes, the color Mom was after the heart attack.

Death grey.

The dizziness that has become familiar to her over the last few weeks washes over her again; a feeling, she imagines, akin to falling through space. She grabs the small medallion of the Virgin Mary that hangs from a thin gold chain around her neck, fingering the raised cameo and delicately ribbed edge. She is always comforted by the contours of the Virgin's silhouette, so peaceful under her thumb. It reminds her of summer evenings on the farm when she was a girl, when the smell of fresh grass and of Mother's prized daphne bush would drift up the porch and in through the screen door. The sweetness would waft in incandescent sheets around the family seated at the dinner table; the scent clinging gently to Mother's skirt as they finished a batch of cookies, the coffee percolating in the corner, while Father helped her two brothers with their homework. There is nothing quite so magical as those years to her—when the family was still together, and the future looked like one endless parade of those warm nights.

The pads of her fingers know every millimeter of the medallion, recognize the hills and valleys of Mary's chipped robin's-egg-blue robe. Fading though the gift may be, it is still as precious to her as the day that she received it. Her mother had given it to her for her Confirmation, as her mother had given it to her, and as she imagined she would one day hand it down to her own daughter. It is one of the few things she has left that belonged to her mother. She rarely takes it off.

She sticks a finger in her mouth and begins chewing. Finding no nail left, she bites her cuticles. She wonders if this counts as eating; when Jake had called to make the appointment, the woman on the phone had told him no food, drink, or cigarettes for at least eight hours before. She'd cheated. She had half a cigarette on the way here, smoked until the nausea kicked in. Inhaling deeply, she resumes counting feet.

Shoes really tell you a lot about the person wearing them, she thinks. She counts mostly sneakers, a couple of pairs of loafers, and one hideous pair of blue suede platforms the like of which she hasn't seen for twenty-three years. Who let these come back into style?, she wonders. The 70's were a hideous decade; she thought so when she was a child. Now, a thirty-year-old woman, she believes it even more strongly. As far as she is concerned, some things are better left dead.

She looks down at her own feet and wonders what her shoes say about her. They are her favorites, a present from Jake for her birthday a couple of years back. Black leather cowboy boots, the gleaming pointed toe peeking out from beneath the faded cuff of her 501's. They are great for New York City, but she never takes them back home with her. Her father, a Montanan all his life, who has been wearing boots since he took his first step, would only tease her.

She misses her father, misses the farm. She hadn't realized how important it was to her to watch the change of seasons come over the land, how much continuity it gave her life. She even misses cranky Mrs. Delvecchio, her father's housekeeper, who, with the full force of her personality anchored behind nearly 300 pounds of dimpled flesh, would always prod Lily about Jake. When was he going to cut out all his tomfoolery and make an honest woman of her, give her a few babies to keep her busy? "It ain't right," she'd say, and with her requisite sigh so expletory that Lily was sure its boom traveled well into the next county, and could be heard over the sound of a tractor on which a farmer was sitting, she would end, "Well, why buy the cow when you can get the milk for free."

Lily does not acknowledge her loss very often. New York is where the Stock Market is, where Jake's career and future are. Where Jake is. New York is where she must remain.

She does have the tree after all. Jake adopted it for her early last spring after a blowout over his refusal to move outside the City. He even helped her build a short picket fence to surround it, to help keep the dogs away. He painted it white and added a small red placard that says 'Mabel', written in green.

Lily now watches the seasons pass through Mabel.

For the first month, she spent at least an hour every day feeding and watering or just sitting on the stoop looking at Mabel. She likes to chart the scarred surface of Mabel's trunk, its gentle curve. It looks as if she is being pulled in opposite directions. Or frozen in some sort of ritual tree dance, saved for when the moon is full and the streets are quiet. A gyration to honor herself, digging her roots deep into the dirt like toes in sand, stretching her branches up and out to grasp at the sky, tickle the other trees, rearrange herself like a new hairstyle.

She remembers the weeks that she watched Mabel's tiny greenish-purple buds slowly open and flower. Mabel giving birth to herself.

She is shivering. It is February but she swears the air-conditioning is turned on. She also has to pee. She has been waiting three hours and has used the restroom nine times. That's three times an hour or once every twenty minutes, she notices. Now she has to go again. It's okay; the bathroom is only twenty-one steps away. She cautiously makes her way across the room and down the hall, careful to avoid eye contact with the others.

Enclosed behind the locked door she feels less conspicuous. She sits on the toilet, wraps her arms around her legs, watchful of her tender breasts, and rests her head on her knees. She counts the small black porcelain tiles on the floor, rocking slightly until someone knocks at the door. She quickly finishes, jumps up, and rushes to the sink to splash cold water on her face, noticing in the mirror how pale she looks, her red-rimmed eyes and auburn hair a sharp contrast to the white skin. The deep bruised circles under her eyes and high chiseled cheekbones give her a gaunt appearance under the shocking 100-watt bulb. A cadaver, she imagines herself. The Walking Dead counting twenty-one steps back to her chair.

She thinks of how, one warm Saturday afternoon in early May, on one of the rare days in New York where you can smell something other than carbon monoxide or urine, the scent of grass had drifted the two blocks from the park to their apartment. Kneeling on the sidewalk, weeding around the lush red peonies at Mabel's base, the buttery smell of the grass hit her nostrils, mixed with the rich odor of damp soil, and Lily remembered. The mystery of life, her mother once told her, is revealed in the kernel of even the tiniest seed.

"Lily?"

She stands and follows.

Obediently, she changes into the thin cotton gown and slippers with the spongy bottoms. She is cold down to her bones, and a raw red rash has broken out on her palms, inflamed by her constant scratching.

This room is much smaller than the last, and only three other women are waiting. Two are chatting amicably, their motivation incomprehensible to her, and besides, it inhibits her ability to count. She closes her eyes instead and imagines that Jake is there holding her, stroking her hair back from her forehead the way she likes, and telling her that it will be all right, soon everything will be back to normal.

Jake is in her blood, as integral to her life as breathing. If it were possible, she would crawl inside his skin and meld sinew to sinew. She would kill to keep him.

"Lily?"

She stands and follows.

Down the bright, sterile corridor she trails the nurse, willing her legs to move and counting each laborious breath. Everything is in slow motion as if under-water. Her vision ripples, and there is no smell, no sound except for the rapid beating of her heart in her ears. Time, standing still, rushes past her like a cur-rent that she cannot get hold of.

She climbs onto the paper-covered table, the cold metal of the stirrups burn-ing into her heels. A frigid, oily sweat covers her body and drips down her fore-head into her eyes. Her hands, like claws, dig into her thighs, and her breath-ing is shallow and rapid; she feels suffocated, she cannot get enough breath. She glances about, desperate to find a focal point, something to count, and finds nothing.

Hovering somewhere above her body and behind her head, she concentrates instead on reciting the alphabet, backward and forwards; then in Spanish. Over the crescendo in her own mind, she notes the motion in the room: the entrance of the doctor, whose cottony hair and portly stature remind her, oddly enough, of Santa Claus; the anesthesiologist setting up and going through the obligato-ry questions about her medical history.

She is jolted back into her body by the chilling stickiness of the lubricant cov-ered transducer being moved slowly and methodically over her abdomen. She clutches at her necklace, and feels its coolness soothe her itchy palm. Convulsively, she hugs herself, and cradling the necklace within her fist, nes-tles it safely at the base of her throat.

"I'm sorry, but you're not allowed to wear any jewelry during the procedure," states the nurse. "Take it off, please. I'll see that it's waiting for you in the recov-ery room."

Lily reluctantly unhooks the clasp and holds Mary in the palm of her hand, the halo and tranquil smile shining up at her through the tarnish. She hands her over, and realizes for the first time that she is nearly naked and very much alone.

The nurse finishes her measurements, wipes Lily's stomach, and pulls the machine back towards the wall. It catches on the electrical cord and slowly swings its monitor around to confront her.

The small screen looms over Lily, screaming its reality. She is pinioned to the table, unable to avert her eyes. Nausea buffets her. She had imagined it would be black and white, like a snapshot, but there really isn't that kind of definition to it, she realizes; just varying shades of grey. Grey that gently shadows and veils. She finds herself tracing its lines, adding the definition, herself.

The fluorescent tube overhead seems to grow brighter, glaring as if it were mad, glaring like oncoming headlights that mark her presence and shift to meet her. She feels blinded. The light sears into her exposed flesh, leaving it raw and tingling. The smell of the crisp, fatty singeing of her body fills the air and gives a smoky quality to the rubbing alcohol that covers the surgical tools lying at her feet. She believes that this is just.

A dark tunnel rises up from the edges of the table to surround her and rushes her past images that dance on her periphery. All a blur, just bits and pieces, like an old home movie whose colors are at once faded and unnaturally intense, its film jerking crazily while rewinding from reel to reel. She makes out her mother's flame-red hair as it passes and she can feel its thick texture in her fingers, can smell the lemon of her shampoo now mixed with the tears on her own cheeks. Speeding through the tunnel, she counts the seconds of each minute of each hour that it takes her to move past each brick in the masonry.

The electric hum of the monitor thumps and pounds in her head. She stares back at the image, and it begins to swell, to undulate, to take on proportions of its own, until it eclipses her own face reflected on the screen. It looks like an interstellar cloud, she thinks. A swirl of grey particles, rotating in on itself, and collecting into a...what's it called? Well, anyway, some kind of hot, heavy mass at its center. A solar system in the making. Or maybe, a Black Hole. She feels pulled by its gravity and struggles to exert her own force against it. Don't they say that Black Holes may be doors to other dimensions? That if we could only find out how they worked, then we could transport ourselves to worlds we have only imagined? That we could transform ourselves through contact with life perhaps older and wiser?

The image stares back at her. It peeps brazenly through the reflection of her own left iris. What makes an interstellar cloud first begin to spin?, she wonders. Is it Fate, or God, or just an accident?

A proto-sun. That's it. There's a proto-sun at the center.

She and the image stare at one another. Lily is suddenly struck by the universe of possibilities beating within the compact inch of cells. A kernel of mystery, she thinks, as she breathes in the thick fragrance of daphne that has begun to permeate the room, so pungent that she swears she is sweating the essence out of her own pores.

Visceral knowledge floats like a bubble to the top of her blessedly still mind. This is mine, she thinks. It belongs to her even more than she belongs to Jake. She need only utter one word to stop this now. One word. One.

White knuckled hands clutching the sides of the table, her heart in her throat, she wrenches her eyes away from the monitor and back towards the ceiling just in time to see the thick grey plastic of the anesthesia mask lower onto her nose and mouth. The smell of daphne is lost in the halothane. From a muffled distance, she hears the anesthesiologist say, "Count backward from one hundred, please."

Okay. Count. I can do that.

THADDEUS RUTKOWSKI
LITTLE BEE
a friend bursts

At the psychiatrist's, I poured forth everything. I reverted to age four, when I had a friend called Little Bee.

He was about two inches long and looked like a bee, the kind you'd see in your back yard, or a bumble-bee fish, the kind you'd get for your aquarium. He was a trusted friend, someone I could confide in.

One day, I left him in the car while I visited the department office, and when I came out he was stealing my battery. He had the engine jacked up and a flood-light attached to the hood. I tried to lecture him on what he did wrong. I was very logical. But he kept trying to run away. I held him between my fingers to keep him from running, but I squeezed too hard, and he burst.

"So should I go to Puerto Rico or not?" I asked the doctor. That was my psychological problem, see, whether I should go to Puerto Rico and begin work on an architectural project or not.

"No," the doctor said. "No, you and Little Bee should go down to Tierra del Fuego and buy some cabbages."

But Little Bee was gone. Burst. Finished. I needed another friend. A little friend. One I could trust. Like an ant.

So I found one. A red ant named Formica. And we traveled, Formica and I, to the South, where the cabbage vendors were unusually abundant.

MAUD NEWTON
WHY I STILL THINK OF MARISOL
life lessons and a search for sexual healing

The last time I saw Marisol, she gave me a pen with a picture of a man in a Santa suit. The kind you turn upside-down and the clothes disappear and the man ends up naked except for the Santa hat. Sometimes I take the pen out and look at the man's body, but it doesn't make me think sexy thoughts. It just makes me think of Marisol.

Marisol had wavy brown hair, green eyes, and a Colombian accent that I only noticed when she got excited. She was 5-foot-10, 3 inches taller than my Dad and she drove a fading red Datsun with orange and yellow stripes. With her rhinestone bracelets, purple eyeliner and kick-ass tan, Marisol was the sexiest girl at the after-school camp where my mom volunteered. She was 16, same as I am now.

The camp was for kids who got caught getting high or running away or hitting their moms. Mainly they only went there if it was their first time in trouble, but Dad said it was one step away from jail. "You keep Ruth away from there," he told Mom.

Mom just rolled her eyes and left the room. When Dad was around, he and Mom ignored each other. I mean, they said hello, but in a mean way, like they really wanted to say fuck you.

Dad was usually out of town on some supposed business trip, anyway. Marisol said he probably had a girlfriend on the side.

"Why do you think your mother does the camp, Ruth?" she said. Then she lit a cigarette and changed the subject.

I don't know if Marisol was right, but Mom gave up on the camp when she and Dad divorced, traded it in for a green belt in karate. And Dad got a girlfriend right away. A girlfriend like a sitcom Dad's girlfriend. Younger and skinnier than Mom. Guess jeans with zippers at the ankles. Purple eyeliner that I guess seemed new to Dad even though it's not in fashion anymore.

Some kids at the camp, including Marisol, had to pee in a cup every week. Social workers came to pick up the pee. They sat in small offices on these big, puke-green couches, and put the samples in tiny, brown refrigerators, and acted like they were interested in what the kids had to say. Nobody knew which day they would show up, not even my mom.

Once, on pee day, this guy named Eddy, who had a Mohawk and an earring and had been caught having sex with a chubby girl named Valerie in a broom closet, touched my cheek and held out his cup. "C'mon, cutie. It's easy for you," he said. He smelled like Halston cologne, Dad's favorite.

But Marisol came around the corner, just as my face was getting hot, and smacked Eddy's hand away. "*Coño, muchacho,*" Marisol said. "Pee in your own damn cup and leave the jailbait alone."

She crossed her arms, leaned against the wall and glared at Eddy until he went in the bathroom and locked the door behind him. Then she looked at me. "Better watch yourself, kid," she said. And then she took off down the hall, her spike-heeled boots clicking efficiently.

When Mom was in charge, Marisol got special treatment. If there was pie, she got the biggest piece. If there was music, she had veto power. Maybe because she was smart and sassy, like Mom wanted to be, I don't know, but Marisol eventually charmed her way out of the sports hour as a trade-off for picking me up from school.

Out of nowhere one morning, Mom said Marisol would come for me and I worried all day about my little-girl bobby socks. After the final bell rang, there was Marisol, zipping up in front of the school. She wore dark sunglasses and drew raised eyebrows from the moms waiting in their cream-colored Audis and Lincolns. I was excited about getting picked up by Marisol, but in a nervous way, like when school was cancelled because of the riots or Hurricane David.

The night David was supposed to hit, I lay awake in my bed. I pressed on my eyelids and waited for the windows to shatter, or at least for the Bahama shutters to sail off down the street, but nothing happened. I remember the Miami Herald was on our doorstep the next morning. "Weak David Plays Hopscotch with the Coast," it said. And even though Mom and Dad actually talked to each other and we all ate pancakes and I got to skip school, I was disappointed. All that nervousness, and nothing even happened, except that a tree branch knocked a tile off our roof and my parents had to pay some guy to fix it.

Anyway, the first time Marisol picked me up, she drove right back to camp. "Hi, kid," she said, "your mom said to buckle up."

No seatbelt on her shoulder, so I didn't wear one either.

She squinched up her eyes and turned to face me. "Are you gonna narc if I have a Kool?"

I shrugged to show I was cool, I didn't care. "No way," I said.

She gave me a serious once-over before lighting one. Then she turned on the radio. That Marvin Gaye song, "Sexual Healing," had just come out, and I tried to pretend I knew it even though I was embarrassed when it got to the part that goes, "get up, get up, get up, let's make love tonight." I wasn't even 12 yet. I didn't know anything about sex first-hand.

It turned out "Sexual Healing" was pretty much always on one station or another, and Marisol just flipped the dial until she found it. After a week I knew all the words, and after two I squinched up my eyes and sang along. At the part where he says, "baby, I think I'm capsizing," Marisol lowered the volume so I was singing alone. When I turned red and stopped singing, she laughed so hard that she choked out a big cloud of smoke and had to pull over. "You like this song, huh Ruth?" she said, finally.

That was the first time she called me by name.

Then she told me about the way sex really happens, how a man's thing points at you when he wants to have sex with you. And the first time a girl has sex it hurts but after that it's OK because your dyke gets broken. "That's why girls who like each other get called dykes, because no man has ever gone inside them," she said.

One afternoon, Marisol took a detour by the arcade so she could meet her dealer, Raul, who wore this bright blue jacket and a skinny black tie. Raul gave her a free quarter bag because she gave him head in the parking lot. I didn't know what that meant until Marisol explained it all to me. She said I could watch if I wanted, but I felt weird about it, so I just played Ms. Pac Man even though I almost never even got past Act I.

When Marisol came into the arcade looking for me, I'd already used up all my quarters, and I was sitting on the floor, reading, like a geek.

I thought she'd laugh at me, but she just said, "No more Ms. Pac Man?"

"Nah, I suck."

"That makes two of us, honey," she said. Then she laughed and all the boys in the arcade looked at her.

I didn't get it, but I laughed because she did.

Afterward, we sat in the parking lot while Marisol smoked a joint, and it was really hot. It's usually like 90 degrees here, anyway, and her car didn't have air conditioning.

While Marisol separated out the seeds from the good stuff, she told me I should have sex before I got my first period so I could see how good it feels without getting pregnant.

"Baby, you can't get pregnant until you get your period," she said.

But I wondered. You have to have an egg inside you before you get your period, and who knows when you'll get the first egg. And wouldn't it be harder to find out that you're pregnant if you miss your first period when you don't even know it's supposed to happen? So even though I sometimes imagined lying down in my backyard with Johnny R. from church, or one of the boys at the camp, I knew I wouldn't really do it because I was too scared of getting pregnant. Plus, Johnny R. was too shy to really try anything.

Marisol's first time was in Colombia, under her grandmother's dining room table after Christmas dinner. "Everybody else was in the next room," Marisol said, "but I got under the table and got it on with my cousin's friend Raul. What a fox."

"Didn't it make noise?" I asked.

"No, he put his hand over my mouth and it was fast. I've had sex with 20 different guys, Ruth, and every one was different."

Marisol was on the pill, so she could have as much sex as she wanted.

After the day at the arcade, Marisol sometimes pulled off the road behind Frankie's Pizza and got high. Then she bought two slices with extra pepperoni and we ate them on the way to camp. "Hides the smell," she explained.

One afternoon, we actually went inside and sat down at a table near the counter. We ate in silence, and I looked out the window at the sign and thought about how bright it looked at night when they turned it on and the little white, neon lights flashed around the word Frankie's.

I told Marisol, and she said, "Sounds like a contact high to me."

I didn't know what she meant, but I didn't want to look dumb so I didn't ask. I just laughed and looked at her dangly earrings.

She frowned at me.

I thought maybe I was taking too long with my pizza. "Do we need to go?"

"Nah," she said. Then she ran her fingers through her hair and said, "Do you think I'm pretty, *querida*?"

I just said yes. I didn't tell her how my mouth sometimes got dry, how my breath caught in my throat when the sun turned her eyes into emeralds, shocking next to her deep brown skin.

My own skin was so pale that when I once got sun poisoning on a family vacation at Marco Island, nobody at school could even tell. "I thought you went to the beach," my teacher said. And then this one kid at school called me "ghost girl," so for a while everybody did.

Anyhow, besides Marisol's skin and eyes, she had nice boobs. I knew they were nice because she showed me in a Hustler magazine one time how the best ones are round on the bottom but they still stick out, and that's how Marisol's were, big but pointy.

Mine were just sprouting then.

"You stand up so straight, like you want to see them bronzed," Marisol said.

The day after we ate at Frankie's, Marisol picked me up from school, as always, but we didn't stop for a smoke break. When we got to camp, there was a sign that said "Congratulations, Marisol!" and a cake, and I gathered that it was her last day. Nobody had bothered to tell me.

At the party, Mom gave Marisol a dumb book for teenagers about taking charge of your life. Making It Happen, I think it was called. And some of the guys gave Marisol candy, with their phone numbers attached. I didn't eat any cake, just sat off in a corner and tried to read my history book.

Afterward, Marisol took me out on the baseball field and gave me the pen.

"Here's what a foxy, naked man looks like, Ruth," she told me.

I was curious to see, but when I tipped the pen over I felt sad. A little bit tingly, but mostly just sad. "I guess I won't see you again, right?" I said.

"Of course you will," she promised, pressing me against her chest.

But when she drove off, her long hair streaming out the window like a flag, I knew she wouldn't be back.

I turned 16 the other night, and I made Johnny R. have sex with me on the golf course behind my house. At first he didn't want to do it. "Ruth, you're special," he said, "and I don't want it to be this way."

Like I said, I know him from church, so that's why.

But when I took off my clothes, he shut up and did what I told him. Like Marisol said, it hurt, and when we did it again it hurt less, but after it was over I just felt lonely and it didn't make any difference that Johnny did all the stuff he was sup-posed to do. He held me close and stroked my hair, and I think he talked about being my boyfriend or maybe marriage, but I honestly don't remember for sure.

I was mostly thinking about Marisol, wondering how come she liked sex so much. Whether she still wore purple eyeliner and smoked Kools. And why sex with Johnny would bring her to mind.

TONY WHITESIDE
HOW'D YOU CATCH THIS THING?
one last summer, a fishing trip

It was a beautiful fish, even an eleven-year-old could appreciate that. A giant rainbow trout with delicate flecks of red and gold. Had to be twenty pounds. Jamal's father brought the monster home from a fishing trip and the boy couldn't take his eyes off of it. This was on a Sunday toward the end of summer.

"Whoa," Jamal said. He hadn't bothered to take off his baseball mitt. His mother strained to lift the giant fish out of a Styrofoam cooler. When she dropped it on the Formica counter, it sounded like old luggage. A plastic fan strained to cool the tiny kitchen, but barely made a breeze. His father stood grinning.

"Zach, how'd you catch this thing?" his mother said. Jamal didn't like the look on her face. It wasn't happy.

"Marcy, what a story. You aren't going to believe this," his father said. He sat at the table, the metal chair squeaked beneath his weight.

"Who all was there again?" she said.

"There was me, Mickey, Ray-Ray and his brother."

"Couldn't you have taken Jamal with you?" she said. She pointed to her son who'd finally gotten his mitt off and was staring into the lifeless eye of the fish.

"Marcy, this was grown up stuff. You understand, don't you little man?" his father said.

"I would have gone," Jamal said.

"I know you would have, son," the father said. "Anyway—"

"Anyway," the mother said.

"Anyway," the father said, "first day out, the only thing we caught was a buzz from Ray-Ray's 40s. Next day, same thing. By noon, I swear we were about to head back, and that's when I felt it: a tug. No, it was more like a big yank. I thought my arm would come off."

"Did you get scared, Dad?"

Jamal's father looked at him the way one would a crazy person. "Hell no, this is why you get on the lake in the first place," he said. "Right, Marcy?"

She didn't respond and instead turned to her son. "Jamal, you never watched me cook before," she said.

"You've never cut up a big ol' fish before," he said.

"Yeah, yeah." His father spoke louder, trying to regain his family's attention. "So, I fought this son of a bitch for an hour. I mean this sucker was strong. It was like a movie. He'd run, I'd reel. Back and forth." The father was gesturing wildly. "But I finally got that big boy in the boat. The fellas even gave me a round of applause."

He waited—for congratulations at the very least.

"That's quite a tale," Jamal's mother said. Then she picked up the knife.

She positioned it just behind the gills of the great fish. In one downward motion, she cut off it's head. It reminded Jamal of a comic book.

Jamal's mother grabbed the fish by the tail and then said, "Your office called."

"On the weekend?" the father said, "What'd they want?"

"Didn't say." She pointed the sharp edge of the knife away from her, across the body of the fish, and began to cut toward the head (or at least where the head used to be). "They said they couldn't find you or that Barbie Doll partner of yours," she said.

She cut into the belly of the fish with the forceful grace of a warrior, removing slippery entrails. The magnificent trout opened like a book. Two hunks of meat held together by graying skin.

"Madison. Her name is Madison."

"Okay, Madison. No cellphone?"

"No reception," the father said.

"Jamal," she said, "you've really never seen me skin a fish before?" The boy had been through enough of these moments to know his mother meant something else by that question. Something he couldn't be entirely certain of until four years later, when he and his mother were living in Aunt Celie's airy house, three states away. He quietly assured her that this was indeed his first fish skinning.

"They didn't say what they wanted, then?" his father said.

"No Zach," she said, inserting the knife between the skin and flesh of the fish. "But they were sure anxious to find you. They even sent Neil out to get you."

"They what? Neil?"

"I thought it was odd, too. Of course, he couldn't find you."

"There's no way he could have," the father said. He was tripping over his words, as if there were one too many sticks of gum in his mouth.

She cut slowly, careful not to slice all the way through the skin. She rotated the knife so that the blade lay almost parallel to the cutting board. With a gentle back-and-forth sawing motion she cut all the way from the tail to the missing head, pulling the skin tightly as she went.

"He even checked the trout farms," she said. "He was funny. He says you don't even have to be a fisherman to catch trout at these places. They keep them in big tanks. All you have to do is bait a hook and they practically jump on."

The fish had been skinned and filleted. Jamal thought it looked just like the tidy cuts of fish on ice at Kroger.

Jamal's father tapped the bottom of his wedding band against the kitchen table, not saying anything at all.

"Hell," he said finally, "trout farms are cheating."

"Only to a purist," she said, stirring a concoction of flour and spices. The mother and father were at opposite ends of the kitchen. Jamal stood halfway between them.

"I suppose I better call the office."

"Good idea," his mother said. "This fish is just about ready for frying."

Jamal's father slipped into another room. His mother's expression became something softer then, something fragile. He watched her dip the fillets into the breading for a moment. She smiled and told him to go back outside and play. There was still time left for Jamal to play.

He wasn't more than halfway through the door, a flash of bright yellow in his thigh-length rain slicker, before he asked, in a low, gravelly voice that sounded slightly familiar, "Do you know who I am?"

"Should I?" I asked, as I stood to greet him, half-expecting him to flash an American Express card to answer his own question.

He put up his hand. "No need," he said in a tone of noblesse oblige, hinting he was a man used to being catered to. Funny, I hadn't known this guy for more than a few seconds and already I didn't like him. I wouldn't say I'm the greatest judge of character—I've made more than my fair share of mistakes—but I can tell when a man has a chip on his shoulder. I can also tell when a man, or a woman, for that matter, is going to rub me the wrong way.

"You will," he said, leaning forward slightly.

"Will what?"

"Know me."

"If you say so, pal. I'm Swann," I said, extending my hand. "And you are?"

He hesitated a moment for dramatic effect, then grinned. "You can call me, James Brown."

"So what can I do for the Godfather of Soul and the hardest working man in show business?" I asked.

Not even a hint of a smile. Instead, he asked, "What's the H. stand for?" alluding to the initial on my front door.

"Harried, hackneyed, horrible, hot-headed, hospitable, hedonistic, hellacious, hog-tied, hateful, take your pick."

"I'm not here to play games, man," he said sharply, and I could tell that he meant it.

"No problem, amigo. It's Henry. Now why don't you take a seat and we'll get down to business."

"Ain't no wonder you use Swann," he mumbled, as he started to move toward me. He was a big man, over six-feet, kind of husky, with a bit of a beer belly. He had a milk-chocolate complexion and he was wearing the worst damned disguise I'd ever seen: a fake mustache, goatee, long side-burns, a curly, yellow Harpo Marx-like fright wig and a wide-brimmed, black Stetson. And although he walked with a slight limp, I noted that he moved with remarkable grace, almost gliding across the room. He sat down on the folding chair in front of my desk and when he gingerly crossed his legs I noticed he was wearing a pair of expensive, hand-sewn cowboy boots.

"So, you're a private dick, right?"

"That's right and the way you say that means I can't very well counter with, 'I've been called worse.'"

"Fact is, I don't like your kind much, Swann."

"There are times, my friend, when I would echo the very same sentiment. Moments of self-doubt, inadequacy, low-self-esteem and self-loathing. But I'll save that for my shrink."

"Good idea. Maybe he gives a shit." He began massaging his knee. "Bad knees, man, and this damp weather don't help none," he explained. "It don't matter how many operations you have, once they go they're pretty much gone forever. But they done me right for a long time, so I can't complain. Anyway, I'll be back in Florida soon, real soon."

"That where you're from?"

"That's where I hang my hat now."

"Speaking of hanging, would you like me to hang up your jacket?" I asked.

"I'm fine."

"Suit yourself."

"Always do. So, enough of the idle chatter. I'm here to see about hiring you to find someone."

"Who do you want me to find?"

"If I knew that, I wouldn't be hiring you."

"So you want me to find someone, but you don't know who it is. Have I got that right?"

"You catch on quick. But first, I gotta know some things about you."

"Fair enough. And by the way, before we go any further, I should tell you that that's the most ridiculous disguise I've ever seen. How's that for a fancy bit of detecting?"

"I'm impressed, man."

"I thought you would be. So what's up with that?"

"I like to protect my anonymity."

"I have no such problem," I countered, knowing that I couldn't possibly be anymore anonymous than I already was. A skiptracer working out of a seamy, broken down office in the middle of Spanish Harlem who had to re-introduce myself to the local bodega owner every time I went in to buy some cuchifritos. No, being recognizable was never one of my crosses to bear. "So, what do you need to know?"

"How long you been in business?"

"Well, I repoed my first car back in '92, so I guess it's over ten years now."

"That's a pretty shitty way to make a buck, man," he said, offering a wry smile.

"I can't disagree, but I've got a calling for it. Finding things is my specialty."

He squirmed in his seat. "Man, this chair is an uncomfortable motherfucker."

"Sorry, but usually folks aren't here long enough for it to bother them."

"Yeah," he said, looking around. "I can understand that. So, ever conducted a criminal investigation?"

"Now and then, though they never quite start out that way."

"What's that supposed to mean?"

"Sloth, envy, greed, lust and coveting your neighbor's wife often make a left into more serious matters, turning them into criminal activities. I prefer to catch them before they do, but sometimes I'm just not quick enough."

"You know, Swann, you talk like someone I used to work with. Someone who used words with more syllables than a cow has titties. Didn't like him much. Man, he got on my last nerve after a while. He's dead now, so he's someone else's problem. But I'm sure his mouth's still goin', no matter where he is, if you know what I mean? You a sports fan?"

"I watch a little baseball every now and then, if that counts."

"That's it?"

"Yeah."

He was pissing me off. In fact, I would have ushered his ass right out of the office except for two things: He was bigger than me and I needed the money and suspected I could hit him up for a pretty penny, because he certainly didn't look like my normal welfare client in search of a wandering husband. "And you? You a sports fan?"

"Golf's my game...now."

"Never could quite get a handle on that," I said giving it a feeble Johnny Carson swing. "Chasing around a little white ball, trying to coax it into a hole."

"Yeah, well, coaxin' balls into little holes is what I do best." He grinned lasciviously.

"Ever been outta New York?" he asked, getting back on track.

"Jersey count?"

"You must be kidding. Jersey don't count for nothing. How about California? Ever been there?"

"Once. Didn't really like it, though. Not enough tall buildings to block out the sun."

"They got lots of cars out there, man. Real nice ones. Maybe you ought to think about it, you being in the repo business and all."

"I'll give it some serious consideration. How about you? Where you from?"

"I've moved around a lot."

"Why's that?"

He shrugged and made a face. "Business reasons."

"How'd you come to choose me?"

"Yellow Pages."

"Smallest ad?"

"Yeah, somethin' like that."

Suddenly, the sound of a jackhammer began to reverberate through my office. I got up to close the window and lingered a moment as I spotted Joe Bailey, the owner of the Paradise Bar & Grill, crossing the avenue, trying to dodge raindrops. Joe used to play some semi-pro football and he moved effortlessly, shifting his hips gracefully as he darted in and out of the late afternoon Broadway traffic.

"This here's a pretty shitty neighborhood," said Brown.

"Yeah, well, the rent's cheap and it feeds into my feelings of superiority," I said, returning to my desk.

"You're in the ghetto, man."

"I guess that's why it's so tough to get a cab up here. But you know, I tell people my office is on the Upper West Side and they seem impressed."

He glanced down at his watch, an expensive Rolex, and my greedy little heart skipped a beat. Without looking up he said, "My wife was murdered. I need you to find the dude who did it."

"I'm sorry, I don't do that kind of finding."

"Don't tell me you got scruples, Swann."

"I won't tell you that because frankly, I'm not even sure what they are. It's just that I know my limits, which is one of my more endearing personality traits. You know, your voice is beginning to sound very familiar."

He smiled.

"So, where do I know you from?"

"Might say I've had my moments in the sun."

"What do you do for a living?"

"This and that."

I realized I wasn't getting anywhere with this line of questioning, so I decided to tackle a more important issue. "You know, I don't come cheap."

He laughed.

"I may look low-rent, but I'm not."

He laughed again. "I got enough to pay you, man, if that's what you're worried about."

"I worry about everything, Mr. Brown. It's my nature. I worry about the diminishing ozone layer. I worry about my cholesterol. I worry about being able to pay my rent. I worry about someone poisoning the water supply. I worry that I'm going to have a heart attack. I worry about the world exploding and I worry about my body imploding. In short, I worry about the sky falling directly on me. So, tell me about your wife."

"She was a slut."

"I take it you were divorced or on the verge."

"Yeah. I dumped the bitch, though she kept comin' back for more. She liked this," he said, pointing to his crotch.

"Obviously, there was no love lost, so why do you care who killed her?"

"That," he said, scratching behind his neck, "is my business."

"Well, it's going to be mine if I decide to take the case."

"You'll take it."

"Why's that?"

"Because I'm going to make you famous, if you do."

"And what if I don't want to be famous?"

"Everyone wants to be famous, man," he said, untangling his legs and crossing them to the opposite side. "I should know. I been there and it ain't all that bad."

"Maybe you should tick off the good points for me."

He snorted. "Well, you always get a good table in restaurants. You get invited to a lot of parties. You get stuff you don't have to pay for. People give you respect, whether your deserve it or not—in fact, the less you deserve it, the more you get. They cut you all kinds of slack. And the women, man, let me tell you, the women are all over you. You'll get more pussy than you know what to do with."

"I didn't know what to do with what little I had," I said, remembering the ex-wife who moved to Vancouver, which was about as far away from me as she could get without leaving the damn continent.

"Yeah, well, you'll learn, man. The Duke here," he said, pointing down below his belt, "likes to get fed…and he got fed plenty…still does. Fame goes a long way, man, and once you got it, it don't just fade away, no matter what they say. But sometimes there's a fork in the road, if you know what I mean. Things just happen…"

"Like a wife getting murdered?"

"Yeah, like that."

"So, you never answered me. Why do you care who killed your wife?"

"Because…they…think…I…did it."

"Did you?"

"Would I be here trying to hire you if I did it?"

"You tell me."

He smiled.

"So, if they think you did it, why aren't you in jail?"

"Because I already been tried and found not guilty, that's why." He straightened up. "But I am not going to rest until the real killer or killers are brought to justice."

"I'm impressed. What were the circumstances of her death?"

"Throat cut."

"And…"

"And then she died."

"There's more to it than that. Tell me how it happened."

"She was with her latest boyfriend and someone got them in front of her apartment building."

"Him, too?"

"Yeah." He ran his finger across his throat.

"Where was that?"

"California."

"Where in California?"

He hesitated a moment. "Ever hear of Brentwood."

Okay, the charade was over. I knew exactly who I had in my office, only I couldn't believe it. The infamous O.J. Simpson, dressed in a fright wig, looking like a refugee from the circus, was trying to hire me to find the killer of his wife, Nicole.

"Listen, O.J. why don't we just cut the crap. I don't know what your game is…"

"I don't have no game anymore, Swann. I'm hiring you to clear my name, so I can get my game back, okay? The Duke," he looked down to his crotch again, "is always on duty and me and him want to come back out into the sunlight. People think I don't have feelings. But I do. You think I like walking around having people whisper and point at me? You think I like hearing 'if the glove don't fit, you got to acquit," over and over again? You think I like never being able to wear a pair of Bruno Magli shoes again? And man, those are some badass shoes. I got to get this monkey off my back, man."

"So you came to me."

"That's right."

"Well, I think if you were serious you'd find someone a little more experienced than I am."

"Yeah, you'd think so, but it ain't so easy to find someone to take this case. I ain't exactly America's sweetheart, you know. And I figure, what does a guy like you have to lose workin' for a guy like me?"

"Not much, I guess," I said, as I reached into my desk drawer and pulled out a notebook.

"You ain't gonna ask for my autograph, are you? Because if you are, it's gonna cost you."

"No. I was just going to take some notes."

He nodded.

"Why don't you take off that head gear and get comfortable?"

He removed his hat and the wig and there he was, in all his glory, O.J. Simpson, one of the greatest running backs in the history of the NFL and one of the most notorious not guilty killers in the annals of American crime. I didn't know what I was going to do, but one thing I wasn't going to do was pass up an opportunity of a lifetime—to put O.J. on the hot seat and maybe have a little fun with him.

"So listen, O.J.—you don't mind me calling you that, do you?"

"It's my name, man. But I've always preferred just plain 'Juice.' "

"Okay, Juice, what's with you and blondes?"

"What's that got to do with anything?"

"Just curious."

He smiled. "The Duke here likes blondes, man."

"Yeah. I know."

"It's the American Dream, my friend. A hot lookin', long-legged, blonde with a nice pair of headlights, a shiny new Mercedes convertible and a bottle of fine Crys-tal champagne. That's my idea of heaven. You got a problem with that? You ain't no damn racist, are you?"

"Nope. I like blondes as well as the next guy," I said.

"That ain't exactly what I meant. So anyway, you gonna take this case or am I wastin' my valuable time?"

"I'm interested. But you know, I gotta say, I watched that trial like everybody else in the country and man, they had some heavy duty evidence that nailed you to the wall."

"And the verdict was...?"

"Yeah, yeah..."

"Twelve of my peers found me not guilty, my friend. NOT GUILTY! In case you don't know, that means I...didn't...do...it."

"It means you got yourself a good set of lawyers, that's what it means."

"Same difference. Hey, I'm the victim here. I'm the one who's gotta slink around in disguise being the most hated man in America. I'm the one who can't get a damn job. I'm the one who's gotta keep it together for two kids who are always gonna ask, 'Hey, Daddy, is it true that you killed mommy?' I'm the one who's gotta hide all his dough so those damn Goldmans can't get their greedy little hands on it. Look at the rest of 'em. Marcia Clark. Million dollar book contract. Got her puss on TV every damn day. The other dude, Darden, another million dollar book contract. Cochran. Book contract. TV. Commercials. The dude's set for life. Scheck? No one heard of him before me, now he's called in on every goddamn murder case in the U. S. of A. I feel like I was a goddamn charitable institution. And me? Nothin'. No one's handin' me a million bucks for my story. I'm not jumpin' over suitcases in airports no more. I can't get no fuckin' job as a sports commentator. Marv Albert—he gets caught slappin' women around and wearing chick's underwear, but now he's back on TV callin' hoops like noth-in' ever happened. What's left for me?"

"I suppose you could team up with Pete Rose and Mike Tyson...Bad Boys, Inc. has a certain ring to it."

"Very funny, man, but it ain't no joke. They piss on me, pal, but that's gonna change, because you, or somebody like you, is gonna find the real damn killer."

"So all this is about money," I said, thinking that if the answer was yes we really would have something in common.

"It's about redemption, my friend. It's about stickin' it to the man. It's about giving that big, fat middle finger to every goddamn, hypocritical, white cracker who's tryin' to keep the black man down. To every goddamn hypocritical football fan who won a bundle bettin' on my ass."

"So you think you're representative of the black man."

"Don't go there, pal, because there's a chance you won't come back."

"Sounds like a threat."

"Ain't no threat. The Juice is a peaceful man." He held up two fingers in the V sign. "I had enough violence to last me a lifetime in pro ball. They unleash the beast in me and it's fine so long as I'm runnin' down the field with a pig's skin under my arm. But now I ain't got to knock any more heads or run over any more people to get my jollies. I'm just warnin' you not to get into a discussion you can't win."

"So you're an innocent man..."

"You hear me say I'm innocent? Who's innocent? You innocent? You walked the straight and narrow your whole damn life? I...don't...think...so."

"How do I know you're not just using me?"

"Using you how?"

"Like tomorrow I see an item on Page 6—'O.J. hires private dick to find wife's killer.' And suddenly there's a little bit of doubt planted in people's minds as to whether you really did it."

"How you figure that helps me?"

"Would a guilty man hire someone to find the killer of a murder they were accused of?"

"Now why didn't I think of that?"

"I think maybe you did."

He flashed an enigmatic smile. "I ain't that smart, man. I'm just a dumb-ass, ex-jock lookin' to get a beer commercial. I want back in."

"Haven't you heard? There are no second acts in America."

"Who says?"

"F. Scott Fitzgerald."

"Sounds like something Cosell would've said. That man was a walking book of quotations and I don't think anybody knew what the hell he was talking about."

"Well, maybe he did say it, but he wasn't the first."

"There may not be a second act, but there sure as hell is a second half, man. They never did call the game off at half-time, far as I know. And sometimes I had my best game in the last quarter, when everyone else was bone-ass tired."

He got up and started ambling around the office, stretching out his knee every once in a while. He stopped in front of a small bookshelf and squinted at the titles. "You like to read, huh?"

"They're mostly for show. I like to give the appearance of being an educated man."

"Oh, yeah? You go to college?"

"Two years."

"Four, for me," he said, grinning. He put the book back and looked at his watch.

"Well, we got a deal or not?"

"A deal?"

"You gonna take the case or not?"

"Can I think about it?"

"I'm leavin' town tomorrow."

"What about I let you know by morning?"

"What do you think is gonna tip the scales?" He took out his wallet, opened it and took out a wad of bills. "You know, the one thing they couldn't take away from me was my NFL pension. And man, that is one fine-ass pension. If I never worked another day in my life, I'd still be in pretty good shape. And they can't touch a penny of it. It's protected. By law. And you know something, I'm a very generous man." He took a bill and threw it on my desk. It was a hundred. "This is for your time, Swann. And there's plenty more where that came from. You do me, I do you. The Juice likes to spread it around. You take this job and your life will change forever. You don't, you'll be sorry for the rest of your damn life. Your choice, man."

He reached across my desk, grabbed my pad and pen and wrote something on it. "Here's my number. You call me by eight o'clock tomorrow morning. I think we're going to work very well together."

He turned and walked toward the door. He opened it and took a step out, then turned back and said, "Swann, you take me on as a client you'll never have to worry about finding other clients for the rest of your life. You'll be the man who worked for O.J. And who knows, hangin' with me you might just get your own book contract and some fine-ass pussy. Won't be long before you'll be callin' yours the Earl. We'll be set for life, my man. The Duke and the Earl. For life."

And then he was gone.

I walked over to the window. It was raining harder now. The wind was blowing so that the heavy raindrops were making a thwacking sound on my window. A moment passed and then I saw O.J. come limping out of the building, listing slightly to one side. He stepped out into the street, which was now fairly deserted. He put up his hand and suddenly, as if out of nowhere, a cab appeared and stopped in front of him. He got in and it sped off.

"Damn," I thought, "a black man scores a cab in this neighborhood. The Duke must be doing something right."

Summer Copeland | **Western Haikus** *Poem*

*Cold February
coffee in bed, laundry pile.
I should have another cup.*

*Who haven't you slept with?
I'm sure
I'll meet them soon.*

*The gas station attendant,
missing her front teeth,
has a contagious smile.*

*Sighs escape from smile
the waitress aches for closing,
remembers herself.*

*The child with the balloon
untied it from his arm
To see how high it would go.*

*He is young and angry and drunk.
I ran my hands down his tattooed arms,
than ran away.*

PHILIPPE STESSEL
A FLY
the unexamined fly is not worth considering

These things happen, Dave told himself. You're in Minneapolis on a business trip with a colleague of the opposite sex, someone you find attractive. You're both young and unattached. You love that strawberry blonde hair. The two of you eat dinner with a customer. You trade looks. Afterwards, you slam a few drinks at the hotel bar, just the two of you. Her idea. The bar closes early but it's too bloody cold to go outside again. Hell, you suggest, there's always the mini-bar in your room. You remember cracking open a couple of beers. That's where things start to blur.

Dave propped himself up on his pillow. What a colossal headache. He swore that if he could just live through this one day, he would never, ever drink like this again. He didn't remember getting undressed or anything. From the looks of the sheets and covers it appeared that a lot of thrashing had gone on. He stood up, but the room tilted him back onto the bed. He sat for a moment staring in disbelief at all the beer cans, pecan shells, airline-sized bottles of Johnny Walker Red and Smirnoff Vodka littering the room. How was he going to explain this mini-bar bill to accounting? What the hell happened last night? Focus. He seemed to remember some moments of affection and tenderness, but it could have been lascivious groping. What time did Valerie leave? My God, she could be down in the lobby, sobbing, talking to the police right now.

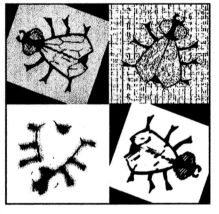

The phone chirped, snapping him out of his stupor.

"Valerie? Hi. Breakfast? Sure. Give me ten, I'll meet you in the lobby."

How bad can it be, he thought, if she still wants to have breakfast with me? Dave splashed his face with cold water from the ice bucket and gave his black hair a quick comb. Thank God it was Friday and they didn't have any client meetings today before flying home to Chicago.

***

Valerie, poised as always, sat in the hotel lobby in her forest-green parka, synthetic timber wolf trim on the hood. Dave did not detect any signs that she might

155

be upset with him. Valerie insisted on leaving the hotel for breakfast. Never mind that it was forty below in a dead calm. The desk clerk at the hotel told her about a place just a few blocks away, had a nice homey feel to it. Whatever. Dave just wanted coffee and some grub, something good and greasy to ease his hangover.

The warm, coffee-laden air of Jimmy's Diner gave sanctuary from the arctic blast outdoors. They took a seat by the window. Everything in the diner was either pink or baby blue. A young waitress in a pink uniform and white apron introduced herself as Brenda. She brought menus and poured them coffee. "It's gonna be a cold one, dontchya know." She apologized for being short-handed this morning. Betty, the second waitress, couldn't get her car started.

Dave looked out the window to the nearly deserted street. "What would it be like if they had never invented windows?" he asked. Valerie gave him a blank stare. Her hair, pushed up and held back by a powder blue headband, looked amazing even under the garish fluorescent lighting. Damn she was beautiful, even with a hangover.

Valerie took a sip of coffee. "Blech! This coffee tastes like dishwater."

"Really?" Dave said. "Tastes good to me."

Valerie flagged down Brenda and ordered tea.

Dave picked up his menu, dog-eared, food-stained and torn. He sighed. A mess. Just like his life. Every time he fell for a girl he ended up doing something stupid, like getting drunk, forgetting what happened and never hearing from her again. On top of that, this was his third job in two years—running around the country selling adhesive products. And, he wasn't any good at it, unlike Valerie who made top salesperson three years in a row. He'd begged Ray, his boss, to give him a chance to work with Valerie, on purely professional grounds. Dave really believed he could learn something, and, in fact, they'd done quite well on this trip. Even though they'd called on all of Valerie's customers and she always did the talking. Dave had tagged along to learn and instead he fell in love.

Valerie ordered two eggs, sunny-side down on whole-wheat toast. Dave scanned the list of items on the menu.

"I'll have two eggs over easy on . . . no, on second thought make that the Everything Omelet."

He asked Brenda if the Everything Omelet really had everything. "You betchya!"

After they ordered, Dave didn't know what to say. He wanted to know what happened last night and how Valerie felt about it. Valerie sipped her tea and gazed out the window, giving up nothing. Their food came. Dave emptied half the bottle of ketchup onto his eggs. Valerie looked on, aghast. Dave asked Brenda for

Tabasco sauce. He slapped half a bottle of that on top of the lake of ketchup already floating on his eggs. Valerie's jaw dropped.

"My God, you're not going to eat that are you?"

He looked down at his plate, half yellow, half red. "Yeah, why not?" He dug in, savoring every forkful. He concentrated on eating, one automatic mouthful after another. Nothing had ever tasted so good. He glanced up at Valerie. She looked so together, neatly and calmly eating her food.

He wanted to say something. Should he apologize, thank her, say he had a good time, ask her how it was, if it was, tell her that he loved her? His fork stabbed another bit of omelet. He began to utter something, he didn't know what yet, when something made him stop. A small black blob worked its way out from among the American cheese, ham, spinach, mushrooms, tomatoes, peas and hash browns cooked into his omelet. What was it? He looked closer. He poked it with his fork. First he excavated the furry leg then the broken wing and finally the listless, glistening eye of a plump, dead fly. By this time Valerie noticed what was going on and cried, "That's disgusting!" She pushed away her plate.

"Yeah, it kinda is."

"Tell them to take it way."

Embarrassed, Dave beckoned Brenda.

"Hi. It seems that my Everything Omelet does have everything—including a dead fly."

She looked at his plate with agony in her eyes. "Oh noo! That's terrible. I'm so sorry. First, I wanchya ta know you're not gonna pay for that." She pulled the order tablet from her apron pocket and ripped up the check. "And I want the owner to see this."

"No, that's ok. Just take the plate away," said Dave.

Too late, Brenda had already bounded half way to the kitchen.

Jimmy, the owner, was also the chef. He stood six foot four over the table. Permanent worry creased his face. His once-white apron looked like an even dirtier version of the menu. Jimmy shook his head and offered his apologies. He didn't understand how this could have happened. The exterminator was just there two days ago.

Dave looked at the fly and all the adults crowded around the table. He thought, in the dead of a Minneapolis winter, a fly lives out its short life in the kitchen at Jimmy's diner. A luxurious existence, never wanting for food nor drink nor warmth, hardly noticed by anyone, except perhaps as an annoyance. Then, one day, no longer satisfied with scraps from the garbage pail, the fly makes a play for the omelet pan. It lands and scarcely has a chance to rub its front legs together and take a slurp when an avalanche of eggs bury him alive. Hopefully, he dies instantly, spared the torment of a slow, scorching death. The fly made a bad decision, but did not die in vain. In death, this fly attracted more attention and consideration than most flies, living or dead. Maybe, this fly was trying to tell him something.

Brenda cleared away the plates and Jimmy returned to the kitchen. Valerie stood up to leave.

Dave blurted out, "Valerie, about last night . . ."

"Don't worry about it."

"Don't worry about it?"

"It was just as much my fault as yours."

"Oh."

Valerie applied some lipstick.

"Listen, Ray called me from the office this morning. He doesn't think things are working out. Of course you can use your plane ticket back to Chicago, but today will be your last day. No need to return to the office. We'll have your desk packed up and shipped to your house. HR will give you a call on Monday to finish up the paperwork. I know it's tough, but that's the way it goes sometimes."

Dave, stunned to silence, helped Valerie put on her coat.

"I probably won't see you since I'm spending the weekend in Minneapolis with friends. It was nice working with you."

Valerie shook Dave's hand and walked out the door as Betty, the second waitress, walked in. A gust of frigid air blew into the diner and slapped Dave in the face. Betty hurriedly took off her coat and hung it on the rack in the corner. Brenda walked up still holding the plate with the fly in the omelet.

"Betty, take a look at this."

Betty, smoothing her hair and apron, looked down at the plate and shook her head.

"Oh noo! Not again!"

SUCH A PERFECT DAY
hunger for love leads to starvation and weight gain

Christina was in her first semester of medical school at NYU when we met. I swept the library floors twice a week for extra money and she was invariably the last to leave.

At the time, I was planning to be a writer, but wasn't doing much about it. I wrote a few sentences each evening and spent a lot of time watching the Knicks and contemplating the meaning of life. Christina thought it was romantic, at least in the beginning. We would sit for hours in my studio apartment on Fiftieth Street and talk about our ambitions. We had a lot of sex.

Christina was a serious student, though, and medical school requires a great deal of dedication. She studied every evening, five hour stretches, and days would pass when I'd hear nothing. At first I didn't mind. I thought I needed the free time to get my own work done, told myself that Christina was a distraction. But I usually ended up going to Grady's on Tenth Avenue. I ate two, sometimes three burgers in a night. I began to gain weight.

I missed her and often went to the library simply to see her study. She hated this, but I managed to keep quiet while she worked. I would stare at Christina's crinkled brow and watch her scribble notes. She had beautiful handwriting and I loved the way her elbow bounced when she wrote.

She pressured me to show her my latest story. She was somehow still under the impression that I was writing. I put her off, said I was working on something big, it would take a while before it was ready. I had nothing to write about, though. I was empty.

Christina noticed I was packing it on. "Why don't you get out more," she suggested. I tried taking long walks. But I got bored and I missed watching Dr. Phil and Cops. I compromised by hiking to a bar with a T.V. and Buffalo wings.

For her, I spent one weekend trying to lose weight. I drank a single Slim Fast shake for breakfast, lunch and dinner. They were delicious. The next day, I drank eleven.

Christina sat on my apartment floor one night. My place was spare in those days, I couldn't afford a couch. She ate Chinese food out of a carton. Her face was lit by candles because I hadn't paid my electric bill.

"Tod? Are you still thinking about law school?" she asked.

I had never thought about it. She only mentioned law school because it was a well worn path to success in her mind. Two of her cousins were lawyers at big firms in the city, worked twelve or fifteen hour days, made good money.

"I just want you to show some ambition," Christina said. "Before it's too late."

I had my whole life in front of me. How could it be too late? And besides, I had her.

Her jaw worked up and down as she chewed her chicken with cashew nuts. The dimple on her left cheek stood out whenever she swallowed. I loved the way she wiped her face: she would close her eyes, like it was a dirty, but necessary job.

"Whenever I'm with you, Christina, my troubles disappear. You're all I need."

She raised her eyebrows.

"Pass me the spare ribs," she said.

I followed Christina to class. It was a Monday. I kept my distance, just enjoyed watching her hair flop up and down. The large lecture hall was crowded, but I managed to find a seat at the back. The professor's voice and the scratching of pens were the only sounds. I must have dozed off and begun snoring. When I awoke Christina was shaking me. People stared. She did that thing I like: grabbed a clump of her hair. How I loved her.

What the hell did I think I was doing? she wanted to know. Didn't I have better things to do with my time? "Look at those clothes you're wearing," she said and touched them.

My jeans had tiny holes at the knees and I wore a red, stained sweatshirt and sneakers.

"What's wrong with you?" she asked. "Do you think you need professional help?"

I didn't think so. I just wanted to be with her, it made me feel good. It made it okay that I wasn't doing anything else worthwhile.

Christina didn't return my phone calls for three days. I figured she was busy with school work. But when I did get through, she said she was in the middle of something and would have to get back to me. That ticked me off. What could be more important than a phone call from your love?

I tried to wait her out. I paid my electric bill. I bought every episode of Dobie Gillis from a specialty mail order catalog and spent two days watching them. I spent a day playing solitaire: I gave myself five dollars for every card I won like they do in Vegas. I finished ahead by thirty bucks and considered this quite an achievement. But it felt meaningless without someone to share it. I needed Christina.

I called a few times and left more serious messages: "Christina, if I don't hear from you soon, it could be trouble between us..." and "My patience is wearing thin with this little game, my love..." I lived off Slim Fast shakes, pizza and beer. I put on ten pounds in each of the first two weeks of Christina's absence. That at least gave me an excuse to go to the Salvation Army for new clothes.

I didn't shower or shave for two days beforehand because I wanted to look as forlorn as possible. I put on my torn jeans, red sweatshirt and sneakers. The woman at the center grabbed my shoulder like we were old college buddies and smiled. She offered me her bologna sandwich (which I took) and escorted me into the back where they keep the "big and tall" clothes. I picked out a pair of baggy brown corduroys, a white sweatshirt and a blue baseball cap. The woman insisted I shower before leaving. I was happy to oblige.

I called Christina and told her all about my exploits at the Army. She didn't pick up the phone, of course. Her machine allowed messages of only a minute and I was forced to call back seven times in order to get the whole story in. I pictured Christina playing them. She would laugh. She would flop onto her couch, hug a pillow to her chest and call me. All would be forgiven.

I tossed and turned all night waiting for the call. Maybe something was really wrong. I cleared the pizza boxes and Slim Fast containers from the center of my living room and began to pace. Maybe Christina didn't share my passion. But we had so much. I knew her favorite place to be kissed. She knew about the night I vomited on my college president's front porch. We were ideal for each other, I had no doubt about it.

There was a day we spent one week after we'd begun dating. It was fall, a Saturday. I surprised her by arriving at her apartment at nine in the morning with flowers and all the ingredients for strawberry pancakes. After breakfast we went to Prospect Park. We watched softball and then took a stroll. We stopped at a pond and threw rocks into the water. Christina leaned against a tree. She held a green leaf in her hand, tore it gently at the stem. I put my hand against her cheek and kissed her. It was our first. I told her my plan. I was going to write novels. Short stories were for the unambitious. I would write a masterpiece, I just knew I had it in me. Money didn't matter. Only dedication. She kissed me so hard she bit down and tore the skin on my lower lip.

"It was a perfect day," she said as we parted in the evening. "I really think you're special."

Three months later, where were we? I examined myself in the mirror. I didn't look too good. I had a tangled black beard that made me look like a bum. My white sweatshirt already had a pizza stain on it and I had packed about two hundred and thirty pounds onto my five foot, nine and a half inch frame. Wasn't love supposed to transcend physical appearance, though? I would have loved HER, that's what I told myself.

I composed a song. It wasn't much, but I thought it really expressed my feelings. The last stanza read: *the sun, the bread, the water, the blade—fly above, juggling pins—blur and clink, a liquid hope—clear, a rainbow—what is it?—It's you*. I read it to her answering machine in the afternoon. I figured she would have to call now. My balls were hanging out there, for Christ's sake. I had said, in not so many words, "I love you." I never thought I would say that, frankly, but I couldn't think of what else to call what I was feeling. I had been with a number of women—not that I'm anything to look at—but had never put myself on the line like that before.

She didn't call that day and by night time I was freaking. My face began to break out in a cherry red rash.

I decided to go to her place and find out, once and for all, what the hell was going on. I began to make a ham sandwich in case I got hungry on the way. There was a soft knock on the door.

She stood in the doorway with a grim look. I tried to hug her, but she pushed me aside.

"You smell terrible," she said.

"Christina..." I was choked up. She was wearing the wool sweater that I had given her for her birthday.

"I'll make this quick," she said.

I bit into my sandwich and sat on the floor. I don't know what I expected her to say. I knew we were having problems. I thought we would work it out. That's what lovers do.

"I don't want you to call me anymore," she said.

"What?" A piece of ham fell onto the floor.

"You're a dreamer," she said. "I just can't be around you anymore. You're a slob. You're fat."

"I love you, Christina." That's all I could think to say.

"You don't know what love is, you selfish prick."

"But we're perfect for each other."

"That's what you think? Perfect? Man, it's all in your head. Perfection? Jesus. Don't you know anything?"

"Christina?"

Who was this standing in front of me? I was stunned into silence. I felt a little spit dribble down my chin.

"Take a fucking shower," she said. Didn't even close the door on her way out.

***

Maybe Christina had a point, I thought after three weeks of sulking. Love isn't about perfection. It exists in a flawed world. Those who fail to see this are doomed to misery.

I started running every day and cut out Slim Fast altogether. I began to eat fruit and I decided to write a novel. I was going to prove to Christina that I understood love.

The novel took me two years. I forced myself to write four hours a night. I managed to hold down two dish washing jobs, earned just enough for rent and food and left time for little else. I was twenty-five when I began and thought when the book was done, Christina would be mine.

***

The book was a love story, although all of the novel's action took place in one day. Christina was the heroine, a pharmacist, a lonely suburban woman who fantasized about finding perfect love. She rejected everyone who tried to get close to her because she thought all any of them wanted was to possess her, like a trophy. She wanted a man drunk on his desire for something inaccessible within her. He would fuck her every evening like a wild animal. Words would be unnecessary between Christina and her love. He could be a mute. That was preferable, in fact.

Tod, a hulking, dim fireman, fell in love with her. He stood on her porch after three margaritas and declared his passion:

"I'm being honest," Tod said. "I can get laid any night. For you, I want to dim the lights, play Lou Reed. I want to kiss your cheek, kiss you everywhere, watch your face as the pleasure ebbs and flows. What will your lips do? Will they clench or purse? Will your eyes be closed? I want to force them open with my tongue, make you watch me. It isn't enough for me to fuck you, Christina. I want to love you."

Christina saw that Tod was not for her. He wanted to possess her like all the others. She went into her house and closed the door on Tod. But this brief encounter on her porch had allowed Christina to glimpse her own true nature and it depressed her. She was living in a fantasy. She would never transcend her mundane little world. She would not find perfect love.

Christina took a bottle of sleeping pills out of the medicine cabinet and ground them in a fine powder. She dissolved the drugs in a tall glass of water and drank them in one glorious, self-indulgent act. She died in bed, arms and legs spread eagled. She imagined that she died for love.

In the morning, poor Tod pounded on the door. When Christina did not answer, he broke it down in burly fireman fashion. He found her lying prone in bed, eyes fixed. He gently kissed her cheek and rubbed her bluish skin. He saw immediately what must have happened: she had been overwhelmed by her passion for him. Tod tucked the body under the blanket and crawled in next to her. He made love to Christina, fulfilling the promises he had made the night before.

Christina's ghost, watching from above, was disgusted. She attempted to pry the rugged fireman off her stiff body. But ghosts, like words, are powerless in the face of flesh and blood. She tried to escape the room, but the walls repelled her. When she covered her face, she saw through her hands. When she closed her eyes, she saw through her eyelids.

Tod fucked Christina's corpse until noon. When he was finished, he rolled over, lit a cigarette and sighed. It was the first sound he had uttered all morning.

Tod imagined he was incapable of feeling a purer passion than he was feeling in that moment. His love was perfect, like a circle, impenetrable. Tod had miraculously achieved what Christina had sought. I intended for this to be ironic.

Christina's ghost touched an odd indentation on the fireman's nose. Tod suddenly swatted the air above his face. The corpse was attracting flies, he thought. It was time to go.

***

I tried to find a buyer for the novel, but no one wanted any part of it. One agent called it the most depressing thing he'd ever read. He wondered about my sanity.

But I hadn't written it for the public and I was sure I was sane. The novel had been like therapy, that's what I convinced myself. I was down to 165 pounds and I was toned.

I called Christina. Blood rushed into my head and I was afraid I wouldn't be able to talk when she answered. But I hoped my love for her would enable me to speak: the words would flow steamy and hot like molten lava. AT&T answered the phone. The number I was calling had been changed. The new number was unlisted.

I went to her old apartment. Victor Lino, a balding man with large biceps, answered the door. He said he knew nothing about the former tenant. I began to cry. I fell on his doorstep and wailed. I pounded the floor with my fists. I kicked a bag of garbage down the stairs. Victor called the police.

Alan Marcellino arrested me. One of the best breaks I ever got. He was tall and resembled Robert Redford, only Italian and not so good looking. He put me behind bars and told me I'd have to spend the night there. But he was sympathetic, he listened.

I said I had lost something, maybe the most precious thing in the world. A true love. Her name was Christina.

The next morning Alan let me out. He told me not to pitch any more fits on the doorsteps of strangers. He said he had once lost a true love, he understood. He winked and handed me a piece of paper: it was Christina's new phone number and address. Alan patted me on the back. I hugged him and promised to send an autographed copy of my novel. I ran out of the precinct.

It was January. I waited outside her apartment in the cold until she came home from work. It was our first contact in two years. I showed her my manuscript and the dedication inside: "To C, My Love." She laughed, tucked it under her arm and said she was late for a dentist's appointment. She looked good.

The first week of waiting was the easiest. The book was three hundred pages and it would take her at least five days. I occupied myself by cleaning. I dusted on the first day. I moved the couch, bent to my knees and scrubbed the grime out of the hard wood floor with a brush. On the second, I removed each book from the shelf and straightened its cover. By Saturday there was nothing left to clean. Two years of dirt, gone.

I looked at the phone. It would be easy to call, it wouldn't mean anything. *Hey, how's it going, sweetie?* No. Too soon.

I went jogging one evening. I stopped at a small grocery store a mile from home, walked around the frozen goods section. I stared at a pint of Ben & Jerry's Wavy Gravy for fifteen minutes.

I rushed home to check my answering machine. The red light was flickering. I felt my face flush with excitement. One call. I put my finger on the button to play the message, but stopped. I wanted to clean up first. I took a shower.

I stood in front of the machine, naked, dripping. I pressed play. It was a message from Sprint. They wanted to know if I was interested in switching from my current long distance carrier. Apparently, they used fiber optic cables for service "clear as a bell."

I shivered. Man, it was fucking cold all of a sudden.

I rummaged through my closet for something to wear. Found my old white sweatshirt.

Maybe just give her a ring, I thought, see how she's doing with the novel.

Maybe she has questions or she's overwhelmed, afraid to call, confused by the welling of two years of emotion. I hung up after one ring. I didn't want to pressure her. Maybe she was really going over it with a fine tooth comb. I blended myself a strawberry Slim Fast and went to sleep.

I woke at six in the morning, sweating. I blended another shake and started pacing around my apartment. Well, what would it really hurt? I thought. Just a little phone call. Just to see. It was my life, after all.

I got her machine.

"It's... Tod... Just wanted to see... well... call me."

I finally admitted that I was desperate. Didn't she see that I understood, finally? I really did love her. Didn't two years of my life dedicated to HER prove that? Jesus!

I waited outside her apartment one night, but she didn't come home. I decided that she was probably working nights. Doctors do that.

You wouldn't think a person could gain fifty pounds so quickly. I thought, just a Slim Fast in the morning to get me going. But the shakes acted like a tonic; they brought back all the memories of Christina that I had been suppressing for two years. I was up to ten shakes a day after a week.

I went to Grady's. The place looked the same, except they had added a big screen T.V. I tried to suffocate my sorrow in grease. One night I sat on the same stool for six hours and managed to eat seven hamburgers. That shot my food budget for a week and I knew I'd have to increase my Slim Fast intake. I told the bartender all about my problem and he laughed. "Women..." he said.

I called Christina's machine three or four times a day.

"I still love you," I said.

I finally caught Christina outside her apartment one night. I carried my walkman. I wanted her to listen to my favorite Lou Reed tune. It could be our song if she would just hear it once. I thought we could spend the night listening and talking about my book.

She was with a tall, muscular man with a gray moustache. She asked him to wait inside for her.

"I don't know what's happened to you," she said. "It's sad. Really. Tod, what..."

"Please Christina..." I could see the moustache poking through the curtain upstairs.

"Don't," Christina said. "Why are you coming around after all these years? Tod, what have you been thinking?"

"Did you read my book?" I was determined to play all my cards. I had come this far.

"Yeah, I read parts. I don't know why, either."

"You read it? Really? Did you...? I love you."

"You love ME? Is that what that story is supposed to prove? Oh, Tod. Promise me you'll get some help. Please."

"But what did you think? The book..."

"It was gross," she said. "I couldn't believe it. It wasn't believable. It disgusted me."

"Don't you... I love you..."

"What? Did you think that horrible thing would make me love you? Tod, Jesus. That story. God. If anything, that book proves you don't know shit. It's just like you to spend two years doing something like that. For love? I haven't thought about you in... I don't know how long. I'm a doctor. What the hell have you been thinking?"

"Maybe we could just go somewhere and talk," I said. I tried to hand her the walkman with the Lou Reed.

She put her finger on my chest. "Now I'm going to call the police," she said. "Get the fuck away from me." She started up the stairs.

I hung around for a few moments. I watched her walk into the apartment. I wanted to remember. It was going to be the last time I would ever see her.

I gained seventy-eight pounds. I couldn't stop listening to Lou Reed. The song I wanted Christina to listen to was *Perfect Day*, written in 1972. My favorite line: "When I was with her, I thought I was someone else. Someone good."

I wasn't, of course.

One day I got a phone call from Larry Gardner, an editor at "Be Your Best Publishing." Alan Marcellino had sent him my novel. Larry thought the book "sucked." But he saw something. Had I ever considered writing self-help? There was something in my writing, he said. I understood human nature. I would be a natural.

I locked myself in my apartment, drank Slim-Fast and let it pour out. I didn't shower or shave. I was determined. Others wouldn't have to suffer the way I had. I wore my white sweatshirt. It would be the last time, but it helped me remember. I wrote down everything I had learned from Christina. I thought about the wonderful times we spent together. I remembered the sex. And it didn't add up to perfection. Or love. That was a lesson. People had to learn that. I thought I knew what love was, thought I could smell it, see it, touch it. But I couldn't. You can't. It's like an electron. The minute you look or grasp, it vanishes.

I finished the book in two weeks and rushed over to Larry's office on Sixth Avenue. He said he was busy, but I forced him to read the manuscript. He couldn't put it down.

"We're going to make a lot of money," he said. He wiped a tear. "A lot of money."

I burned my sweatshirt and threw away my blender. I started jogging again.

My first self-help sold a million copies and was a best seller for fourteen weeks. "A Love Supreme."

I moved to a penthouse apartment on Park Avenue. I bought a Mercedes. My mother started bragging about me to her friends. George Steinbrenner, the Yankees owner, called me for advice on trades and his love life.

Last month my doorman stopped me and asked for an autograph. He held out a copy of my second book, "Touched by Tenderness." He grabbed my shoulder and said, "Man... no one knows more about love than you. How'd you get so fucking smart?"

"Wait for my next book," I said and patted him on the head. "It's an autobiography."

"I can't wait," he said.

I still think about Christina once in a while. But sometimes you have to move on in life. My new girlfriend is Japanese. She's smart and artistic, she paints watercolors and sings to me in the evenings. She's in her third year of medical school.

CHAPTER 4: PROFILES

CHARLES SALZBERG
PAT COOPER
you can't handle my truth, my friend

I am ten minutes early for my lunch with comedian Pat Cooper. But Cooper is even earlier. As I pass by Sammi's, a popular, downscale Chinese restaurant on Sixth Avenue and 11th street, I spot him through the window, seated comfortably alone at a table, facing out toward the street. But once inside, when I approach him from behind and introduce myself, I see he is not really alone. But then again, as I soon find out, Pat Cooper is never alone. An audience is only a joke, a wisecrack, an insult away.

Our lunch has been arranged by a mutual friend who's known Pat for years. "I'm doing you a big favor," she tells me. "Pat's perfect for a book, and you could write it with him. You're going to owe me..."

Although I've never met him before, I know who Pat Cooper is. As a kid, I watched him perform on Ed Sullivan with other comedians like Bob Newhart, Jack Carter and Jackie Mason. As an adult, I've watched him on Carson, Griffin, Letterman and Leno. He was always funny, outrageous, on the edge, and for some reason he always seemed angry about something or, more precisely, angry at someone. Now, at age 70, his career has undergone something of a resurrection—or at least taken a different turn in the road—after appearing with Robert DeNiro and Billy Crystal in "Analyze This," and being discovered by a brand new audience with his numerous appearances on Howard Stern's radio and TV shows, as well as Don Imus' radio show. And now, after being in show business for over fifty years, Cooper is busier than ever, working 40 weeks a year, appearing in Vegas, where he lives most of the time, Atlantic City, Florida, and anywhere else they'll have him. The man lives to work.

"WhattamIgonnado, retire?" he says, his voice rising, the words spilling out of his mouth as if they're stuck together with Crazy Glue. "Then what? I love what I do. But when I don't have it anymore, I'm finished. Goodbye. I'm not gonna be like Bob Hope. Ninety-something. They put him in one of those K-Mart commercials. Guy couldn't say da-da. He's worth half a billion dollars if he's worth a quarter. He had to do that? Bobby, it's over! I loved Henny Youngman. I *loved him*. He was working in a wheelchair. I said, "Henny, how the fuck can you do this?" I shocked him. "He says, 'I'm a sick man, you shouldn't say that.' If he's a sick man, what was he doing on stage, reading cards at 90 years old? You're telling me that's not a disgrace to my fucking business?"

But Pat Cooper is not Bob Hope and he's not Henny Youngman. He can stand up on his own and he does, as often as he can. In fact, tonight he tells me he's headlining a fundraiser for a friend, a New Jersey politician who needs dough to run for Congress. "He's a lawyer, a singing lawyer, who has stage fright," Cooper tells me. "I told him, 'Whaddya do in front of a jury? You got stage fright there?' He says, 'No. I'm fine in the courtroom.' So I tell him, 'Then just make believe you're singing in front of a jury.' I don't know why the fuck he wants to be in politics, but he's a friend, so I'm there."

Pat Cooper's latest audience is smaller than he's used to; but what the hey, a laugh's a laugh, isn't it? Seated at the table next to his are six young guys, late twenties, early thirties, their sleeves rolled up, their sport jackets hung on the backs of their chairs which have now been angled to face Cooper, who is holding court as if Sammi's has magically been transformed into an impromptu dinner theater. And make no mistake about it, Cooper has got them in the palm of his hand and he's working the noontime crowd as if he's getting paid for it. I can't quite make out what he's saying, but he has these Gen Xers in stitches and I hesitate to break up their party. As I wait for a break in the action—which I soon realize may never come—I feel like an intruder. But I feel odd just standing there, as if I'm a waiter at the Carnegie Deli waiting patiently while a customer decides on pastrami or corned beef, so I introduce myself. Cooper, without missing a beat, looks up, holds out his hand so I can shake it, and announces, "Boys, here's my date."

"You're better looking than I thought you'd be," cracks one of the young men, but Cooper doesn't hear him. He's the main attraction and he's not about to hand over the stage to some amateur pipsqueak trying to crack wise.

"What's your name?" he asks me.

"Charles," I say.

"You don't look like a Charles. You look like an Anthony. Maybe you should change it."

I sit down and before I can say a word, Cooper launches into a non-stop monologue, peppered with profanity and profundity.

For the next hour or so, he doesn't shut up. Rat-a-tat-tat. Words are ammo, his mouth an assault weapon and it seems as if he never has to stop and reload. Numerous times during the next hour various diners glance over and recognize him, some lean in to tell him how much they love him. From their ages, I surmise it's more likely they know him from Howard Stern than from Ed Sullivan. The stories that come out of his mouth, about his tough childhood, his family, how he got into the business, working with and knowing Sinatra, Tony Bennett, Steve and Edie, and other comedians who are his contemporaries, like Shecky Green, Buddy Hackett and Soupy Sales, are hilarious, and no one, not even Howard Stern, is immune to his acerbic wit.

"I told Howard, 'Howard, your wife's going to leave you.' 'Why?' he asks. 'Because you're cheating on her.' 'I don't cheat on her!' he says. 'Sure you do.' I say. 'You talk about this ones tits and how you're gonna bang that one. How do you think your wife feels about that? That's cheating, my friend. You're cheating on her and she's not going to stand for it.' 'You're crazy,' he says. And look at what happened..."

Somehow, no matter what the subject, the conversation always gets back to those who have done Pat wrong, or the phonies he's worked with. And inevitably, Pat Cooper cuts them down to size.

"I worked with Tony Bennett. He'd always say, 'Frank Sinatra says I'm the best. Frank says I'm the best' I said to him one day, 'Tony, my friend, I hate to tell you, but Sinatra never said that. I worked with Frank. I asked him. I said, 'Frank, did you ever say that Tony Bennett was the best singer?' He told me he never said that. Come on, would Sinatra ever say another Italian was the best at anything? Italians don't do that, my friend. We don't help each other. We're not like the Jews. The Jews help their own. Not the Italians."

Cooper, even while seated, is in perpetual motion. I've never seen a man with so much energy. In the middle of telling a story, he will often stand to act out a scene, and he often punctuates his tales with wild gesticulations. At one point, he swings his arm out wide and knocks over a glass of water. Quickly, he apologizes and starts to wipe up the mess. A waitress notices the mishap and quickly appears with a bunch of napkins. "Look what he did," he says, pointing at me. I smile sheepishly, as Cooper grabs a couple of napkins all the while aiming a steady stream of words at the waitress. "You're a sweetheart," he says. "That's why I eat here all the time...My friend here, he's very clumsy..." It's no wonder I feel guilty, even though I had nothing to do with the water spill. Once the waitress leaves, Cooper quickly gets back on track.

Although Cooper is 70, you'd swear he was no more than late fifties, early sixties tops, and it's probably because he hasn't given the aging process time to catch up to him. He's too busy talking, telling anyone who will listen "the truth."

"I don't give a fuck," he says. "I'm not going to sit here and lie about people. I went on Tom Snyder and I told the truth. 'Pat, you can't do that,' they said. But I did. I told everybody that Lola Falana was a cheap bastard. That Jerry Vale stole from me. That Steve and Edie didn't pay me. They're all cheap bastards. What the fuck do I care?"

Cooper has worked as a comic for over 50 years, ever since the days he was Pasquale Caputo of Brooklyn. "I came out of the womb funny." He was born in Brooklyn. His father was a bricklayer and to hear him tell it, his mother was the meanest s.o.b. in the free world. "She'd whack us around but good. She'd sit there in her rocking chair and no matter where I was in the room she'd reach out and smack me in mid-rock. She could reach me from any angle, that's how good she was. Italians, they say, 'Your mother hits you because she loves you.' The more she hits you, the more she loves you. I'm 14 years old, she puts my hand over the burner on the stove. I go outside. A neighbor sees me. She asks, 'What's wrong?' I tell her what my mother did. She says, 'Your mother puts your hand over the burner because she loves you.' I say, 'Yeah, then why don't you go inside and let her hold your hand over the burner to show you how much she loves you.' I guess your mother runs you over with a car, she really loves you."

"Once she threw a plate at my father. He says, 'I gotta go out to the store, I'll be back in a few minutes. He goes to Italy. Eight months later he comes back and says, 'You got any more dishes to throw?' Another time, she decides to buy a building without telling him. He finds out. He says, 'Now you can fuck the building.' He walks out, checks into the St. George Hotel, and that's where he lives for the next 36 years.

"I'd run away and they'd never even send anyone after me. I'd come back two weeks later and I'd put forty bucks on the table and they'd say, 'Where've you been? We missed you.' "

Cooper changed his name as soon as he began to perform publicly. "My father hated that I changed my name. I betrayed him. I betrayed my heritage. But people still know me by that name. On the way over here, a truck driver sticks his head out the window and yells, 'Pasquale Caputo!' like it's some kind of poetry." Pat Cooper, or Pasquale Caputo is one of the people. He speaks for them. And if he's angry, it's because he is carrying the angst and pain and the day to day humiliation for all of us.

Cooper has three sisters, but he doesn't speak to any of them. One, he hasn't spoken to in 20 years. One night, he's in Morton's, having dinner and a woman comes up to him and says hello. "Who are you?" he asks. "I'm your sister," she says, "don't you recognize me?"

"Get the fuck outta here," he says. "My father dies," he explains, "and she puts the announcement in the paper saying he left three daughters. Doesn't mention me at all. I don't exist in the family? I don't exist, they don't exist. I don't got three sisters."

Cooper makes no apology for his forthrightness. "That's who I am. That's who I'm gonna be. If you're born a dog, you don't die a cat."

Though he was funny all his life—his humor obviously a way to deal with the pain of his childhood—his first professional gig didn't come until he was 15. "My sister was a singer. She entered a contest at the Fox Theater in Brooklyn. She was going to sing 'Ave Maria.' I went along with her. She comes up to me before she goes on and says, 'They've got an open spot. Why don't you go on and do that thing you do with your mouth, making noises to go along with music.' First prize was twenty-five dollars. Second prize was a watch. I won the twenty-five bucks. My sister wanted to dig my grave. She sings this religious song and I win the dough for making noises with my mouth. After that, I had to sleep with one eye open in case she came at me with a knife one night."

Cooper found his calling and nothing would deter him, certainly not having a formal education. "I only had one week of high school, and I was absent that week," he cracks. He began working small clubs in Brooklyn and, when he was lucky, in Manhattan. But at the same time, he was working as a bricklayer, just like his father.

One night, he was working a place called The Living Room, in Manhattan, and a manager by the name of Willie Weber happened to be in the audience. "Usually, there were two shows a night and I just went up there and did twenty minutes on anything that came to mind, and then did the same thing again. But at The Living Room there were three shows a night and I had to change my routine for the second show, so I came up with this routine called 'The Italian Wedding.' It killed."

After the show, Weber approached the kid and said, "I think you've got talent, and if you let me help you by shaping your act, I think you can go places."

Cooper thought, why the hell not, and so, with Weber's help, he shaped the act and one day he called Cooper and told him he'd been booked for the Jackie Gleason Show. "I didn't believe it," says Cooper. And he really didn't believe it when he was waiting to go on and the Great Man himself passed by.

"I was standing there, my back against the wall, and Gleason passes by. I was scared to death. He stops, looks at me and says—and remember, this is before he'd ever heard my act, 'Kid, you're the greatest. You know how I know that? Because I'm the greatest, and if you're on my show, then you must be great, too.' And then he just kept walking."

The show was taped for the following Sunday and Monday morning Cooper, who was back on his day job laying bricks, received a call from Weber. "Kid, the Copa wants to book you."

Cooper couldn't believe it. He was so shocked, so unbelieving, that he refused to quit his job as a bricklayer. "I had a family to support. Who knew how long this was going to last," he says. But there was a slight hitch. The Living Room, now with a hot commodity on their hands, didn't want to let him out of his contract. Weber said, "No problem. We'll buy your way out." "So," says Cooper, "we paid them a hundred bucks a week so I could appear at the Copa."

And that's how Pat Cooper got to rub shoulders with all those people he now tells the truth about. At least it's the truth as he sees it.

Bam. Bam. Bam. No one is safe from his biting tongue, nothing is sacred, not even the long departed. "I worked as an opening act for the singer, Sergio Franchi. We used to appear together all the time. Franchi dies. His wife misses him terribly. She comes to me and says, 'Pat, how'd you like to open for Sergio?' "

"Sweetheart," I say, "I hate to tell you this, but Sergio's dead."

She says, "Yeah, but you go on, you do your act, then I bring out film of Sergio..."

"Sweetheart," I say, "you think I'm gonna open for a fuckin' dead guy, you're crazy."

Although Cooper has been in the public eye for thirty, forty years, he's never quite made it to the rung of a Hope, a Berle, or a George Burns. "I'm not a star, my friend," he says proudly. "But I don't fuckin' wanna be a star. I don't wanna work that hard. Listen, in a horse race does that horse care if he comes in first? Hell, no! You come in last, they still feed you, they still put a roof over your head, they still bathe you. Same thing with me."

"Money means nothing to me. I make it, I spend it. I'm having lunch with you, dinner with you, I pay. If I don't have the money, I borrow it and pay, and you'd never know I didn't have it. DiMaggio, he was a cheap bastard. Never picked up a check in his life. He'd say, 'Pat, I wanna sign some balls for you.' I'd say, 'Joe, I don't want any balls. What am I gonna do with a bunch of fuckin' balls?' He says, 'I'll sign 'em, To Pat: Best Wishes, Joe DiMaggio.' I say, 'just sign 'em, Joe DiMaggio, forget the Pat.' He says, 'Then you'll just go out and sell them.' Cheap bastard."

"I said to him, 'How come you didn't get one more hit in that 56 game streak? You woulda made a million bucks. Fifty-seven straight games. You woulda been all over those Heinz ketchup bottles, the relish, everything.' I'd tell him this every time I saw him. I used to make him crazy."

Money is one of Cooper's favorite topics—although on second thought everything is one of his favorite topics, because one thing Pat Cooper does not lack for is opinions. "One time I got this check and a manager I had signs my name on it. Steals the fuckin' money. That's fraud. I press charges on him. One day I go into this fancy restaurant on Park Avenue and a friend of my father's"—Cooper presses one finger to his nose, a finger on the other hand to his ear, bending both of them out of shape, leaving little doubt that this guy was "connected"—"is there with this deadbeat. A big fella, he goes over to this guy and says, 'You owe Pat money, you pay him. You don't pay him, I'm gonna take care of you," and he punches him in the face. The guy goes down. There's blood all over. I look around. I don't want any trouble. I say, "Listen, it's okay..." The fella says, 'You drop the charges, Pat. This guy'll pay or else he'll get more of this...' badda-bing!, he hits him again. I'm afraid he's going to kill him, so I say, 'Yeah, I'll drop the charges. Don't worry about it." So, I drop the charges. But it was all a set-up. The guy was willing to take a couple punches if I'd drop the charges. I never saw a fuckin' dime."

Cooper doesn't hang out with other comics, primarily because he finds them depressing, insecure. But he is a student of comedy. "You gotta have a gimmick. I told this one guy, 'Tell people you're the worst comic in the world'—and he was, believe me, he was—'then you play a college and they come to see you and they walk out and they say, 'Yeah, he is the worst comic in the world.' Then word gets around and you're a hit. Everyone wants to see the worst fuckin' comic in the world."

What Cooper does have is a wife, whom he's been married to for 36 years and who lives in Las Vegas with him, when he's not on the road—which is about 40 weeks a year—two kids and several grandchildren, whom he adores.

"So, Pat," I say, finally able to crowbar in a few words while he digs into his chicken dish, "about the idea of doing a book, what do you think?"

"I think, my friend, the time is right. And you know, I'd get out there and sell it like crazy. Let me tell you a story, my friend. I had a record come out with my routines on it, including 'The Italian Wedding.' It came out and it just sat there. The fuckin' record company wasn't doing a thing. So, I picked up some Massachusetts phone book and I copied down a whole bunch of addresses and I sent out a mailing, telling them all about my record. The record started selling like crazy. I went there and they gave me a fuckin' parade. Can you believe it! A fuckin' parade. And that's what I'd do to sell this book."

At the end of the meal—a meal he insists on paying for—Cooper says, almost apologetically, "Look, I entertained you for an hour, right? Nothing comes of this, at least you had a good time."

And he's right. After all, that's what Pat Cooper has been doing for over fifty years—making sure people go away feeling they got their money's worth.

RICHARD GOODMAN
WILLIAM BURROUGHS
on books, movies, sex and dinner

I arrived at Burroughs' London flat off Picadilly in the early evening. Burroughs opened the door, and I saw a smaller man than I had expected from the photos, with thin grey hair pushed over to cover baldness. He appeared to be in his late fifties, but it was difficult to say exactly. He wore slacks and a turtle neck, both of which were too large for him. We shook hands, and he motioned me in. He seemed shy, even a bit awkward, as if I were perhaps the host and he were the guest.

His apartment is sparse, with plain adequate furniture and pleasant. He has a living room, bedroom, bathroom and kitchen. All our conversation took place in the small living room. He has only a few books, and these are mostly copies of his own works. A few other authors, including Terry Southern, are represented.

A "young man" named Johnny was there. He was English and wore tight slacks and a turtle neck. He was friendly, obviously not a student of the arts. He served the drinks, lit the cigarettes, emptied the ashtrays, and for the most part was content to stand and not say anything. Occasionally, he would add a Goofy-like affirmation to something. He left, with a pound note from Burroughs. about an hour after I arrived.

Burroughs sat on a stool in the center of the living room with a cigarette almost always pressed to his lips or dangling from his hand. Ashtrays seemed to grow hills of butts quickly, and quite soon the room was very smoky. Though Burroughs was silent to begin with, almost forcing me to prod him, he answered all my questions politely and sometimes anecdotally. He carries with him a flavor of formality. He speaks with an inflected drone, and he did not always look at me when he spoke. I began by asking him what his latest project was.

"I'm writing a novel. It's over there." He pointed to the desk next to the window.

"I just got back from New York. I flew over there with the film script of *Naked Lunch*. A producer said he was interested: I think he does 'The Dating Game' or some quiz show. So, Terry Southern and I flew out to LA at his expense. When we arrived, this big black shiny Rolls-Royce met us at the airport, *whisked* us on into town. Well, it turned out he wasn't interested. He was worried about all the sex and violence. He said we'd have to cut out all the sex scenes and a lot of the scenes with violence. But what's *Naked Lunch* without sex and violence?" He spread his arms to indicate "nothing."

"Terry and I did *some* cutting, but he still wasn't satisfied, so we gave it up. When we went to leave the Rolls had shrunk considerably, down to some kind of *mini*. I said to Terry, 'We'd better get out of here fast before he decides not to pay the hotel bill.' "

Did he have anyone specific in mind for parts in the movie version of *Naked Lunch*?

"Yes. We wanted James Taylor, Mick Jagger, or Dennis Hopper for Lee. Taylor and Jagger said no, and Hopper was all set to go, but it was dropped since there was no financing. We wanted Groucho Marx for Dr. Benway, but he wouldn't hear of it.

"It's *terribly* difficult to get backing for a film. Distribution's a problem, too. Most of the time you end up not making any money on the damned thing, so you have to get everything on that first sale. After that, baby, it's *gone*. I've got several other film scripts here. Some just in idea form and some full shooting-scripts. I did one on the life of Dutch Schultz. But I'll never sell that. Too expensive to produce. Too many scenes." What did he think of the movie *A Clockwork Orange*, very popular in London at the time? He had praised the book.

"I thought the movie fell apart exactly where the book did. In the middle. Everything goes along quite well, then you come to the middle section. During that whole prison sequence I kept wondering what the hell Kubrick was doing.

"Did you see *The Godfather*? I liked that. Very good. But Pacino stole the show. That scene when he comes out of the john with the gun hidden, and the guy thinks *something* is wrong for that split second, but he's too late. Then *bam!* two slugs in the belly.

"I wanted to see the film, because an old friend of mine's in it. One of my former customers. That was in New York, *years* ago. He was a member of the Mafia then, and they didn't like the fact that he was on junk. They said he was a disgrace to the family. So, they told him either get off junk or else. Apparently, this frightened him into his senses, and he quit. I saw him recently, and he told me 'Baby, I don't need junk. I don't want it.' I thought he did pretty well in the film."

He picked up a thick volume and handed it to me.

"Here. Take a look at this." he said.

It was the full report on the President's Commission on Pornography, replete with color photographs. It had been given to him by Terry Southern.

"When I was in New York, I saw a lot of pornographic films, about twenty of them, mostly gay films. All around the Times Square area. And very good quality, with close-ups *both* oral and genital. Good-looking models, too. The fact is, if you can't perform, you just *don't* make it. You go in someplace. and immediately you're in front of the camera; if you can't do it. baby, they can get somebody else.

"Those animal pictures are disgusting, aren't they?" he said in reference to some of the harder hard-core photographs.

"I'm going back to New York in a few months. They've asked me to be a judge in the Erotic Film Festival. I'll be there for about a week. But I don't like New York. Can't *stand* it. Can't get out of there quick enough."

Now that the subject of sex was about, I asked Burroughs what he thought about homosexuality. I thought I had discerned a conflict in his writings: While it is obvious that he is much more interested in homosexuality than heterosexuality, he often satirizes his homosexual characters and their behavior, even to the point of overtly putting them down. There is one long sequence in *Naked Lunch* in which a "straight" boy is mocked and mentally tortured into making homosexual admissions by a mad doctor. Why? Did he have a negative view of homosexuality...

"Nooo. "

But what about the satire?

"Well, I say so when they get a little out of hand. But that's not my view. No, not at all.

"We know that the brain can be electronically made to produce any response," he said in reference to the *Naked Lunch* sequence I had mentioned.

I asked him about Jack Kerouac. Kerouac and Allen Ginsberg had been "students" of Burrough's back in the early Beat days. Did he miss Kerouac?

"Oh, Jack, Jack. Well, I hadn't seen him for *years*. I saw him briefly in New York in 1968 after I had returned from Chicago (Burroughs was covering the Democratic National Convention for *Esquire*) and was staying in the Hotel Delmonico writing the article for *Esquire*. He came up to my hotel room and brought his three Greek brothers-in-law with him. They ran up a two hundred dollar liquor bill. *Esquire* didn't want to pay the bill, but I told them they had to, and they ended up paying.

"They asked Jack to debate William Buckley on television. He was champing at the bit. But I said to him, 'You can't go on there. You'll be cut to ribbons.' They wanted me to go along as a spectator, but I wouldn't have any part of it. So, Jack went on, and it was a farce. That was the last time I saw him."

What about Jean Genet in Chicago? Genet had also covered the Convention for *Esquire*. Did Burroughs have much of a chance to talk with him?

"Oh, yes. Quite a bit. He doesn't speak a word of English, and my French is very limited. But we got on somehow."

I had read that Genet had escaped a beating from the Chicago police by simply, well, *shrugging* his way out of the situation.

"Well," said Burroughs, "what *happened* was that he was being chased by a cop, and he turned around and shrugged as the cop was about to hit him with his club, and the cop veered away. But more cops were coming, so Genet took refuge in the nearest apartment building. Then he just knocked on the first door he came to. It turned out to be a student's apartment. This guy with a beard opened the door. and Genet said. 'Je suis Monsieur Genet.' And the guy said. 'Oh, great. Come on in. I'm doing my thesis on you."

What, if anything, did Burroughs miss most about America?

"The food. It's impossible to get a decent meal here. I miss Horn and Hardarts. For about a buck-fifty you can get a really decent meal. I could eat there every day of the week."

Why was he living in London?

"Taxes, Baby. I get off much better here than I would in the States. It's purely monetary. Oh, London; well, I don't much care for London itself. No, I could just as well live somewhere else. The services here are terrible. If I want an electrician or a plumber, I have to practically start a war before I get him. Awful. The trouble is that they don't pay those people a damn thing."

About seven o'clock, a young friend of Burroughs' named Miles dropped by. He immediately made himself at home, lying on the couch to Burroughs' left. Miles is a collector of Burroughs' work. He is presently, at Burroughs' request and under his supervision, putting together "The Archives." This is a collection of Burroughs' books, articles and letters, along with pieces published about him. The collection will eventually be sold to the highest bidder. Miles, quite affable, often added to Burroughs' conversation, addressing Burroughs as "William." Miles showed B. what he had done that day on The Archives. B. examined the small file Miles handed him and pulled out a few items.

"I don't think we'll include the laundry slips," he said as he eliminated an item.

When I heard that his personal letters were going into The Archives, I told Burroughs that I hoped he would soon publish more of his correspondence. (B., I found out later, makes a carbon copy of every letter he writes, He does plan to publish more of his correspondence.) I told him that I liked *The Yage Letters* very much (a book consisting of an exchange of letters between Burroughs and Allen Ginsberg) but that I didn't like Allen Ginsberg's contribution. I thought it was self indulgent and petulant.

"Oh, well," he said. "Allen has this idea that the whole world is love. Everyone is everyone's brother, that kind of thing. He's always felt that way. But I have a different view. I think there are sinister people about, trying to do you harm."

I thought of Burroughs wandering through Mexico and Central America in the early fifties. Had he met any Joseph Conrad-type Germans in the jungles?

"Oh, yes. Real Joseph Conrad Germans. One character in a mountain village claimed he had the only existing map to the secret treasure of the Spanish monks. Something like that. He told me all we had to do was to go out and dig it up. It was just waiting for us. He wanted some money, but I didn't give him anything."

What about the revolver the character Lee (an early pseudonym for Burroughs himself) carried in *Junkie*? Did Burroughs himself ever carry a gun?

"Ohhh, yeah. When I was in Mexico City. I used to have this big ol' .380 automatic. Used to stick it in my pants, right here." He pointed to his stomach-belt area. He was talking like a cowboy now. "I remember one day I went into this *pissoir*, and I was waitin' for my turn, when this man comes in—a typical Mexican punk—and he pushes his way in front of me. So, I opened my coat and tapped the handle." Pause. "He didn't go into that *pissoir* ahead of me."

A little later another friend named John dropped by. John had long white hair: he might be fifty or he might be forty. He sat down at Burroughs' right, and he and B. bantered each other about why B. hadn't called him that day as he had promised. This was well past the time when we had begun drinking Burroughs' liquor, and B. was loosening up a bit.

"Well, look, Baby, I did," B. said. "I've got the number right here." He got up, walked to his desk, and began searching for the number. "I called you this afternoon, five o'clock, Baby. But the only person who answered was this Italian waiter. I mean, I'm sure he's very nice, but he wasn't you."

"Well, I'm sure I gave you the right number, William," John said.

"Baby, It *couldn't* have been the right number, because all I could get was this goddam Italian waiter who spoke Italian, and I don't speak Italian. Now, just wait a minute while I get that piece of paper you gave me with the number on it."

After this was finally settled—John had mistakenly given Burroughs his "old" number—John proceeded to explain to me that he was the first person ever "cleared" from Scientology. A sort of black belt achievement. He talked about that and reincarnation and his appearances on the Joe Pyne television show.

"This is not my first life," he said. "Oh, yes, my last life was very good, very interesting. But it was so good to be able to finally say good-bye, to lay my body down and just give it all up. But I *loved* working with all those silent film stars. They were wonderful, kind people. When I was on the Joe Pyne show, Joe asked me. '*Were* you Rudolph Valentino in your last life?' I wouldn't say yes, and I wouldn't say no."

He and Burroughs then talked about personal matters for a bit.

About nine o'clock, B. had a little *entourage* in his apartment. There were murmurs of, "I'm hungry," and, "Let's get something to eat." Someone suggested a Mexican restaurant in Soho. Everyone agreed, but Burroughs maintained control.

"Ok, now let's not go into this thing too hastily," he said.

Finally, he had the plan. We all got up to leave, and immediately someone was reaching for Burroughs' coat, while someone else went for his hat. After one person had helped him put on his coat and another had given him his hat, he turned to me and said with a wry smile, "Around here, I'm known as 'The Don.' "

We took a cab to Soho. It was a good restaurant and a good Mexican meal, but Burroughs wasn't talkative. He preferred to sit back easily at the head of the table and listen to the talk of Scientology and reincarnation. I felt it was a waste. I asked him about Norman Mailer.

"I like Norman," he said slowly and precisely, "A lot of people say they have trouble with Norman, but I don't. Get along with him quite well."

He seemed distant, so I left him alone.

The check arrived, and Burroughs examined it carefully.

"Ok, boys," he announced, "looks like we've run up quite a bill here."

We paid and strolled out into the street. It was about ten-thirty. Pub closing time, nearly. Although Burroughs hates pubs, he suggested we all go to a gay pub. So, we walked on, Burroughs in command. Most of us had had our share of liquor by then. The talk on the way over was easy.

The pub itself wasn't at all like some of the gay bars in America: no overt theatre, no whining sweet-sarcastic voices. Burroughs struck up a conversation with a friend of a friend, and I talked with Miles.

"William's amazing," he said. "He must do three or four versions of each work. I'd say he only publishes twenty percent of what he actually writes. The other things are mostly first, second and even third drafts. He works very hard. Eight hours a day, I'd say. Often more than that."

When we left the pub it turned out that Burroughs was going one way and the rest of us were going another. Burroughs seemed a bit wobbly to me, and I was worried that he might have trouble finding his way home. He was going to walk. He shook my hand warmly.

"Ok, Baby." he said. "You've got my address. Next time you're in London, look me up."

He waved and ambled off down the street. We watched him disappear into the blackness of the night. Then we turned away and began walking.

"Will he be all right?" I asked Miles.

"William? Oh, sure. Somehow he always seems to find his way home."

RYAN VAN WINKLE
THE STREAKER
go streaking with our intrepid reporter

Just maintain eye contact, I tell myself, *Don't look away. No fear...* No fear and then we're off into the fleshy madness. Joel screams, "Let's GO! Naked guys, naked guys running at you!"

It's Halloween and the grain alcohol and adrenaline are warming parts of me that have never seen the sun—never mind the Syracuse cold. We're huffing fast down the street—past Clintons, nuns, Lewinskys, flappers and pirates. Joel's thin, graceful frame is directly in front of me, arms flailing bare feet pounding pavement as the crowd cheers. Some gasp, others laugh. Some move out of the way quickly, some are frozen in place and are told by Joel, "Naked guy touching you!" Men scream from a dark porch, "Put some clothes on! Freaks! We don't want to see you!" My lungs are burning, my chest is heaving and Joel is about to high five me. He's in much better shape than I and is doing a dance in the street saying, "You're great man, that was fucking great. Oh man—you're awesome. That was awesome!"

I now understood why Joel streaks: the adrenaline rush, the raw logic of lunacy. The crowd watched us get back into costume and began saying things like, "I can't believe you guys! What were you thinking? How much have you had to drink?" My excuse was easy—"it was a once in a lifetime experience." Joel is the professional. Joel is the man who has run naked through restaurants and 8 mile golf courses. Joel is the one bouncing on the balls of his feet, hanging like a noose, yelling "Freedom!" at the gawkers.

Joel is the first to admit that he's completely insane. He warns me as he reclines on a couch, "If your going to get into my mind, it's going to get scary."

Max Klopell, a friend of Joel's, tells me after I agree to the Halloween streak, "You know if I did any of the stuff Joel asks me to do I'd be in jail."

But I had to go with Joel because his rationale was so appealing, "It's an idealist thing. Because life is so monotonous. Sometimes you don't feel alive and I want to make *my* life extraordinary. I've got to do something crazy sometimes or I fear I'll become one of them."

"Them" being the people at Syracuse University where we are both students. Joel finds "Them" to be anal and prissy. It is the most anal place he's ever been and it's certainly more uptight than his home of San Jose California. Everybody, he says, is worried bout passing the social grade and saying and doing the right things. So they do nothing. Many times during our conversation Joel simply says, "Do something, do anything."

Joel has done a lot. He's a Senior majoring in both Philosophy and Television, Radio and Film. He's on the wrestling team and participates in many campus groups. He's also streaked in dozens of places dozens of times. Like on the University quad the night Freshmen were treated to a free showing of "The Birds."

"The Quad was great," Joel explains, "Because it was freshmen, they're insecure of themselves and aren't going to boo. It's the upperclassman, getting ready to go into the capitalist, greedy society that can't deal."

It's a good response that makes a streak successful. The worst was an unbearable experience at the "asshole neighbors" party. There had been tension between the houses all year. Joel and his roommates would keep the windows open and loudly discuss masturbation. The neighbors would call Joel a prick and flick him off. So one night Joel and his girlfriend ran naked into their party and began using the dance floor. According to Joel, people just turned and walked away. "C'mon let's party," Joel cried, jumping up and down trying to excite the crowd. The music was turned off—silence. They didn't mind his girlfriend being there but they told him he had to leave—but quick.

Joel spoke to one of the house members later that year and the guy just didn't get it, "He said, 'I just can't understand that. Why? Why?' Some people can't understand I'm doing something out of the ordinary. They're so set in how they think things should be."

Joel knows he's different, "got a couple of screws loose." His thought process is amazing. When you say to most people, "Wouldn't it be funny if somebody's suit came off during a swimming race?" they laugh and pass it off. Not Joel. And that is how this illustrious streaking career began. In front of 2,000 people in one of California's statewide swim meets. As soon as the joke was made, Joel explains, he was ready to do it. His friend looked him straight in the eyes and said, "You will not do this." But there was no question in Joel's mind—he was going to swim naked. "It just touched my ego. Carpe diem. Just experience for the hell of it." His only worry was *how*?

It's ironic, he says, that there is no thought as to whether or not he should streak—only ways to pull it off. He had to formulate a plan.

He practiced diving in repeatedly with his suit untied to make sure it would fall off at the right moment. He went to the 50 meter relay team and demanded he swim the last leg. Then there he was, on the blocks, "just dying and smiling." He dove in and it worked. "I almost drowned, I was laughing so hard, swallowing water, the suit down to my knees like a parachute." They lost the race but a streak addict was born.

Wanting the entire crowd to get a show Joel lifted his lower torso out of the water while doing a flip turn, hoping that people would notice the Speedo-Free Joel.

"It really bothered me not knowing if anybody saw me." He soon found out that his teammates (they walked away without commenting) and his coach (he shed a tear) saw the softer side of Joel. But what about the audience? At his Senior prom he asked some people who were at the meet if they saw "that naked guy swimming?" and many said they had, which led Joel to believe that about half the crowd caught a satisfactory glimpse.

"It's all about the reaction," he says, adjusting himself in his gray sweats, "If I saw someone doing something crazy I'd love it. It transcends our fears, let's us know that life isn't dismal. I don't do this because I want people to say, 'oh I'm scared!' and then call the cops."

Joel's encountered a cop a few times. Once after running naked through a Denny's in California and once on rollerblades in Syracuse. His blue eyes flash with the retelling of the story he calls, "The most legendary."

He used a rope to tie himself to a car, tossed on a ski mask, lit a cigar, and stuck about a half dozen roman candles in his belt. The car took off and there was Joel in all his glory putting Roman Candle to cigar and exploding up and down the streets of Syracuse. People started coming out of their homes to see Joel flapping by, "I heard cheers," he says smiling and scratching his spartan red beard, "It was like a whole bunch of people doing the wave all down the street." And then there was a stop sign. Not wanting to rear end the car Joel let go of the rope and headed on down the street sparking up his last fire work—pointing it straight ahead, watching the wick to see when to release. When he looked up he saw a police officer directly in front of him. Joel was no more than a few feet away when the cop shoved his hand out of the way and bear hugged him, "and I'm naked and he's like what the hell are you doing? Saying, 'Put your hands on the car—take your hands off my car!' and all I could say was, 'Officer do you want me to put pants on now?' "

Joel wasn't worried, "I knew the consequences and I didn't care. If I go, I do. Things don't affect me. You could chop half my finger off and I'd be okay. I figure, this is new, I might as well enjoy it." He wasn't arrested that night. It is the way things go, he says, once the cops get over the initial shock and anger they usually think it's pretty funny. They know he's not hurting anybody and he explains to the cop what he's been explaining to me, "I wanted to live a bit."

"I'm just a regular guy," he insists, "I don't do drugs, I don't get angry or violent." Joel only battles the monotony of life by getting crazy. "I have done so many stupid, asinine things," he smiles struggling to remember the best. He's soon pointing a finger illustrating how he held up McDonald's with a zucchini. Then he's cracking up about the time he ran onto a driving range dressed as Santa Claus yelling, "If you don't hit me you're going to get coal in your stocking!" Then there's the time he and a friend decided to act like monkeys in the school dining hall. They were banging trays, jumping on tables, screeching and rolling around. They were ignored. Even when they'd go under tables and play with people's shoelaces, they were treated like they weren't even there. Eventually an employee told them they had to leave and they stayed in character and had to be shooed out the door the whole time, rolling on the floor, running back and nipping each other.

"What helps me do this is the thought, 'What if I died tomorrow?' None of this shit matters. If I do it, I'll feel better. It's the same with asking a girl out—what's the worst that can happen?"

I think, "embarrassment, mockery," comparing my lumpy-in-the-wrong-places bod to Joel's trim one. He encourages me, "People think it's cool if you aren't great looking or well hung. Listen, I wasn't getting all that much drag when I was swimming, you know? They know you're not showing off." He was right, people are still mentioning Halloween to me. "We miss out on so much opportunity. It's training for getting out of a rut. At least they'll remember you."

"Everybody should do it once," he says, convincing me in his living room. It is stark, there are no pictures on the white walls, just a few couches and a TV. "It's definitely a risk. You risk arrest, social rejection, catching a cold," he laughs pulling off his Mickey Mouse cap, "It gets people out of their comfort zone. It always works to shock people."

His biggest ambition, streaking wise, is to get naked and run around in the Carrier Dome during an SU football game, but he's worried that he'll get his diploma revoked. More importantly, he wants ultimately to incite social change. "Nihilism will kill America," he predicts. In other words, "Do something. Do anything." But love doing it.

CYNTHIA EHRENKRANTZ
BETSY
alzheimer's: a vanishing history revealed

"I don't know what I am, who I am or where I am" Betsy wails. "What am I doin' here? I want to go home. Why won't you let me go home?"

"You are home Auntie Betsy" I tell her. "This is your home and you know who you are. What's your name? "

"I'm Betsy Wolfe" she answers.

"Almost right, Auntie Betsy. What's your name?

"I'm Betsy Watson. Mrs. Watson."

She is quiet for a few moments and then she says again, "I don't know what I am, who I am or where I am. What am I doin' here? I want to go home. Why won't you let me go home?"

Betsy is sitting on the edge of the bed. She wears a navy blue and white print polyester dress, no bra, knee-highs sagging around her surprisingly trim ankles and shapeless shoes. Her wispy white hair is combed flat on her head and her teary eyes are large and limpid behind thick lenses. Although it is a cool, breezy day, her forehead and thick nose are shiny with sweat and she dabs at it often with a tissue. We are sitting in her sunny room in Heatherdale House, the assisted living residence she moved into two years ago. Her ample frame makes a deep valley in the bed which is covered by a bright golden yellow bedspread. There are pictures of family and friends on the bureau and her window looks down on a rose garden in full bloom.

I am re-arranging her photographs in a new pocket album. The old one has become so tattered that the pictures are getting dog-eared and falling out into the lumpy handbag she carries with her everywhere. It's hard to know what to bring her when I fly over once or twice a year from New York to London to visit but the little photo albums I pick up for her in the drugstore are always a good bet. I've brought gummed labels and I paste one on each picture. "Mother in the garden at Palmers Green", "Your sister Rose", "Cynthia's grandchildren." Occupying myself with this task, and showing her the photographs, I try to distract her from her agitated state.

"Let's go for a walk, Auntie Betsy." I say and we walk down the corridor together, hand in hand, Betsy lumbering along, rolling slightly from side to side like a sailor newly ashore. Other residents greet us.

" 'Ullo Betsy" they say. "Is that your niece all the way from America?" and at last, she smiles.

"Yes," she says. This is my niece, Cynthia."

I sigh with relief that she remembers my name. Her deterioration into the nightmare of Alzheimer's disease is slow but relentless and I know that, one day, I will come and she will have no idea who I am.

Betsy is my mother's youngest sister; the last of my grandmother's five children. She is ninety three. No one in the family has lived so long.

She was born in 1910. At thirty two, my grandmother, Rivke-Leah, had thought that her childbearing days were over. The first four children had been born, "steps and stairs", every two years. When Betsy came along Fan, the oldest in the family, was twelve and Rivke-Leah pressed her into service as baby-sitter and general household help.

Although she was only four when Betsy was born, my mother, Tilly, became her caretaker while the older children were in school. Tilly didn't start school till she was seven when word leaked out that the Wolfe family had another child at home who was ready for school and the truant officer came calling.

Monday was wash day. At 5.30 am Rivke-Leah attached a garden hose to the kitchen faucet filled the huge copper boiler, and lit the gas jet underneath. When the water started to heat up, she dropped in a cube of "Reckett's Blue" , filled the boiler with the white clothes and sheets and, stirred them with a sawn off broomstick. She baled steaming hot water out of the galvanized tub on the stove into the kitchen sink and she started scrubbing the diapers on a washboard before she added them to the copper boiler. As soon as all the diapers were boiling, she picked up the baby, sat on the rocking chair and nursed her. But when she put Betsy down in the cradle, she refused to settle.

"Tilly", she called " Come here."

Tilly came in from the girls' bedroom, dragging her feet. She'd been playing with a rag doll—a dishtowel rolled up to look like a real baby—and resented the interruption.

"You can be a big help to Mama. How would you like to take Betsy for a walk?"

"Do I have to, Mama?" Tilly pouted.

"Yes you do." Rivke-Leah insisted. "See if you can get her to go to sleep. I think she has a tummyache."

With the baby tucked snugly into the carriage, Tilly started off down the street. She soon forgot her resentment and she felt really grown up pushing the carriage, just like the mummies in the neighborhood or the nursemaids she sometimes saw in the park. She started to skip down the street, playing a sort of hopscotch, hopping first on one foot, then on the other. She lifted her hands from the carriage, only for a moment but the street had become a steep hill and the carriage started careening down, bumping on the cobbles. Tilly forgot hopscotch and started chasing after the runaway carriage, a huge lump in her throat, her cheeks turned flaccid and limp. In no time at all, the baby carriage was all the way at the bottom of the hill and, oh my, it had tipped onto its side and Betsy, swaddled in blankets, was rolling over and over in the gutter. Tilly reached her charge and tried to pick her up but the baby was heavy and awkward wrapped in all the blankets. A woman stopped, sized up the situation, and accompanied the sobbing babysitter and her charge back to the house.

"I remember how terrified I was," my mother told me. "I watched the carriage bumping over the cobbles, and I could hear Betsy screeching. If that kind woman hadn't taken me home, no-one would have known about it. I would have been too scared to tell Mother."

When Betsy was about ten months old, eleven year old Rosie decided to surprise Rivke-Leah by getting the baby ready for bed before her mother came home from marketing, heavily laden with bags of fish and potatoes. Rosie put the galvanized tin tub on the stove and filled it with water. After about ten minutes, she tested the water temperature with her elbow just like her mother did. She asked her brother Goody to help her lift the heavy bathtub off the stove and onto the kitchen floor and she undressed Betsy and gently lowered her into the lukewarm water. But when she put Betsy in the tub, the baby screamed and refused to sit down. Rosie held Betsy's arms and tried to push her into a sitting position, but the slippery baby writhed out of her grasp and struggled to stand up, slithering all over the tub. Of course, the bottom of the bathtub was red hot. Twelve year old Fan summed up the situation immediately, pulled Betsy out and tried to comfort her before her mother came home.

The worst accident occurred when she was about fourteen months old. One Thursday afternoon, Rivke-Leah went marketing and left Fan in charge. Betsy was in a large cradle on the floor next to the fireplace and Fan was trying to rock her to sleep. But Betsy insisted on sitting up in the little bed and rocking herself violently. Suddenly, the cradle tipped over and Betsy fell out, hitting her head hard against the brass fender that surrounded the open fireplace. She lay on the floor, limp and silent. After a few moments that seemed like an hour to the other children, she stirred and started to cry and, much to Fan's relief, she soon lay back in the cradle and fell asleep. Fan instructed the other three children:

"Don't tell Ma. I'll give you each a ha'penny if you promise not to tell." Goody, Rose and Tilly swore they'd keep the secret and when Rivke-Leah came home Betsy was fast asleep. She slept an abnormally long time, not waking till 10 the next morning. Rivke-Leah was glad to have uninterrupted time to complete her chores preparing for the weekend. But when Betsy did wake up, she cried inconsolably and kept on hitting her head with her fist. Nothing would calm her. By Tuesday, when this behavior had continued for four days, Rivke-Leah took her to the doctor. He felt the huge bump on Betsy's head, saw that the baby's eyes were not focusing properly and asked Rivke-Leah what had happened. My grandmother couldn't answer him. She explained that she often left Betsy in Fan's care and he told her to ask Fan how Betsy had banged her head.

When Rivke-Leah got home, she asked, "Fanny, How did Betsy hurt her head?"

"I dunno," Fan answered, looking down at her feet.

Rivke-Leah stood the other three children in a row and asked them the same question. She was weeping now, rubbing her hands on her face, clutching the fractious baby to her breast.

"What happened to her?" she sobbed, "My poor Betsy-leben, My poor Betsy-lovey."

Tilly had spent her ha'penny already. "I know what happened" she piped up.

But knowing the cause of Betsy's concussion didn't do anything to heal the harm that had been done to her. After a couple of weeks, she stopped hitting her head with her fist but, whenever she misbehaved or did poorly in school, people would say "Well, what d'you expect? She was dropped on her head when she was a baby."

Betsy soon assumed the special role of family troublemaker. The other four children were good students, obedient and well behaved. Rivke-Leah and her husband, Shlomo-Zalman were proud of their four good looking, high achieving children. Betsy, however, floundered in school. She was inattentive and uninterested in her lessons and she soon learned that she could attract a lot of attention by misbehaving. She became a frequent truant and a glib liar. She habitually stole money from her mother's handbag and escaped from school to the comforting darkness of the local cinema where she loved to lose herself in the breast-heaving romances of the silent movies. By the time she was thirteen, she'd made her name for herself in the family as a "wild child".

"I used to loved goin' to the cinema," Betsy told me when I was a teenager. "But I was always in trouble. Once a boy took me to the pictures and gave me a box of chocolates. When I got home, I offered them round to everyone and Ma said, 'where'd you get those?' I told her a boy had given them to me. Ma said that a boy doesn't give you such things for nothing. She told Daddy and he took the belt off the sewing machine and beat me with it. Ooh, it didn't half hurt."

I asked my mother how her parents could have been so mean to Betsy.

"Mean?" my mother said. "What did she tell you?" I repeated Betsy's story. "That's not how it happened," my mother sniffed. "Mother emptied Betsy's pockets to wash her dress and she found a condom. She didn't know what it was, so she showed it to Daddy. He'd never seen anything like it and he took it to Goody. Poor Goody was so embarrassed having to explain what it was. That's when Daddy took the belt off the sewing machine and beat her. My parents didn't know what to do with her. They were at their wits' end."

When she was fourteen, Betsy left school. My grandparents expected her to apprentice to one of the needle trades—dressmaking or tailoring. But Betsy hated sewing and she had no talent for it. She begged to be allowed to learn hairdressing and my grandfather reluctantly agreed. She enjoyed the work and became an expert at Marcel waves and permanents

She was still a constant worry to her parents. Even though the other children had left school at the same age, they read serious books and were interested in politics, opera, and the theatre. Betsy stayed out late and ran with a wild group of flappers and their beaus.

One day, Goody was invited to a party. As he was getting ready to leave, Rivke-Leah asked him to take Betsy with him. He must have been terribly resentful at being asked to take his fifteen year old little sister to a party where most people would be in their twenties but Goody, always the dutiful son, agreed to take her along.

It was usual to play parlor games at such gatherings; charades and word games were popular and, at this party, they decided to play "Think, Word, Letter," an elimination game in which you set up a clapping rhythm, and go around the circle in turn. The first person might say "Think, elephant, R." The next person in the circle would have to think of a word beginning with "R" so they would say "Think rattle T." and the next person would say "Think Triangle P" and so on. First the rhythm is established and, as the game progresses, it gets faster and faster. This is an elimination game, like musical chairs. The first person unable to think of a word, or who breaks the rhythm, is "out". Betsy sat down with the others to play but Goody looked over to her and said "Don't you play this." He knew she would be hopeless at this game.

"I wouldn't 've minded being the first one out if he"d let me play. I was so ashamed when he made me leave the circle so that he could play with all his clever friends."

Pushed aside by her family, Betsy found her own level. Her friends were children of janitors or costermongers who had stalls in the vegetable market. She borrowed money from her sisters which she never returned. She often came home in the wee hours of the morning and her parents were deeply concerned that she would one day get pregnant.

Betsy and I have a cup of tea and a piece of cake in the dining room and we walk along the sunlit corridor hand in hand. Back in her room, I pull out a big, black photograph album with a scuffed cover. It is full of snapshots of Betsy on vacation in the Channel Islands in the early 1930's. She is very slim, wearing shorts or a sagging bathing suit and every picture shows her with a different young man. Her arms are often draped around their necks or she is leaning over them, lips pursed ready to give her partner a juicy kiss. Finally I find the picture I'm looking for.

"Who's this?" I ask her

"That's Jim," she says. "Jim Watson. Isn't he handsome?" The photograph shows a square jawed man in his thirties. He has a thin, slightly turned up nose and a shock of wavy blond hair. His teeth protrude slightly like a doll's. This is my Uncle Jim.

Betsy met Jim when she was vacationing on the Isle of Jersey in 1935. He lived in London and worked as a janitor of a large corporate office building in Islington, a tough, neighborhood in North London. Jim was from a poor, working class family. He'd been in the navy in World War I and, when his ship was torpedoed, he'd clung to a spar in the icy water for more than twenty four hours. This was the reason given for his stammer.

It was a stammer like no other I have ever heard. Combined with an almost unintelligible Cockney accent, each sentence was painfully, long-windedly spoken.

" 'Allallallallallall-ow, Cyn-cyn-cyn-cyn-whasaname-cyn-cynfia," he would greet me. " 'ow-'ow-'ow-'ow-'ow-'ow-'ow-whasaname-'ow-'ow are yer?"

And, of course, he was not Jewish.

No-one in the Wolfe family had ever married "out." Unlike their parents, Rivke-Leah and Shlomo-Zalman who moved exclusively in Jewish circles, the children had Christian friends who they met at work or on vacation but Betsy's sisters and brother wouldn't consider dating any of these friends. They knew how grieved their parents would be if they were to marry a gentile and all four of them were extremely dutiful children. The commandment, "Honor thy father and thy mother", was not a hollow saying to them. It was a creed.

When Betsy and Jim came home from vacation, they started seeing each other regularly but she never brought him home to meet the family. Finally, in 1937, they were secretly married in a registry office ceremony. Betsy continued to live at home in my grandmother's house. (My grandfather had died ten years earlier) and, on weekends, she would tell her mother that she was going to stay with one of her girl friends. After a year and a half of this routine, my Aunt Rose begged Betsy to tell her mother about the marriage and to bring Jim home to meet everyone.

It was the custom to "sit shiva" for a child who had married out of the faith; to treat them as if they had died, mourn for them and then to cut them off from the family entirely. But my Grandmother couldn't bear the idea of cutting off her child. When Betsy finally brought Jim home and confessed that she was already married, I remember my Grandmother, grief-stricken, rocking back and forth in a kitchen chair, wiping her swollen red eyes with a corner of her apron, and sobbing, "If he vanted to marry me, I vouldn't hev him."

Jim was putty in Betsy's hands. After she had introduced him to the family, she asked him to convert to Judaism and in 1939, at the age of forty two, he went

191

into hospital to be circumcised and he studied for conversion with a liberal Rabbi who performed a Jewish wedding ceremony in my Grandmother's living room

But, in spite of his efforts to join the family, my mother's sisters and brother were united in their attitude to Betsy and Jim. They were uniformly ashamed of them. Although they were always included in gatherings of the immediate family, they were never invited to weddings or other large family celebrations. Our extended family was now entering the professions. My cousins became doctors, lawyers and CPA's and they married "well." Betsy and Jim were treated like double skeletons in our family cupboard

Jim was hard-working and conscientious at his job and he was promoted to the position of head housekeeper. They moved into an apartment on the top floor of the building where they lived till he retired. He appeared to be a model, if somewhat boring husband.

One day, when I was fourteen, I was on my way to the theatre and stopped in to visit them there. When it was time to leave, he took me down in the elevator and, in the overheated, cramped space, surrounded by mirrors reflecting the glaring light, he groped for my breasts and pressed wet, panting kisses on my face while I tried to reach the button marked "G" so that I could escape into the cool air of the London evening.

I look at his picture and shudder slightly and I find a picture of a smiling, tow-headed baby but I turn the page quickly before Betsy can see it.

It's time to clean out Betsy's weighty handbag. Bags of boiled sweets, a cheese and tomato sandwich dotted with blue mold and wrapped in a napkin, and then, at the bottom, a doll with real hair and a jaunty smile and a little teddy bear.

"Aren't these nice!" I say. "Who gave them to you?"

"I don't remember," she replies.

"You always liked dolls, didn't you, Auntie Betsy."

"Yes. I love dolls." She says, dully.

It's time for me to leave. I kiss her clammy cheek.

"Will you come back?" she asks.

"Yes." I say. "I'll be back the day after tomorrow."

Two days later, I find Betsy, sitting by a window, reading the "Daily Mirror" and whistling a little tune.

"Hullo darlin'," she says. "Are you here for your holidays?"

"Yes. But I'm going home soon. Back to New York. Look, Auntie Betsy. I've brought you a present."

I pass her a big shopping bag and she pulls out a baby doll with a dimpled, smiling face and eyes that open and close.

"Ooh!" she says. "Thank you so much, darlin'. How lovely. I love her." She kisses the doll's face, lifts it up to her shoulder and pats its back gently. "She's goin' to be so spoilt." She says and her eyes fill with tears. "I don't know why," She says. "I'm so happy that you brought her and I do love her, but I feel sad too. I don't mean to but I just do." She sits dreamily in her chair, patting the doll gently. Then she cradles it in her arms.

In 1940, Betsy became pregnant. Although my grandmother was not resigned to Betsy's marriage, she was excited at the prospect of a new baby. As Betsy's time drew near, my grandmother and her friends guessed the sex of the child. Carry high and it would be a girl; low and it would be a boy. A needle was suspended on a thread over her belly. Swinging in a circle signified a girl; if it swung back and forth, it would be a boy. It was hard to determine the pattern so opinions were evenly divided. When her time came, Betsy was in labor for more than twenty four hours and her baby girl was delivered stillborn. The next year, she was pregnant again. The atmosphere around her was electrically tense and this time, when the baby was born, the cord was wrapped around his neck and he died also. It was 1943 now and Betsy was thirty three —getting old for bearing children—and now she found that she was unable to conceive. Jim said to my mother, "Uv-uv-uv-uv-whasername-uv-uvver women jist 'as to lif-lif-lif-lif-lif-whasername lif-lif-lift their skirts and they gits pregnant."

Finally, my cousin Martin was delivered by Caesarean section on July 24, 1946.

Martin was a sunny-natured baby with white-blond hair and his father's china-blue eyes. My grandmother and aunt Rose doted on him and baby-sat with him often. My brother, a year older than Martin, was a colicky baby who cried most of the time. He had a stubborn nature and temper tantrums. The contrast between the two cousins was palpable and Martin was clearly the favorite.

Betsy was thrilled with her newborn but, soon after Martin's first birthday, when he began to assert his independence a little, she became very impatient with him. If he didn't obey her, she smacked hit him often. He soon became a mass of nervous tics and, when he began to speak, he stammered. By the time he was two and a half, his behavior had become rather bizarre. He flapped his hands, rocked back and forth, and poked his finger in his eye with a twisting motion. As he grew older, he became obsessed with the timetables of London Transport and, by the time he was eight, he could give you directions to any location in London, telling you where to change buses or get on the Underground. I believe he was mildly autistic and that he may have had Asberger's syndrome—a manifestation of autism which includes nervous tics, difficulty socializing with others, and obsessive "idiot savant" type of learning. Betsy took him from one doctor to another to try to find treatment for his unusual behavior but no-one seemed to be able to help him. Betsy sent him to a Jewish day school and he grew up to be good at mathematics and conscientious at any job he took on—just like his father. When he was twenty, he decided to move to Israel where he lived on a kibbutz and his good work habits were valued. He would have stayed there but Jim became very ill with emphysema and he came home, moved back in with his parents and never left. After Jim died, Martin became Betsy's constant companion. She still shouted at him if he didn't do as he was told but he clearly adored his mother, called her "My lamb" and seemed content to live with her and chauffeur her to the supermarket or Bingo games. Living at home, doing sedentary work and taking virtually no exercise, he became obese and, when he was forty two, he dropped dead on the floor of the living room where Betsy found him when she came home from her Bingo game.

Betsy holds the doll tight on her shoulder patting it rhythmically.

"I always wanted a baby of my own." She says. "I didn't have any children did I?"

"No," I lie. "But you can take care of this one now."

I am amazed that Alzheimer's disease can be a blessing

DOMENICK ANGIELLO
CINDY
loneliness at the shopping network

Cindy is a character. I can see that right away. She lumbers into my awareness as I sit, at 3:45 with my son Jack and his girl, Tina, on the porch of Al E. Gator's in Fort Pierce. Having delayed lunch this long, we've decided to cool our heels a few more minutes and have Early Bird, which starts at 4:00. The kids introduce me to the heavy, thirty-something woman as someone they know from TVC, the shopping network, where they and half the retired people in Palm Beach County work part time. The effect of seeing Tina and Cindy together is comical. Tina is one of the world's doll-like miniatures. You could make another three of her out of Cindy's extra body mass. Cindy's rapid, continuous speech is like the bubblers people have in their swimming pools down here, so much like them that I entertain the whimsical notion that being near them a lot has influenced her speech. Maybe I entertain this fantasy because she doesn't seem to have quite mastered the pace yet. Occasionally, she runs out of breath and there is a slight hitch in a wrong place.

Cindy tells us that the food in Al E. Gator's is really good, but the service is slow. "They keep you waiting forever for your water, for your bread, for everything, and you're left just sitting there." We aren't daunted. Even if the meal takes a while to come, it sounds like it will be worth the wait. Anyway, it's still fifteen minutes to Early Bird, and Jack is on his cell phone taking care of business as he paces the porch, so Tina and I have been relaxing on the bench in the shade of the porch roof. But Cindy has a plan for us. She thinks we will be more comfortable inside, where she says we can just get a table and wait for Early Bird. Cindy says, "Be sure to sit in Crystal's section, though. Crystal is a wonderful waitress. Really she is the only good one in the place. She sets you up with water and rolls and butter as soon as you sit down and she takes your order right away. I mean Crystal is wonderful. The rest of them keep you waiting forever." Like most people, I guess, we go along with Cindy more to avoid hurting her feelings than because we are so worried that the service of anyone but Crystal will be unsatisfactory. Then too, Cindy's detailed knowledge of the place suggests to me that she works in Al E. Gator's and knows the ropes, so I am willing to take her advice.

Tina tells me later that Cindy has nothing to do with the establishment except that she lives in an apartment just behind the restaurant and eats Early Bird there daily, filling out the online Quality and Service Survey afterwards to earn the complimentary dessert the next day.

Jack says that, in the coffee room at TVC, Cindy complains constantly to her fellow workers about the low salary and announces she is looking for a job with much better pay, say $30 an hour. She tells them that she has $75,000 worth of furniture stored in Toronto, where she made big money as a "credit card manager." She tells others of her lucrative job as a "department store buyer" in

Dallas. I could be wrong, but it seems to me she talks too fast and too much to be fastidious about the truth. How much truth can there be, after all? My suspicion about her veracity makes me think of my mother's comment on an aunt whose accounts of events always varied from my mother's memory of them. Mom was a stickler for the truth, but my aunt embellished her accounts—maybe just for the creative exercise. She seemed never satisfied with people's obvious and ordinary motives, so she shaded her reports to add the interest of jealousy or anger or magnanimity. Mom said, "Your Aunt Alice is a big fabricator of small truths."

As we are making our way to a table in Crystal's section, Cindy tells us that the paragon of service is on her way and will be on site in a few minutes. Danger signals go off in my head. *This will not turn out well*, I think. As we sit down, with Cindy standing right beside Tina's seat, a waitress comes over to take our drink order. Cindy tells her we are waiting for Crystal. The young woman looks puzzled but doesn't comment, and turns to her other customers. *This* waitress seems bright-eyed enough to me.

Apparently to kill some time while she awaits her personal waitress, Cindy sits down at our table and launches into a frantic account of how you can make up to $700 a month charging merchandise from the SmartMart circular. She only charges $200, but that's just because she doesn't want to put $700 on her charge card. But you *could* make $700 if you *did* put that much on your card. "See, you order this, and this, and this," she says, indicating items in the multi-color direct-mail piece she's holding. "You can always use this item, right?" she says excitedly, "And this? And then you mail in this coupon and, a month later—Boom!—you get a $200 check in the mail." Her explanation—which clarifies nothing—goes on, mantra like, to the point that I strongly suspect she must be selling some pyramid scheme.

I study my menu ferociously, hardly able to process a word of the descriptions of the "Florigator Fritters" and the "Trash Can Tortillas" because Cindy's voice is making my head spin with indignation. I am hiding behind Tina, in a sense, since, as a man, I might be excused from the charge of rudeness on the basis that I needn't be a party to a conversation between two women about shopping. Jack seems to be exercising the same strategy. Tina—little Tina—must bear the brunt of this onslaught. She says at one point, "I would never use that," and repeats this assertion several times. Cindy says, "Oh, you can always sell what you don't want to your friends at TVC."

Three separate times Cindy takes her leave of us, saying how nice it was to run into Jack and Tina, how nice it was to meet me. I can't see how she has met me at all. Finally, she takes a seat alone at the table just behind ours.

There is plenty of Cindy overlapping the seat—enough for half a chair more on each side. At one point, she asks from there if we were expecting someone else. There is an unoccupied seat at our table for four, and I feel my shoulders tense involuntarily as I anticipate that Tina or Jack may suggest Cindy join us.

As I realize they will not, my shoulders relax. I hope I haven't visibly cringed. I realize by this time that Cindy is just trying to make friends, and I wouldn't want to hurt her feelings. I think she may have had her fill of rejection.

As we all sit waiting for Crystal, a family seated after us is being served. I catch the eye of the waitress who tried to serve us twenty minutes earlier. She comes over and takes our order for drinks and appetizers, and summons a busboy who fills our water glasses and promptly brings hot rolls and butter. We are halfway through our meal when Crystal arrives to take Cindy's order. Crystal is a beautiful eighteen-year-old. She is a Florida pattern: almost blank good looks under the usual blond hair pulled straight back but with jewel-like blue eyes. Except for her eye color, she looks like Julia Stiles. When she is not sitting with Cindy, she is working either in tandem with our first waitress or at odds with her. Even though we have lingered over our Early Bird, we are finished long before Cindy is. As we leave, I glance over my shoulder at the expanse of Cindy's back.

I associate her isolation at her table with what the kids have told me about their jobs at TVC. They say that each of the telephone people at TVC has his or her own desk. On one floor, a hundred of them occupy a room the size of a football field, but the ceilings are low, so the place doesn't feel like a stadium, and each operator is separated from the person at the desk ahead by a screen.

Although the pay is small, they find TVC a pleasant place to work. It is clean and well lit. The work schedule is very flexible. The people are pleasant, too. I gather that, in this area, where so many of the residents are new, the coffee room at TVC substitutes for familiar neighbors, family, the crowd in the neighborhood bar back home. It must serve as a place to assuage the nagging loneliness that some of the transplanted people had even at home, maybe, but since their move here, have become acutely conscious of, many having come long after mid-life to this new place that was swamp and subtropical forest only twenty years ago and then a *tabula rasa* and now a community—to use the term loosely—the result of a master plan developed by engineers. It seems to me that working in the windowless building TVC occupies would be a sort of practice for the mausoleum or for interment, but featuring electronic contact with the world of the living. When people in the outside world—really all over the world—see an object on their TV screens that stirs their concupiscence, they call in and someone—It could be Jack or Tina or Tina's parents or Cindy or any one of the many people who answer the phones there—sets in motion the computerized process that will soothe their urge for possession.

Most of the shoppers' calls are cut and dried. The operator's greetings and responses are scripted, and there are guidelines about how to conduct a telephone contact. For instance, they are to answer the phone with the appropriate greeting for the time of day and then say their first name—never their last—and request the item number the caller wants. They are never to use the customer's first name even if the customer urges them to do so.

As we drive back to the kids' apartment, I think of Cindy answering calls at TVC, what her conversations must be like, her part in them regulated and scripted but conducted in the bubbling voice I have just heard for the first time that afternoon. It must be a pleasant telephone voice, and Cindy has an impulse to kindness, which would come through in an acceptable way over that medium. Most people call with a need she can easily satisfy. They are ordering an item, the receipt of which she can facilitate. She can send one or many, according to their wishes; she can send it to their address or any address of their choice; but she cannot vary the price or modify the product. Cindy can be accommodating within those limits, and she is often genuinely enthusiastic about her callers' choices. Someone wants two of those lovely dragonfly pins for cousin Hope, the ones with the genuine diamond chips. "Oh, she will just treasure them! They're so elegant!" Cindy says. Another orders the genuine opal ring with solitaire setting in sterling silver: "I got that for my mother. Opal's her birth stone, and she *loved* it." Another wants the old-fashioned wicker hamper which comes in a choice of decorator colors. Cindy exclaims, "That is *such* a good buy! I've seen them for twice the price."

Sometimes Cindy works in the middle of the night, partly to earn the fifty-cent premium for the overnight shift, but mostly to avoid contact with her mother, who is calling every hour on the hour at home and leaving messages on Cindy's answering machine. Mother is very ill, and Cindy would like to help, but instead, she is accumulating guilt by avoiding the sick old shrew, who is always hurting Cindy's feelings by comparing her unfavorably with her married sister Lois, who lives in San Francisco and is a stockbroker and very successful but wouldn't lift a finger to save the infant Jesus.

The small hours after midnight is the time certain men call, their tongues thick with drink. They can't decide what to order or which of their girlfriends to get it for. Cindy asks questions about these women and forms a picture of each of them. She tries to help. Often these men order nothing. Usually they can't remember their girlfriends' addresses or phone numbers. But by the end of their calls, often they wind up declaring their love for Cindy. "What's your name again, Honey? I know who you are. I've spoken to you before. No, no, no. I know you're the one. Why won't you ever tell me your last name? Why do you keep calling me Mr. Gunderson? Please call me Carl. I feel I know you better than I knew my wife. Where *are* you anyway?"

A little piece of her dreams of telling them and seeing what would happen. She can see the tabloid headline: TRUE LOVE TRIUMPHS AT TVC.

In the middle of the night, men from Nebraska threaten to drive to wherever she is. "How can you deny our love?" they wail. They want to marry the understanding woman with the charming, effervescent voice.

She understands their loneliness.

I grew up in the suburbs of Massachusetts in the early 80s, when most teenagers adored rock idols like Bruce Springsteen, Madonna and The Rolling Stones. But I was a trumpet player as were many of my friends. Thus, we ate, drank and slept the trumpet. Our heroes were players like screech trumpeter Maynard Ferguson or members of the Canadian Brass Quintet. And, naturally, we listened to the Boston Symphony Orchestra and its new, exciting principal player, Charles Schlueter. We were all blown away by his rich, round sound and by the force of his playing. How could he get so much air through the trumpet?

As I became interested in other endeavors after high school, the trumpet became more of a hobby and I didn't think much about Charlie and his playing. I certainly never imagined that I'd get to meet him. However, a close friend of mine from those days, Michael Butler, continued studying the trumpet and eventually, after many years, began taking lessons with Charlie.

A few months ago Mike invited me to sit in on one of his lessons. Charlie met us on the porch of his home in a suburb of Boston. He was quiet and friendly and, at 62, moved energetically. His practice room in the basement of his house is small and filled with trumpets and parts of horns. During the lesson, Charlie made small corrections in Mike's approach to the music and Mike always responded—they were speaking the same language.

I enjoyed the lesson very much and had many questions, but, unfortunately, Charlie had another student scheduled immediately after Mike. So after returning to New York, I emailed Charlie a long list of questions. He generously responded to all of them and what follows is our version of an interview, email style. Charlie is still the Principal Trumpet of the Boston Symphony Orchestra, a post he's held since 1981. Prior to that he held the same post with the Minnesota Orchestra, the Milwaukee Symphony and the Kansas City Philharmonic.

How did you get started playing the trumpet?

When I was ten years old I wanted to play accordion, probably because my next door neighbors' grandchildren each played. When my parents took me to the local music teacher, Charlie Archibald, he talked me out of the accordion and suggested I try his cornet, which I did, and I liked it, so I started taking 2 lessons a week from him for $0.75 each!! Charlie was a very interesting person. He had been director of bands in both elementary and high school in DuQuoin; he had worked in the coal mines for many years (that's probably how my father knew him); he was self taught—on all band instruments and he played a little piano also. I'm pretty sure he had absolute pitch (though I didn't know what that was at the time). He had had polio a few years before I studied with him. He was not expected to live; and then when he did, the prognosis was that he would never walk. When I began studying with Charlie, he was walking on crutches about five miles a day, on dirt roads, and before long was using only a cane. This was all when he was 70+ years old.

Why the trumpet and not something else?

I'm not sure why I didn't continue on the cornet; when my parents bought me my own instrument, it was a trumpet; I have no idea who made it. On the bell, it said "Elkhart Model," made in Elkhart, Indiana.

When did you first know that you might be good enough to make it in this highly competitive field? Did you feel confident or did you always feel you'd make it?

I'm not sure if that was ever a conscious thought. I think Charlie assumed that I would become a band director, so he began teaching me to read bass clef, but as if I were playing a trombone or baritone horn—in other words as a non-transposing instrument.

After studying with Charlie for about 3 years, my father had his first of many heart attacks, and was unable to work after that, so even lessons at $0.75 was more than I could afford, so there was a period of about 4 months that I had no private lessons. About the same time, a new trumpet teacher, Don Lemasters, moved to DuQuoin and started teaching at the local music store-The Egyptian Music Company. (Southern Illinois is known as "Little Egypt"—hence the name of Southern Illinois University's teams are known as the Salukis). Don was from St. Louis, and had studied with Joe Gustat, who played first trumpet in the St. Louis Symphony for over 25 years, and Ed Brauer, who was on staff at NBC Radio. I had heard about Joe Gustat from Charlie Archibald because they had played together when they were growing up. He had always spoken very highly of him, but by the time I started playing, Gustat had retired and moved to Florida. Joe was the trumpet "guru" in the midwest—like Max Schlossburg was on the East coast and Louis Maggio on the West coast. But Joe was the teacher who players went to study with if they had some problem—like Dizzy when he sort of blew everything out, Buddy Childers, when he got out of the army and had some problems, Raphael Mendez, when he injured his lip (though I understand he attributed his recovery to Maggio).

Don was getting $2.50 for lessons. For me that was an astronomical fee!! As fortune (or good luck) would have it, just before Christmas, The Egyptian Music Company had a coloring contest in the DuQuoin Evening Call, the town newspaper, which I won and it entitled me to 10 free lessons with Don. He sort of overhauled my playing: he changed my embouchure and taught me about breathing (which had been Gustat's specialty). I must have shown some promise, because after the 10 free lessons, he continued to teach me for free, for the next 5 years. He also arranged for me to study with Ed Brauer (when he felt it would be beneficial for me to work with Ed) also for free. I applied to (and was accepted at) the New England Conservatory, but Ed said that if I could get into Juilliard and study with Bill Vacchiano, and got his "blessing," that I could almost be assured of having a successful career in the orchestral world. I guess he certainly was prophetic, though when I left Juilliard, I didn't know whether or not I had Bill's "blessing."

So I applied to and was accepted at Juilliard, but even then a lot of people said to me: "Be sure you get your Music-ed degree, because it's not possible to make a living playing!" I didn't know how good it was necessary to be to "make it," because in DuQuoin, I think I just assumed that since I played better than my colleagues, that it would always be that way. So I don't know if I had confidence or if it was the confidence that my teachers had in me that caused me to forge ahead.

Symphony orchestras were not that "stable" as a means of employment—even the New York Philharmonic only had about a 32 week season in 1957; The St. Louis Symphony had about a 20 week season at about $75.00 a week. The major radio/TV studios in all large cities—NBC, CBS, and ABC had staff musicians—the most famous of course, was when NBC in New York created the NBC Symphony for Arturo Toscanini. It started out as being made up of the "staff musicians" and then others were hired from other orchestras. Before Harry Glantz left the New York Philharmonic to become 1st trumpet in NBC, Benny Baker, who was on staff, was the 1st trumpet. Even Bud Herseth finished his Masters Degree from the NEC, by correspondence, after he became first trumpet in the Chicago Symphony, probably because the season was only around 28 weeks.

You must have been driven. What motivated you to work so hard? What was your practice schedule like? How much do you practice now?

I don't know if driven would be the word, but since I wasn't any good at any sports, playing the trumpet was something that was fun and it was mine! I practiced a lot from the time I started; with 2 lessons a week, I always had to be ready for the next lesson; I can't remember any more what days—seems like Monday and Thursday. I didn't really think I had any special "ability" on the trumpet—to me at the time it seemed that I had to work hard to keep up. Practicing was also a kind of "escape mechanism." It could make the time go quickly; I could use it to get out of doing "chores." Later at Juilliard, I could rationalize not doing homework for other classes by "having to practice." I didn't have much money or many friends, so practicing took my mind off of being hungry or lonely, so I put in 6-8 hours a day. And also, my father had said, "If you learn how to play the trumpet, you won't have to work in the coal mines." So that was probably very high on the motivational scale!

I don't practice that much any more and since I have been using Monette instruments (18 years) and mouthpieces (16 years) so much practicing isn't necessary. I am a firm believer in taking time off from the instrument. If I have 3 or 4 weeks off, usually I don't even look at the trumpet for at least 2 weeks. I don't think in terms of "getting back in shape." I pretend I haven't taken any time off—and with Monette equipment that is very easy, since I don't have to distort and contort the muscles to make things work.

Since you mention Monette, can you talk just a little bit about how you discovered them and what makes them special?

Dave first contacted me when I was still in Minneapolis. I think either Doc Severinsen or Sandy Sandberg (then VP of Conn) suggested that he get in touch. At that time, Dave was working in Salem, Oregon, repairing instruments, and beginning to make some modifications on existing trumpets. He called to ask what I had done to Bach C trumpets that improved intonation, response, etc. So I gave him the specs on the leadpipe. A short time later he sent me some pipes that he had made for me to try. At that time my response was that I didn't notice anything special. About 2 years later, when I had moved to Boston and Dave had moved to Bloomington, Indiana, he came to see me in Cincinnati when the BSO was playing there on a US tour. I tried the leadpipes once again and one of them felt great. He made a temporary fit of the leadpipe to my Bach C and I used that combination for about 4 months, until Dave started making the whole trumpet. I got my first Monette C (#005) in July, 1983, and the rest is history. I never played the Bach again! Even still using a Bach mouthpiece (at that time a plain #1 (now a #1X) with a #16 hole,) the Monette was superior in almost every way—sound, response, intonation, evenness through all valve combinations and keys. When he started making mouthpieces in 1985/6. that made me a complete convert. Every trumpet player has always looked for the better mouthpiece that would enable the player to have a better sound, better intonation, articulation, range, endurance, more comfort. Once he figured out the mouthpiece issue, he was able to make the first Raja I trumpet (integrated mouthpiece). This was 1988; in 1991 he made the first Raja II, and in 1993 or 1994, the first Samadhi.

Why did you choose classical playing and not something else? Or do you even make that kind of fine distinction?

Although I had played in the Southern Illinois Symphony, (which was part of SIU, and consisted of professors, students and people from the area) when I was in high school, only because my high school band director, Mel Siener was principal bass and good friends with the conductor, I had never heard any really good orchestras until I got to New York. I didn't own a phonograph until I got married, so I hadn't even heard recordings. When I got to NYC, I tried to make up for lost time by going to every concert I possibly could: I tried to hear the New York Philharmonic almost every week—they also broadcast every Sunday, Boston (they used to play in NYC once a month), Philadelphia, National, Chicago, and many more. (Chicago played in Carnegie Hall for the first time in 40 years in 1959. I had never heard Chicago even though I grew up 300 miles from that city!)

When I was in DuQuoin, I played in dance bands in night clubs as well as with my own group for high school proms and homecomings, but I didn't play jazz, probably because without a phonograph, I never had the opportunity to hear the great jazz players, like Dizzy, Miles, Clifford, Charlie Parker, etc. Although I did get to hear Louis Armstrong once when I was in high school. I played lead in a Latin Band during my last year at Juilliard and also in the big band at Juilliard, (the Jazz Workshop, as it was called). I never thought it was possible to work in the studios, because I was under the misconception that you had to be able to improvise in order to break into that part of the profession.

Who were some of your musical idols when you were growing up? How were they important to you?

I don't know if I thought of them as idols, but I suppose my teachers were my trumpet role models; Don and Ed, and certainly Bill when I got to NYC. I actually had heard Armando Ghitalla on the radio, playing with the Cities Service Band of America even though I didn't realize it at the time. Certainly he became one after I heard his Town Hall recital in 1958. Harry Glantz wasn't playing much by the time I got to New York, but I listened to all the NBC recordings I could get my hands on. I heard recordings of the BSO with Georges Mager; Fritz Wesenigt in the Berlin Philharmonic (again on record); Bud Herseth. I didn't consciously try to imitate them, but I was certainly influenced by them.

What is the most important aspect of playing for young trumpeters to keep in mind when they're practicing?

I don't know if it's possible to focus on one aspect. Music is the obvious answer; that is the reason for playing any instrument. And of course music is primarily sound, so it is important to be aware of the kind of tone one is creating. Young players should try to listen to fine players on all instruments, not just trumpet, in order to develop a concept of a beautiful tone, which can influence their own. Breathing is most fundamental, because air is the raw material without which it will not be possible to develop a really good sound; Insufficient air will almost surely cause inefficient playing habits to develop such as embouchure problems, articulation, endurance, range etc.

I've heard that you have some unique ideas about breathing technique. Is this so? Can you expand on this a little?

That could take a few days! Basically I believe it's important to always inhale to the maximum. I know there are a lot of players who suggest to only take in the amount needed, but I maintain that you have the same amount of tubing in which to make the air vibrate at the appropriate speed in order to produce whatever note but also to have the potential for having the maximum resonance, dynamic control, range of color (timbre), as well as phrasing and nuance. It is also necessary to provide the body (and brain) with the oxygen necessary to function efficiently. It's been my experience both personally and with students, that all playing deficiencies can be attributed to insufficient air. I could go on in more detail but I hope this gives an overview.

I noticed that hilarious New Yorker cartoon in your practice room (the one

depicting the trumpet player sitting on the therapist's couch). **What tickles you about that cartoon? Why do you find it "appropriate," as you said.**

I often feel like I'm doing some sort of therapy when teaching. I seem to spend most of my time trying to convince a student that he or she can play better than he or she thinks possible.

Many of us may feel pressure to perform at a high level, to succeed at whatever we are doing. The trumpet, for me, is a metaphor for this kind of struggle—putting the self on the line. So I'm curious to hear about this aspect of playing from a professional. Do you ever feel the pressure of playing in front of a large audience, particularly when you're playing the most prominent instrument in the orchestra? How have you learned to deal with that pressure and stress? Do you practice any particular techniques to help you concentrate?

First of all, there is no "product" in what we do. Good or bad, it's gone, as soon as we play it. So for me, process is more important. It may sound selfish to some, but it's important to play for oneself. That is, your first responsibility is to yourself. It's too big a burden and creates greater anxiety to try to play for your teacher, your parents, the conductor, the audience, colleagues, audition committees, even for the composer. If I can come close to my own standards, then that includes an awareness of context which is also part of process, for which only I can be responsible.

Have there been any particularly embarrassing moments in the orchestra? How do you feel afterwards?

I remember one time in Carnegie Hall playing the Wedding March from Mendelssohn's Midsummers' Night Dream, and I couldn't remember whether it was the first or second time through a repeated section and guessing wrong!

Another time, also in Carnegie, my third slide fell out in the middle of the Bruckner 9th Symphony, and I was scrambling trying to pick it up in time, which I did, but it sure must have looked funny to the audience.

I would have appreciated a large trap-door into which I could have disappeared!

Do you still enjoy playing in the orchestra? Do you ever yearn to do more solo or quintet work? Talk a little about your latest album.

Orchestral playing is still my first love. I get my share of solo and quintet playing when I go off to various places to teach and perform.

My new CD is on the KLEOS label and I think has a nice variety of repertoire: 2 works with piano (Honegger and Enesco), 1 with cello (Chardon), 1 with horn and trombone (Poulenc), 1 chamber work (Saint-Saens) and 1 with organ (Svoboda). Since my previous CD, BRAVURA TRUMPET, has not been available for a couple of years, I have another CD that will be out I hope early next year, on which I re-recorded the 2 works by Robert Suderburg and the Sonata of Hindemith, which were on BRAVURA, as well as the Sonata by Jean Hubeau, all of which are trumpet and piano. Deborah Dewolfe Emery is the wonderful pianist on both CDs.

Do you have any favorite pieces to play?

I suppose Mahler Symphonies are at the top of the list, but I try not to have favorites as such.

Would you like to talk a bit about your foundation? Why did you found it? What's it's purpose? What inspired it?

The easiest answer is to give the Mission Statement:

The mission of the Charles Schlueter Foundation is to foster the enjoyment of music, promote music education, assist in the training of talented young brass performers, encourage improved brass pedagogy, and support the creation of new literature for brass instruments.

The goals are: to establish international collaboration in the field of musical performance; to celebrate and preserve the cultural and artistic heritage of the trumpet and its repertoire; to bring the artistry of trumpet virtuoso, Charles Schlueter, to young instrumental students in their schools; to support and encourage the creation of new solo and ensemble literature for the trumpet; to inspire and guide emerging talented trumpet performers toward professional achievement; to support Mr. Schlueter in his efforts to record important trumpet repertoire for posterity; to promote music as an essential part of school curriculums; to maintain an effective liaison with various schools, communities and national organizations that have allied interests in music and music education; to understand and demonstrate how music serves as a means of communication across a range of cultures throughout the world.

Who are some players, classical or jazz, you admire now? What do you like about their work?

I'd hate to leave anyone out, but I've always admired Doc Severinsen, Maynard Ferguson—I mean they are still doing it after all these years—talk about total commitment! Wynton is doing wonderful things as a player, composer, teacher. Terrence Blanchard, Marvin Stamm, Lou Soloff, Brian Lynch. All great players and totally committed to their art. I have many students who are making their own glowing reputations, which makes me proud. My apologies to those I've omitted.

Are you still improving as a player? How is that even possible?

I hope so. Trying to find imaginative ways to play old familiar repertoire as well as new.

What kind of music do you listen to besides orchestral? What inspires

you about it? What do you look for in a piece of music of any medium?

String quartets, singers, any group or individual whose approach is musically satisfying.

I read an article in which you said that players should take risks, even if it means missing a few notes. Do you still feel this way? Is this, for you, a metaphor for anything larger? A way of living?

If accuracy is the primary goal, then there will often be a lot else that is missing.

You've been at this a long time. Any thoughts of retiring?

Not yet!

What do you plan to do on your sabbatical this year?

About the same as always, except playing with the BSO. I have a full studio at NEC. I went to Brazil for the month of October and played and taught in 7 cities. I will be going to Japan in April. I plan to work on the book I've been at for many years, with the hope of finishing it. Probably a few recital programs and solo appearances.

To find out more about Charles Schlueter, check out his website: www.cschlueter.com

RACHELLE MEYER

Joelle Hann | **Gutting Trout**

*Roughly the flesh resists
then the head pops open
a silver-red rose forced to flower.*

*I'm glad you are dead.
Your deflated fins lay against my palm
like a hushed-up baby;
each of your speckles
once part of the black and yellow lake
flash like codes.*

*Killing was like a game, but it wasn't.
The bolted handle of the knife
clubbed you dead. I used to watch his expert
    hands.
I learned to kill
by splitting myself in two—
one shrieking, as the blade
shrank into the skin,
the other standing back in a smirk—*

*Your filmy lake-water back
slaps the sink,
my father's knife seems to know you.
—here's the white bucket for your innards
the silver tap to flush you out.*

*"Intestine," my mother says. "Digestion. Waste."
I scratch your black intestine with my thumbnail
'til each vertebrae is articulate.*

*Then I open you
without disgust, adult-like:
lost are all the organs that propelled you
    towards me;
I relate to you perfectly. Your scoured inside
is my ideal self, gutted and clean*

no mess in my all-reflecting eyes.

BUSKERS ON THE BOWERY
a johnny fox's freakatorium

I stand outside the Freakatorium with my face pressed against the glass, something that many Lower East Side residents and passer-by have probably done. With an intriguing name and an amazing collection of oddities, human and otherwise, even when closed and only marginally illuminated, it's mesmerizing. It's in this Peeping Tom position that I'm discovered by Johnny Fox, the proprietor. He saunters towards me in a newly-acquired leather studded cape that he later describes as "Liberace meets Evil Kenieval."

It's no surprise that this man would appoint himself the historian for dime museum and side show history. He has lived the story of the human oddity as well as preserved it. With an ability to swallow sixteen swords at once (a world record if not a Guinness Book's; they closed the category after the previous record holder slid down a mere thirteen), and a long run living in a school bus while travelling from street fair to street fair, Johnny Fox has settled in close to the Bowery and made the region's peculiar history his own.

Johnny throws his cape over a wax figure of Mao Tse-Tung and lights a cigarette. It isn't long before another pedestrian comes by, holding a two-year-old child up to look through the glass. She raps on the window even though the door is locked. Johnny lets them inside briefly, giving the little girl a finger puppet to entertain herself. You'd think that the fascination with this atmosphere belongs in childhood: the sideshow, the circus, the sleight of hand magician who pulls a coin out from behind your ear and startles you into crying. It takes a special perseverance to take that fascination through adulthood and adopt the lifestyle as your own. Johnny found something lacking from all comic books he read as a kid, and started looking for around him for living breathing heroes to emulate. "I thought, 'I want a real superhero,' and my dad bought me a Houdini book and said, 'Here's a real superhero, no jail cell could hold him.' And I read the book and thought, 'Yeah it's cool, but he's dead. I want a real superhero, who's alive.' "

But beyond the obvious influences you find dotting the walls of the Freakatorium, he also credits storytellers like Spalding Gray, Garrison Keillor, and Eric Bogosian for shaping his life. And his love of history and storytelling is evident as he continues on about the history of dime museums and his own personal history, either gnawing on the edges of his fingernails or blowing smoke rings towards me, which dissipate around my fingers as I try to penetrate them.

Though he spent close to twenty years in Colorado, Johnny Fox grew up closer to the influences of the Bowery in Hartford, Connecticut, and even learned many of his magician's skills from Slidini, a local performer known as the godfather of closeup magic. He would stay up until three or four in the morning practicing these tricks. But the calling of sword swallowing followed soon after.

"I was doing the magic act in Aspen. And one of the ways we'd get people into the restaurant was to go out and perform and gather a crowd, and say, 'Hey, you guys wanna see the good stuff follow me back into the restaurant.' And I started getting more interested in street performing, and thought I could see the world this way."

He hasn't retired his act while maintaining the Freakatorium. He still keeps a vigorous touring schedule, as well as donating his talents for worthy causes. "I do a show every year for kids. Every state has a burn camp for kids that are severely burned and burn survivors. And once a year the fire fighter's union, the AIFF, they do a national burn camp in western DC, and they bring in one kid from each camp around the country and provinces of Canada. It's happened six times, and I've done every one of them. As a kid, I had this thing about never growing up seeing sideshows and superheroes, you know, that thing. Anyone who's got the courage and bravery to stand up in front of anybody and say, 'This is me, this is how I am, and I'm comfortable with that.' "

The Freakatorium itself is a tribute to that spirit. The current site located on Orchard Street is a prototype he wants to relocate to the Bowery, the original home of the dime museums, where human oddities exhibited themselves before there were sideshows. Johnny points out one of his favorite acquisitions—the wood pieces carved by The Armless Wonder, Charles Tripp, with his feet. And as I look around the shop, at the poster for the Fiji Mermaid, at the two-headed troll dolls, I sympathize with these people eternally consigned to the status of 'Freak!' Scenes from The Elephant Man where the unwanted and abused are exploited or starved for affection flash through my head.

Johnny disagrees with that portrayal. "There were some people who seemed like they were being exploited. For JoJo there was a concocted story, they would say he was captured by trappers in Siberia he doesn't speak much, he just grunts and growls a little bit. In reality, he was fluent in five languages. He was not being exploited. It might have appeared that, but sideshow performers were making a fortune. There were also pinheads, microcephalics. Mentally retarded. Whoever was their manager was taking care of them; they were making them good money. There was no way they were going to mistreat them or abuse them. They wanted them to be healthy, they wanted them to be happy. They taught them simple little magic tricks and they were entertaining people. And people were laughing at them, and they would introduce them saying they were Aztecs, a lost tribe. So after sideshows stopped doing that, what happened to these microcephalic pinheads? They went into institutions. And I believe they were much happier entertaining people. So is it exploiting if someone is happier?"

He does concede that some sideshow performers were mistreated. "Sometimes it was unfair. The managers were taking the lion's share. Like in the case of the Siamese twins Daisy and Violet Hilton." But when it comes down to it, some people choose this sideshow lifestyle, and will willingly participate in it and memorialize it like Johnny. "This is a part of New York history that isn't being preserved that there is so much interest for nowadays."

The interest has extended to media coverage, including a story by ABC news and a feature by Time Out during The Freakatorium's year-and-a-half existence. "I think the media wants to see it happen. I don't know why people would give me free advertising like that except that they'd want to see it turn into something. So they're giving me the tools to use and see what I do with it."

And the project is still in the making, involving valuing and inventorying his collection, and presenting a business plan to possible investors in the hopes of buying a building on the Bowery. In the new home of the Freakatorium, Johnny envisions combining the resources of his sideshow artifacts with a small beer and wine garden. And of course there would be performances. "When I first started the place the vision was to have a theater, to do the theater shows and to have the lobby of the theater to be a mini-museum so the show would start as you walked into the theater. The inside of the theater would be decorated with old sideshow banners, and present some illusions that were done, like Spidora, the head of a human being and the body of a spider."

It seems like an awesome task to bring this project together, but Johnny's years of busking and street performance have given him a Darwinian approach to business, and his passion for the sideshow freak an ability to isolate that unique quality and become its foremost expert. "I think we're all freaks. We all have something that's unique and unusual about us, whether it's the way we think about things, the way we react to things, the way we dress. There's people that are freaks about their looks, they go and get plastic surgery and they don't have to. You know, there's so many different types of freaks. Some people admit it, some people embrace it, some people hide from it and deny it." And some appoint themselves to keep its history alive.

This article originally ran in December 2000 in plasmotica.com.

The freakatorium is located at 57 Clinton Street between Stanton and Rivington. For more information visit www.freakatorium.com

CONTRIBUTORS

Domenick Angiello, one of four brothers, was born in the Bronx, N.Y. in 1940 of first generation Italian-American parents. He attended PS 95, then Fordham Prep, and finally Fordham College, where he specialized in tippling and eking out what was then called "the gentleman C." Nevertheless, he managed to go on to earn an M.A. and a Ph.D. (in medieval English literature) from Fordham. He is now a professor at Mercy College in Dobbs Ferry. In 1980, Dom added general contractor to his resume, more or less in imitation of his idol, Geoffrey Chaucer who, for a time, had charge of construction and maintenance projects for Richard II. Having no royalty to serve, Dom has built and remodeled castles for the aristocracy of Westchester, N.Y. A few years ago, despite his best efforts, Dom's poetic urge reemerged-metastasized as a desire to write memoir. "The Store" is a symptom of that disease.

Nicholas Bhasin is a comedy writer and screenwriter. He studied improv comedy at the Upright Citizens Brigade Theatre of New York.

Bill Bilodeau is the editor of a daily newspaper in New Hampshire. He studied creative writing at Harvard and is currently at work on a novel. He is married... with children.

Kathleen Boland is a freelance TV Segment Producer living in Los Angeles. She studied improv at the UCB Theater in New York and now performs at IOWest in Hollywood.

Hillery Borton is always an editor, sometimes a writer, and most recently a maven. She has worked for major publishing houses and now offers her services through her own company, Maven Media. She used to write criticism, when asked by TheSimon.com, but her assessments were hardly objective and never hard hitting. Now she keeps to writing the personal essay, which is what she was really doing all along.

Laura Buchholz has written for A Prairie Home Companion with Garrison Keillor and Comedy Central. She can be seen every Sunday night at New York City's Juvie Hall in the sketch show Saturday Night Rewritten. She has collaborated on two short films by Please Stop Stealing My Bike Productions and is the former humor editor for Ducts.org.

Jennifer DeMerritt is a humorist, pseudo-intellectual, and amateur hack psychologist. She has written for BUST Magazine, Nerve.com and Glamour, and performed at theaters, dives and art-holes throughout the city. Her hobbies are watching bad performance art and spanking her cat Tatiana a.k.a. Fat Tati or Tati the Body.

Cynthia Ehrenkrantz is a retired specialty food and confectionery broker, living in Westchester county, N.Y. She was born in England in 1933 and came to the United States in 1957.

Gideon Evans is a Producer on Comedy Central's The Daily Show with Jon Stewart. He is also a playwright, actor and voice over artist. Gideon resides in Brooklyn, N.Y. where he wanders the streets looking for new friends.

Thomas Fast, a.k.a. Naked Man, teaches English and Spanish at a private high school in Japan. Originally from small town, Oregon, he studied art history at New York University. He has traveled and lived throughout Europe, Latin America and Asia. His photographs have appeared in articles and magazines, and have been exhibited in Japan. He also makes occasional guest appearances as a DJ at his local coffee house in Okayama City. FYI, his nickname is an homage to the "Hadaka Matsuri" or "Naked Man Festival" that takes place in his Japanese hometown every winter. He himself only rarely appears naked in public, but as a "Hakujin" (white guy) in Japan, Tom draws a lot of attention either way.

Last we heard, **Robert Flanagan** was living on a tiny island 800 miles south west of Hawaii. With a Masters Degree in English and no job prospects he accepted a commission as an Army Lieutenant, a Reconnaissance Platoon Leader. He published a short story in Rosebud Magazine, a literary quarterly, and teaches English on the island.

E.B. Gallardo is a free-lance writer currently at work on a collection of Fairy Tales. She holds a degree in English from Hunter College, CUNY. Her work has been published in both Ducts.org and MOXIE. She lives in New York City with her Chihuahua, Esmeralda.

Eric Gillin was born in Randolph, Mass., and works as a staff reporter for TheStreet.com. He is also the founder and editor of Blacktable.com.

Mark Goldblatt has published op-ed columns in the New York Times, the New York Post, the Daily News, and Newsday, and has written feature articles for Travel and Leisure and book reviews for Reason and the National Review. Mark resides in New York City.

Richard Goodman is the author of French Dirt: The Story of a Garden in the South of France. He has written on a variety of subjects for many national publications, including The New York Times, Creative Nonfiction, Commonweal, Vanity Fair, Garden Design, Grand Tour, salon.com, National Gardening, Saveur, Ascent and The Michigan Quarterly Review. He has twice been awarded a fellowship at the MacDowell Colony. In 2003, he was awarded a fellowship at the Virginia Center for the Creative Arts. He created, wrote and narrated a six-part series about New York City for Public Radio in Virginia. He contributed extensively to The Mavens' Word of the Day Collection, a book on words and word derivations published by Random House. He has taught creative writing in New York City for a number of years, most recently with the New York Writers Workshop. He also works as a landscape gardener in Manhattan. He teaches creative nonfiction at Spalding University's Brief Residency MFA program in Louisville, Ky. Recently, he wrote the introduction for Travelers' Tales Provence, and his essay about Paris appears in the new collection, The Best Travelers' Tales 2004.

Stephanie Hart teaches writing at F.I.T. and the Parsons School of Design and is the former Children's editor at Ducts.org. She has published a young adult novel. Her short stories have appeared in the magazines Caprice and And Then, as well as the anthology, Mondo James Dean. A personal essay appears in the anthology, Self Portraits: Language Learners in a Multicultural World, published in 2000 by Teachers College Press.

Margaret Hundley-Parker's writing has been published in the New York Times Book Review, Time Out New York, and Travel & Leisure to name a few. Her book, The K.I.S.S.

Guide to Fitness came out on Dorling Kindersley Publishing in 2002. She is currently the New York Editor for American Woman Road & Travel. "I Ain't Proud" is an excerpt from her first novel, Below the Belt.

Patricia Kinney was born in Seattle. Having earned a living as a writer and teacher of writing for over 15 years, she has been a journalist, columnist, screenwriter, photographer, playwright, comedienne and editor. She studied writing and literature at The Evergreen State College in Olympia, Washington and is currently obtaining her MFA in Creative Writing from Antioch University in Los Angeles. The mother of six boys (two are writers) recently relocated to Portland, Oregon. Kinney has been published in The Sun, Hipmama, Bellowing Ark , Poetry Motel , Poetry Magazine , Steam Ticket , Slightly West and various other journals and anthologies. Kinney is editor and publisher of 4th Street, a poetry bi-monthly.

Ross Klavan wrote the screenplays Dark Fields for Miramax, and the adaptation of Tom Clancy's Without Remorse for Paramount. His critically acclaimed original screenplay Tigerland was nominated for the Independent Spirit Award. The film, based on Klavan's novel of the same name, was directed by Joel Schumacher and released by 20th Century Fox. A TV movie, Deathwork will soon be shown on TNT. Klavan's short fiction has appeared in Zing Magazine, Pierogi Press, and on the BBC.

Jonathan Kravetz, President, Editor in Chief, Ducts, is co-founder of Ducts.org and founder of the New York based reading series, Trumpet Fiction, held each month at KGB Bar in the East Village of New York City. He has an M.A. in Cinema Studies from New York University and studied fiction and screenwriting with a variety of New York teachers, including Alice Eliot Dark and the late Fred Hudson.

Mitchell Levenberg has published short stories in FICTION magazine, The New Delta Review, The Cream City Review, Fine Madness and others. He teaches writing at New York University and St. Francis College.

Katrina Markel is a graduate Broadcast Journalism student at New York University. She also has a degree in acting from NYU. Over the last few years, Katrina has directed a number of off-off Broadway plays and recently completed a feature length documentary about her hometown, entitled Homecoming.

Daniel McCoy is a freelance writer and actor. He is a regular contributor to the Brooklyn humor magazine Jest, and his work has appeared in Modern Humorist and on the public radio programs Rewind and Morning Edition. He studies improvisation at the Upright Citizen's Brigade Theater, and performs with the troupe Robotski.

Rachelle Meyer is a freelance writer and graphic designer who lives, and sometimes works, in New York City.

Maud Newton grew up in Miami, Florida, where she was often mistaken for a tourist because of her pallid complexion. She now lives in Brooklyn and is a graduate student in creative writing at the City College of New York. Beyond Ducts, her writing has appeared in Swink online, Story South, Mr. Beller's Neighborhood, Eyeshot, Pindeldyboz, and elsewhere. She's working on a novel about Evangelical Christianity in 1980's South Florida.

Elliot Ravetz, who resides in New York City, writes about classical music, books, and ideas.

Harilyn Rousso is an educator, social worker, psychotherapist and activist who has worked in the disability rights field, with an emphasis on issues of women and girls with disabilities, for more than twenty years. She is also a writer and painter, incorporating disability-related themes into her work. Harilyn is the author of the book Disabled, Female and Proud! Stories of Ten Women with Disabilities, co-editor of a text on gender issues for students receiving special education services, and contributor to a variety of journals. Largely a self-taught artist, she has been a resident at the Millay Colony for the Arts and Vermont Studio School, and has had individual and group shows in NYC.

Thaddeus Rutkowski grew up in central Pennsylvania and lives in Manhattan. His novel, Roughhouse, was published by Kaya Production, New York. His fiction was nominated for a 1998 Pushcart Prize. He has read his work at many New York spaces, including the Nuyorican Poets Cafe, where he has won the Friday poetry slam.

Charles Salzberg is a New York based freelance writer and teacher. He has published a wide variety of fiction and nonfiction books. His writing has appeared in the New York Times Arts & Leisure section, Redbook, New York Magazine, Travel & Leisure and many others. He is a founding member of the New York Writers Workshop and he is the nonfiction editor for Ducts.org.

Philippe Stessel has attended school, lived and worked in Manhattan 24 years and in only two apartments. He scaled the corporate ladder, producing everything from Japanese television commercials to investment bank Web sites, until he jumped off. He is currently drawing down his retirement fund and working on short stories and a novel.

Ryan Van Winkle, the poetry editor for Ducts.org, is 24 years old and lives out of a back pack. He has no permanent residence and is a happy freelance writer. He spends as much time naked as humanly possible.

Tony Whiteside is a creative supervisor at a large advertising agency. His writing has appeared in The Stamford Advocate, and he's recently sold his first photographs. He holds an M.A. in American Cultural Studies from Columbia University, and lives in the Connecticut woods with his wife, daughter and catnip addicted cat.

Helen Zelon's writing has appeared in The New York Times, Cosmopolitan, Family Circle, Brooklyn Bridge and Scientific American: Explorations. A proud booster of her adopted hometown (New York), she is a nonfiction contributor to Totally Brooklyn.